AROUND THE WORLD IN
WANDERER III

HALF WAY ROUND
From a remote Fijian island Susan looks out towards
WANDERER *at anchor in the quiet lagoon*

AROUND THE WORLD
IN WANDERER III

ERIC C. HISCOCK

Author of
Wandering Under Sail
Cruising Under Sail
Voyaging Under Sail
Beyond the West Horizon
Atlantic Cruise in Wanderer III
Sou'West in Wanderer IV
Come Aboard
Two Yachts, Two Voyages

WITH 62 PHOTOGRAPHS BY
THE AUTHOR
9 CHARTS AND 3 DIAGRAMS

S

SHERIDAN HOUSE

This edition first published 1997
in the United States of America by
Sheridan House Inc.
145 Palisade Street
Dobbs Ferry, NY 10522

Copyright © 1956 by Eric Hiscock

First published 1956 by Oxford University Press
Published 1987 in paperback by Sheridan House
Reissued 1997 by Sheridan House

Printed in Great Britain
ISBN   1-57409-040-2

To

All those people along *Wanderer III*'s
route whose friendship and hospitality
encouraged and refreshed her crew

CONTENTS

ILLUSTRATIONS

The last photograph in this list (facing p. 241, bottom) is reproduced by kind permission of Mr John Owen, Newport, Isle of Wight.

CHARTS

PLANS

The plans of *Wanderer III* are reproduced by kind permission of her designers, Laurent Giles & Partners, Ltd., of Lymington, Hampshire, to whom the author and publisher express thanks for their co-operation.

1

DEPARTURE

'YESTERDAY afternoon Mr. and Mrs. Eric Hiscock left Yarmouth, Isle of Wight, on the first stage of a voyage round the world in their 30-foot yacht *Wanderer III*. The voyage is expected to take three years.'

The voice of the B.B.C. announcer, reading the six o'clock news, came clearly from the loud-speaker in the cabin out to where Susan and I sat in *Wanderer*'s cockpit, watching the faint grey line of the English coast vanishing headland by headland into the distance astern.

This was the great moment for which we had schemed and worked and struggled for so long, the moment of our departure. But although we both got a thrill from hearing ourselves mentioned in the news, and knew that now there could be no return, no calling off of the adventure on which we had embarked, I do not think either of us realized it to the full just then. We were more concerned with the business of finding our sea-legs, for the wind was fresh and our little ship was sailing fast as though she was in a hurry to reach warmer latitudes, and her motion was considerable.

For a long time Susan and I, who are both well used to the handling of small sailing craft, had wanted to make a long voyage. This was chiefly for the satisfaction of achieving something by our own unaided efforts and by the practice of such skill as we might have acquired; but also we wished to see a little of the world, which we could not afford to do in any other way, and to gather copy and photographs for the books and articles which are our livelihood. In 1950 we were fortunate enough to be able to make a voyage out to the Azores and back in our previous yacht, the 24-foot cutter *Wanderer II*. That trip was so successful that we decided to go ahead with the plans for a longer voyage, right round the world if we could

A.W.W—B

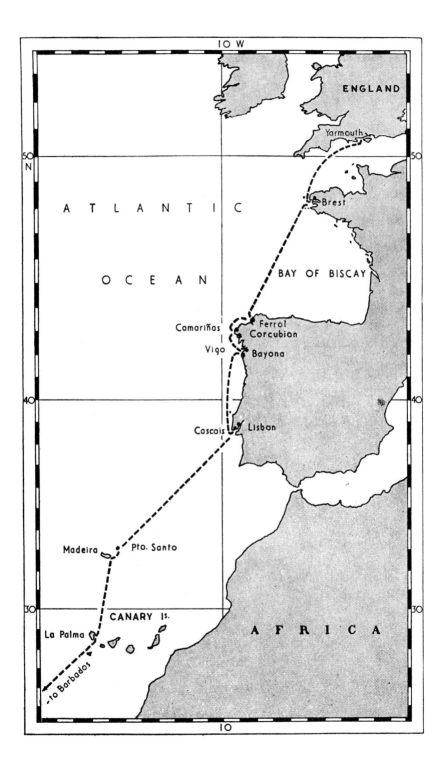

possibly manage it. We sold our beloved *Wanderer II* as we considered she was too small to live in for a period of three years, and she had not the space needed for the stowage of all the provisions and photographic equipment we wished to take with us. We also sold other possessions, and so amassed sufficient funds to have a 30-foot yacht designed and built especially for this long voyage (see Appendix 1).

For eight months we lived at Burnham-on-Crouch watching her take shape, delighting in the skilled and honest workmanship of William King's good men; checking this, altering that or adjusting something else, as she grew from a pile of sweet-smelling timber into that most lovely of all man's creations—a sailing vessel. Her sides were enamelled gleaming white with a broad green topstrake, her decks were pale green to be cool and easy on the eye in the sunshine of the tropics, and her bottom was sheathed with copper to protect it from the dreaded teredo worm. Then one quiet and misty day in the spring of 1952, Susan broke a bottle of wine on her bows and *Wanderer III* floated in her natural element. (*See p. 4.*)

There was then much to do to prepare her for the long voyage ahead. We took her on a trial cruise to south-west Eire, looking for a gale in which to test her seaworthiness and learn how to handle her in bad weather, but all we found were winds so light that they barely stretched our new red-brown sails. After that, working to a list which had been long in preparation, we fitted her out with charts, books and navigational equipment; with tools, wire and hemp rope, and spare parts for all the mechanical gear, such as lamps, galley stove, w.c., motor and winches. Also, so that we could develop our films on board and enlarge them to whole-plate size, in order to supply illustrations for the articles I hoped to write as we went along to pay for the venture, we took aboard a large stock of photographic materials and darkroom equipment. But the bulkiest and most important items of all were water and food. In three separate galvanized steel tanks we carried seventy gallons of fresh water, which should be enough for drinking purposes for ninety days. We were each allowed to take out of England only £25 of foreign currency for the first year, and unless we called at Gibraltar, which we did not wish to do as it was some way off our planned route, we would not reach a sterling area until we arrived in the West Indies in November. Therefore, as we were to start the voyage in July, we filled every available locker and shelf with tinned provisions, and by the time *Wanderer* was ready to leave, she was a good six inches deeper in the water than ever Jack Giles, her designer, had intended.

We hoped we had thought of everything, but it was too late now to worry about that, and as we hurried along over the crested sea we soon had other things to think of. With nightfall the wind freshened; heavy dollops of water started coming aboard to cascade down the helmsman's oilskins, and it was necessary to reduce sail. I groped my way forward with the reefing handle, while Susan ran the yacht off before the wind so as to keep me as dry as possible, and at the mast, where the roaring of the bow-wave sounded louder and the phosphorescent wake looked broader and faster, I struggled with the unfamiliar job of rolling down a deep reef in the mainsail. We sailed more easily then, and Susan went down to her heaving galley to cook a meal on the swinging stove.

Most people can learn to sail a boat, and anyone with an elementary knowledge of arithmetic can learn to navigate; but to prepare and cook a meal in the confined space of a small yacht's violently lurching galley, where the cook and his pots are liable to be hurled from one side to the other, and there is a grave risk of burns from boiling water or cooking fat, is the most difficult of all the arts concerned with cruising under sail, and is more conducive to seasickness than is any other occupation. Susan, who is not immune from that complaint, is therefore the heroine of this story, for she cooked all the meals except breakfast, and not once throughout the voyage did she fail to produce at least one hot meal a day, no matter how bad the weather was. On this occasion we each took one Avomine pill to help keep the scrambled eggs in their proper place; but, like most seasick remedies, Avomine has a soporific effect; so in the early hours of the morning, when we raised the coastwise lights of France, we could scarcely keep our eyes open long enough to time them, and steering a compass course with eyelids heavy as lead was agony.

PLATE I

Wanderer III, our 30-foot sloop, on trials after building at Burnham-on-Crouch.

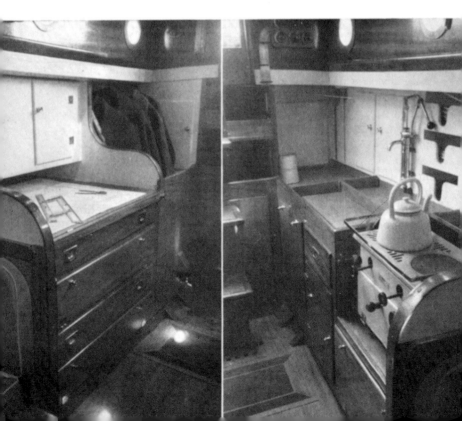

Our intention had been to pass outside Ushant and head direct for a Spanish port; but with dawn the wind died. It seemed pointless to remain drifting in the busy steamer lane when the crusty bread and good cheap wine of France lay near at hand. So we altered course for the Chenal du Four inside Ushant, and there, drifting, ghosting and sometimes using our tiny auxiliary motor, we just saved our tide. Entering the Rade de Brest, we eventually anchored in the delightful Anse de l'Auberlach,where the drone of a distant threshing drum lent a drowsy air to the warm afternoon.

Our stay in the Rade and its neighbourhood lengthened into nearly a fortnight, as the calm continued for some days and was then replaced by a strong south-west wind. Although we would, of course, have to face bad weather at some time during our voyage, we did not wish to force a passage to windward across the Bay of Biscay with the yacht so deeply laden and untried. So we waited for an improvement in the weather, or at least for a change in wind direction. Although this delay so near to home was something of an anticlimax, we much enjoyed ourselves, for several of our cruising friends, returning to England from cruises on the Brittany coast, came in for shelter or a rest and we had many a gay reunion with them; but we did feel a little sad and lonely when they had all sailed on.

We had not visited the town of Brest since before the war. We remembered it well as a busy and crowded place, its cobbled streets congested with trams and other traffic. Now all was different; a new town had risen from the ruins, with wide, smooth streets, towering new buildings and chromium-plated shop fronts. But it seemed a city of the dead. The streets were empty and silent, the shops and offices unoccupied. During the wartime air-raids the shopping and business centre had moved out to the east where we found it still—noisy, crowded and thriving; although the fine new town was almost completed, some difficulty was apparently being experienced in persuading people to go and work and live in it.

PLATE 2

Top: The cabin has sleeping accommodation for two (see plan on page 260) and the forepeak can be used as a darkroom. *Bottom left:* Aft is the chart table with stowage space beneath it for 400 charts, and opposite (*bottom right*) is the galley with stainless steel bench, swinging stove, pantry, and fresh water pump.

So far as bad weather was concerned we might just as well not have waited in France, for no sooner had we been tempted out to sea by a light, fair wind and a rising barometer, than we encountered a small depression, the centre of which passed over us with sudden shifts of wind. At 3 a.m. the wind was strong from north-east; at 3.15 there was no wind and we were slamming about in an abominably uneasy and confused sea; at 3.30 a gale was howling at us from out of the south-west and we had to heave-to for five hours under the close-reefed mainsail.

Two days later we met much worse weather, a 40-knot gale which raised a heavy sea, and again we had to heave-to. The Bay was certainly living up to its evil reputation, which until then we had always thought unjustified, for we had often sailed there before and found the weather no worse than it is elsewhere on the same latitude. As the close-reefed mainsail was too large for so strong a wind, we took it in and set in its place the trysail, a sail of heavy flax canvas measuring only seventy-five square feet in area. Simple though that job should have been, it took us nearly two hours to complete, for we were not then familiar with the best way of doing it, and the violent motion added to our difficulties. As that was our first real gale in our new and untried yacht, it was not without interest; but for a time we were a little apprehensive. Shortly after setting the trysail a heavy crest broke aboard, filling the self-draining cockpit and the deck, so that for a moment nothing on the deck except the upturned dinghy and the four ventilating cowls was visible. No doubt the crest came aboard because *Wanderer* was moving too fast, for we had not then discovered the best position in which to lash the tiller. After some experiment we got the yacht safely hove-to, and then there was nothing to be done but go below to the snug, dry cabin and wait for an improvement in the weather.

With the approach of night the gale freshened, and its moan in the rigging rose to a shrill whistle; the rain drove horizontally, and every now and again there was a muffled crash as a crest broke close alongside and a deluge of spray rattled on deck. But our little ship seemed to be making reasonably good weather of it, shipping no heavy water and moving slowly in a direction at right angles to the wind. There was nothing much to worry about, for we were well inside the Ushant to Finisterre shipping lane, and any French or Spanish fishing vessels in our neighbourhood would probably be hove-to also. But we slept little that night, for we both felt tense and apprehensive, a condition we have now learnt to expect in any gale at sea, although reason may insist that there really is no danger. 'Suppose,' we say, 'in spite of all, we are nearer the lee shore than we think we are? Maybe there is some as yet undiscovered weakness in hull or gear. Perhaps metal fatigue will develop in one of the rigging screws and the mast will go. What then?' So we lay awake listening to the noise of wind and sea, longing for the dawn.

After two weary days and almost sleepless nights had passed the gale moderated. The note of the wind in the rigging dropped and the sea became less steep and crested. Fitfully from out of the breaking cloud-mass the sun shone wanly; we were able to fix our position by observations of him, make more sail, and steer a course for El Ferrol, the naval harbour on the north coast of Spain. We entered it in the dark and found an anchorage off the town, having taken no fewer than six days to cross the Bay of Biscay, a distance of not much over 300 miles. But we had learnt that *Wanderer* is capable of looking after herself when properly hove-to.

The Spanish coast between El Ferrol and Vigo is one of our favourite cruising grounds. Its people are friendly and pleased to see one, it abounds in fine scenery, has many excellent anchorages in its deep inlets, and its port officials are courteous and do not bother one with a lot of unnecessary paper work. Fruit, vegetables and fish are remarkably cheap, and that is largely due to the favourable rate of exchange given to visitors —110 pesetas to the £ instead of the usual sixty. However, our visit that year was only a short one as we were in a hurry to get south after our various delays, and we stopped only three times on the way to Vigo.

In the vicinity of Finisterre we had expected to pick up the Portuguese trade wind to hurry us down the coast. But it was not in evidence, except on one day when we had an exhilarating sail in a strong wind and bright sunshine to the lovely Ria de Camariñas; there, tack and tack, we beat our way in to an anchorage, with a rainbow in the bow-wave spray and our faces rough with salt. For the rest of the time there were only light variable airs, and on one memorable night, when we were approaching the mouth of Vigo Bay, a calm and a thick fog. All that day we had crept slowly down the coast from Corcubion, only getting an occasional glimpse of a mountain peak through the haze; so when the fog closed in at nightfall we were not quite sure of our position. Fearful of being run down, for we were in or near the approaches to a busy port, we hung our 300-candle-power paraffin pressure lamp in the rigging, and had the foghorn ready for use if we should hear

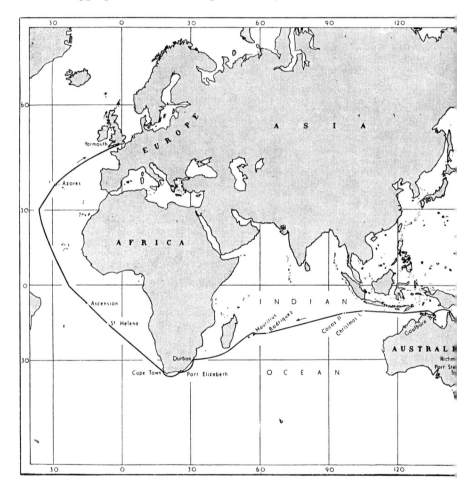

another vessel. It was an eerie sensation lying there in the centre of our own small circle of fog-bound visibility, with ears strained to catch the faintest sound. Several times we heard voices and the throb of a motor, but mostly the only sounds were the dripping of moisture from the sails and a noise as of distant clapping. This last was caused by the jumping in unison of countless small fish, their bodies gleaming silver for a moment as all broke surface together in the light of our lamp and then fell back, leaving a pattern of tiny ripples on the pale green water. Often as they jumped, terns, using our light to fish by,

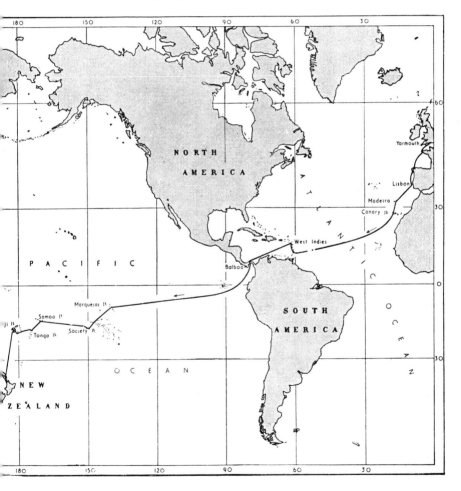

swooped down for a meal among them. Twice during the night, when the sound of breakers shoreward grew unpleasantly close, we started our engine and motored out to sea for a mile or two, for apparently a current was setting us towards the land. We were indeed thankful when dawn brought a breeze to clear the fog, revealing the Islas Cies and the entrance to Vigo Bay ahead.

The long bay looked very jolly in the early morning sunlight as we sailed peacefully up it. The only quiet berth for a small vessel at Vigo is in the yacht basin beside the Real Club Nautico. That is convenient for the town, but unfortunately it is indescribably filthy, for one of the sewers discharges there and the local motor boats frequently pump out their oily bilge water. But we went into it because we wished to collect our mail, which the kind secretary of the club was holding for us, fill our water tanks and buy some fresh food.

On one of our shopping expeditions a young priest decided to join company with us, partly, I think, because he wanted to practise his English. Until then we had been a little shy of the fish market, which is an enormous building packed with women all shouting at the tops of their voices, and many of them carrying baskets of fish balanced cleverly—but precariously to our way of thinking—on their heads. If you stop to listen outside you might well think that a hundred highly successful cocktail parties are being held within. And the smell! I imagine whatever fish is not sold is just thrown on the floor and trampled under foot and that the place is rarely, if ever, scrubbed out. However, the fish for sale is fresh enough, so we told our priest that we would like some sardines. Gathering his robe round him and clasping a handkerchief to his nose, he took a dive followed by Susan and me, and we came out unscathed with some fine fish, which were delicious fried, and some very dirty change for our money.

On leaving Vigo Bay we turned south once more and from then on for the rest of our cruise we sailed in waters new to us. The trip down the long, straight and almost featureless coast of Portugal, on which the Atlantic swell was breaking heavily, was uneventful and slow, for the wind was so light that it could not keep the sails asleep; again and again as *Wanderer* rose to a swell, the mainsail and spinnaker were thrown aback and then filled again with a crash a moment later. We passed outside the Ilha Berlenga—the graveyard of many a fine ship —and not until we had reached Cape Roca, the most westerly point of Europe, did we pick up a good breeze, and we were soon beating swiftly into Cascais Bay at the mouth of the River Tagus against a strong north wind which came to us hot and sweetly scented from its journey over the land.

There is no harbour at Cascais and the bay is open from south-west through south to south-east; but it is considered to be a reasonably safe summer anchorage, for the wind then blows mostly off the shore. A fall of the barometer, or the sudden departure of the sardine fishing fleet which makes Cascais its headquarters, may give a little warning of the approach of bad weather, and then the shelter of the Tagus lies not very far away. But even so we did find it a little unnerving to lie there with nothing except sea between us and America.

The little town looked attractively southern, its red and orange roofs glowing brightly in the intense sunlight against the cloudless blue sky, its houses colour-washed in every pastel shade; the red-gold beaches of the bay were thronged with holiday-makers from Lisbon. The noise ashore was considerable, for every vehicle, including the electric trains, hooted long and loudly on the slightest provocation. The sun had greater power than we had ever known before, but out in the bay the boisterous wind blowing through the yacht day and night with hardly a pause kept her cool and sweet.

Cascais is one of the collecting places for long distance voyagers about to spring off on the Atlantic crossing. Peter and Anne Pye's *Moonraker* and the Dutch yacht *Harry* were lying there, both bound for British Columbia; also in the bay was *Ling* on her way to New Zealand and *Viking* manned by Sten and Brita Holmdahl, a charming Swedish couple attempting, like us, a circumnavigation of the world. It was a great pleasure to meet these yachts and to discuss with their people, whose ideals were so similar to ours, the practical side of cruising and the plans we had all made.

There is in Portugal a body of men known as the International Police. To judge by the behaviour of some of these people they may well have been trained by the Gestapo. Their job appears to be to watch and worry the foreigner, and that they do efficiently and sometimes with discourtesy. On arrival we had hoisted the international code flag 'Q' which means: 'My vessel is healthy and 1 request free pratique'. This is the proper signal to make on arrival from another country, and usually brings off the customs, port doctor or some other official. But at Cascais nothing happened for two days, and then we were peremptorily bidden to an interview with the police. For four hours they kept us waiting, and at the interview, during which our interrogators sprawled in their chairs, Susan was not even offered a seat. No interest was shown in our ship's papers, but our passports were seized. I would have objected to that in any event, but it struck me as being a particularly stupid action when the owners were living aboard a yacht at anchor in an open bay from which they might have to depart at a moment's notice if the wind were to come onshore. So I protested.

The senior policeman then rose to his feet and spoke for several minutes. Through a member of the yacht club, who was kindly acting as interpreter, I gathered the theme was:

'Either we keep your passports or you leave Portugal at once.'

These were strange words in a country which has often claimed to be Britain's oldest ally.

'All right,' said I, 'we will leave your country now and go to some more friendly land.' But Susan whispered in my ear:

'We can't go now. I've sent the laundry to be done.'

So we had to put up with what A. P. Herbert calls 'passportery', and although often under the cold, unfriendly eyes of the International Police, we spent ten quite enjoyable days in the Lisbon area.

The most interesting place we went to was Seixal, a little village up a snug creek on the south side of the Tagus. The waterfront houses, all painted in gay colours, were only partly hidden from our anchorage by a fine avenue of trees, and the creek was enlivened by the comings and goings of *frigatas*. These picturesque trading vessels, which do much the same kind of work as used to be done by our own Thames spritsail barges,

PLATE 3
A River Tagus *frigata*. Even the inside of her hold is elaborately painted.

are all gaff-rigged cutters with great rake to the mast so that it can be used also as a cargo derrick. Of sixty or seventy tons I judged most of them to be; none had engines, and all were superbly handled by their crews of two or sometimes three men. But it was ashore that we discovered the most remarkable thing about these fine vessels. Two were lying alongside the quay where they had just finished unloading their cargos of pit props, and we saw that even the insides of their holds, ceilings, beams, deckhead, everything, were painted in elaborate patterns (*see p.* 12), paints of many colours being used. No doubt a rough cargo would spoil much of this decoration, but always the crews seem to have their brushes at work.

Also at Seixal we met the cod-fishing schooner *Julia Primero*, only that week returned from her five months' fishing expedition to the Newfoundland and Greenland banks. She is of particular interest as being the last of the Portuguese schooners to have no auxiliary power, and she is more than 100 years old. At the invitation of her owner, we moved up the creek and spent a night in the little dredged pool where she lay with a chain of women unloading her salted cod—pressed flat and stiff as boards—into the fish-curing factory, and we were entertained on board by her skipper and mate to biscuits, port wine and cod fried in batter. A fisherman's life on the banks is a hard one; in *Julia*'s forecastle thirty-five dorymen lived, three sharing each bunk which is five feet square.

Having returned to Cascais for our passports, we set off for the Madeiras and had a perfect passage, the kind of sailing one dreams about, or even buys or builds a boat to get. The wind was on the quarter and never faltered for a moment day or night. We carried the whole mainsail and spinnaker most of the way. All day long the sun shone from a clear blue sky, and at night there was bright starlight and a blaze of phosphorescence in the disturbed water of our wake. In three and a half days *Wanderer* covered the 485 miles to Porto Santo, a small and not often visited island some thirty miles to the northeast of Madeira, her best day's run being 145 miles. After we

PLATE 4
The island of Porto Santo, Madeira's near but unspoilt neighbour. *Top:* Fishing boats. *Bottom:* Loading an open boat through the surf.

had cleared the steamer track from the Berlengas to Cape St. Vincent, the sea was empty of shipping, but there were schools of tunny about, the fish in line ahead jumping clear out of the sea, their bellies showing pale yellow as they did so. One forenoon when I was steering, I heard a sudden hiss on the quarter, and there followed a patter as many small bodies struck the mainsail and spinnaker and fell to the deck. My first thought was of flying fish, but I soon saw that I was wrong, for these were a type of jet-propelled squid, eight or nine inches long with short tentacles at their forward end. Where each fell on deck, and I picked up fifteen, there was a black stain from the ink which these creatures eject when frightened or defending themselves. They looked so disgusting that I threw them overboard, but we have since been told that they make excellent eating.

At sunset on our third day at sea we caught a glimpse of Porto Santo's peaks ahead, and we reached the anchorage off the island's southern shore during the night. Fishing boats were lying there without a light among them, and we found our searchlight of great assistance in selecting a clear berth. At dawn we had our first real look at the little island, which is only six miles long and three miles wide at its broadest. It looked sun-baked, light brown, and without a touch of greenery to be seen anywhere except on one of its jaunty, conical peaks, which had been planted with trees in an attempt to induce rain to fall. The bay in which we lay, extending for the full length of the island, was bordered by golden sand on which the swell was breaking white, and the water was the clearest and the bluest we had ever lain in. This was a romantic island indeed, and we were glad to learn later that it had been discovered some time before Madeira, and that Columbus married the Governor's daughter and lived on the island for two years before making his discoveries to the westward.

It was with some misgivings that we launched the dinghy and rowed in towards the shore, for that was to be our first attempt at landing through surf, and a 7-foot pram dinghy of aluminium alloy is not the best of surf boats. We both wore shorts, but as Susan knew well by then how disapproving the Portuguese and Spaniards are of unskirted women, she carried round her neck a small waterproof bag containing a skirt;

and I, in a similar bag tied well up under my chin, carried one of our cameras. Oars, baler and shopping bag were secured to the dinghy with lanyards. Just outside the surf I turned the dinghy and waited for a succession of large breakers to expend their energy, and then backed quickly in. As soon as the dinghy touched bottom, we jumped out, but we did not manage to get her clear of the sea before the next breaker half filled her. But at least we kept ourselves dry. We tipped the water out, and as the dinghy weighs only 50 lbs. we soon had her up above high water mark. Susan put on her skirt, and we walked along the coast track, crossing the dry and dusty watercourses, to the village to pay our respects to the Captain of the Port. He was charming, refused to take down any particulars, and pressed the local wine upon us with considerable alcoholic effect, for it is potent and we are not accustomed to taking wine at three o'clock in the afternoon.

Bearing in mind the island's nearness to crowded Madeira, which is one of the most densely populated rural areas in the world, it is surprising that Porto Santo has not become an annex and been spoilt; but the fact that it has no harbour (although it has a Captain of the Port), and that the crossing can be a rough one, is probably responsible for that. Its chief export is wine, 600 pipes a year; the vines are trained so that the grapes lie on the hot, sandy earth where they are almost toasted, with the result that the fruit matures to a greater extent than in Madeira, and the natural alcoholic content is greater. Water also is exported, for Madeira water lacks in mineral salts, and lime. We watched sacks of lime being carried down the beach on men's backs and loaded through the surf into an open boat—a lively, picturesque scene. (See p. 13.)

After spending two rolly nights off Porto Santo, we sailed across to Funchal in Madeira where, as is usually the way no matter where we go, the inhabitants, and particularly the British residents, were very good to us.

Mr. Cox, the British Consul, and his wife, had us to many meals in their lovely home, and drove us up into the mountains to relax in the cool, thin air, to gaze on the heights of Pico Ruivo, and to look down a thousand feet or more into a crater where a tiny white village, like a toy, lay shadowed by the mountains, a place where the stranger dare not stay because of claustrophobia. Noël Cossart showed us over his wine lodge and asked us to sample various blends of Madeira—a most confusing but delightful occupation—and he presented us with a small cask of our choice with '*Wanderer III*' engraved upon it. The Creed Miles had us to dinner, along with the Pyes and the Holmdahls who had arrived the same day as ourselves, on the verandah of their house which overlooks the bay; the fairy lights of Funchal were spread out below us and the moon shone serenely down. The meat was roasted on open fires before us, and while we ate, a party of men and women from the hills sang and danced for our entertainment; the words of the song they sang varied, but the melody was always the same; it had an elusive quality, and it haunts us still. We from the little ships, making our brief visits, see and hear things which are not always vouchsafed to the ordinary traveller, and we are grateful.

Everything we wished to buy at Madeira, except broad-brimmed straw hats, proved to be expensive, so we decided to sail on to La Palma, one of the Canary Islands, to buy vegetables and fruit for the Atlantic crossing. The Pontinha at Funchal was not an easy place to leave that day, crowded as it was with lighters and small craft, and with a fresh east wind blowing straight into it to set us all rolling and pitching. But the International Police, having reluctantly handed over our passports, insisted that we go before nightfall; so we went.

All through the night we hurried on our way for La Palma, while the pinprick lights of Funchal slowly waned, and we wondered who was dining in the Consul's gracious house where we had been made to feel so much at home. The wind fell light at dawn, and not until the third night did we creep in beneath the pall of heavy black cloud which hung over the island, to reach an anchorage in the harbour of Santa Cruz.

The harbour has a flashing green light at its breakwater end, and we picked that up without difficulty; but we were perplexed by a white light flashing an equal number of times, but at irregular intervals, beyond it, while the swell on the rocky shore boomed sullenly. It was not until next day that we discovered that the coast road there runs through a tunnel, the seaward side of which is pierced by large windows or ventilation holes, and the flashing lights we had seen came from the headlamps of passing motor vehicles seen momentarily through each opening in turn.

La Palma is an island of about the same size as Madeira and rises to a height of 7,000 feet. The picturesque little town of Santa Cruz is unsophisticated and rather charming. It has a cinema, the films for which are selected by the Church, which in most other respects as well appears to rule the island in a sombre, heavy-handed kind of way. Any film containing the most innocent sort of love interest is banned, but oddly enough the more gruesome type of horror film is permitted. Although the climate is hot the women are stuffily dressed in black, so Susan wore a skirt ashore. But one evening when we were watering ship, which meant taking our cans through a little surf on the beach to the one and only waterside tap, where we queued with the inhabitants of the town, some of whom not only filled their pitchers at the tap but washed themselves also, she dressed very sensibly in a shirt and her most demure shorts. So great was the interest shown by the passengers in a passing bus, a converted model T Ford, that the vehicle was nearly capsized as its human freight moved bodily to one side for a better view of this amazing sight of a woman with legs. Nevertheless our reception was friendly, and there was no official fuss. We called on the Captain of the Port whose staff was reading paper-backed books with somewhat suggestive pictures on their covers. He received us courteously and offered us the freedom of the port, while the Captain of Police, a jovial little man with a huge paunch, a chain-smoker of cigars, became a friend although we could scarcely speak a word of one another's language.

I fear that in spite of our general decorum we became one of the sights of the port, for it was so windless and humid in the lee of the mountains where we lay at anchor, that we always ate our evening meal under the awning on deck by the light of our powerful pressure lamp. This was too much for the islanders who just could not ignore our oasis of radiance in the blackness of their harbour, and a constant stream of small boats circled us slowly as we ate. As the island is Spanish, fresh provisions are plentiful and cheap, and we remained for a week laying in stores and generally preparing ourselves and *Wanderer* for the long Atlantic crossing which lay ahead.

OUR FIRST OCEAN CROSSING

As La Palma's barren mountain peaks faded out of sight astern, we wondered what the Atlantic held in store for us and how long it would be before we next sighted land. According to all that we had read, the crossing by the southern route from the Canaries to Barbados, which is the outrider of the West Indies, could take a sailing yacht of *Wanderer*'s size anything between twenty-two and forty-four days; a few had taken longer. But it was now mid October, and the pilot chart for that month showed nice long arrows flying from north-east and east-north-east, and as most of them had four feathers, meaning that their average strength would be force 4 on the Beaufort scale (a moderate breeze) we thought we ought to take not more than thirty days for the 2,700-mile crossing. It may seem strange that although we much enjoy sailing, almost the first thing Susan and I do on dropping the land is to work out our estimated time of arrival at the next port. But I believe that is a common trait among sailing folk, most of whom prefer to arrive rather than to travel hopefully, and one of the greatest interests on an ocean voyage is in getting the best performance out of the yacht and trying each day to improve on the previous day's run.

The two most important considerations when planning a long voyage in a small sailing vessel are to avoid dangerously bad weather, and to make the greatest possible use of fair winds. The North Atlantic and the Pacific and Indian oceans have at their western sides areas which are subject to hurricanes, cyclones or typhoons, all of which are revolving storms with winds often in excess of 100 miles per hour. These occur, with very rare exceptions, only at certain times of year, and one therefore plans to pass through those areas during the safe months. The summer months, in particular August and September, are the danger months in the West Indies area, so we had planned our cruise with the intention of arriving in November. Similar considerations were to govern our time-table in the Pacific and Indian oceans. To obtain the greatest benefit from fair winds, we would, throughout our east-to-west voyage round the world, remain as much as possible in the trade wind belts, which extend approximately from the equator to 25 degrees north and south latitude. North of the equator the trade wind blows mostly from a direction between east and north-east, and in the southern hemisphere from between east and south-east. Except during the hurricane months, and in one or two places where they are replaced for a period by a monsoon or by light variables, the trades blow almost constantly throughout the year and the weather in their areas is usually fine and settled. The doldrums, a belt of calms, squalls and rain, separate the north-east from the south-east trade wind.

As the Canaries lie outside the northern limit of the north-east trade wind, we headed at first in a south-westerly direction when we left La Palma instead of direct for our destination, so as to get down into the heart of the trade wind as soon as might be. For nearly a week we worked hard, shifting and trimming our sails to make the most of the light and variable winds which were all we had; and then, when we had reached a position where, according to the chart, the trade wind should blow steadily throughout the year, we were becalmed.

Wanderer lay without steerage way rolling idly above her own reflection in the sea which, except for a long, low swell, was so smooth that it had the appearance of oil, and one could scarcely tell where the horizon lay, for sea and sky were of the same pale blue. Out of the cloudless sky the sun blazed down relentlessly, making the deck so hot that it was not possible to stand on it barefooted, and the cabin temperature rose high into the nineties. After we had stowed the sails, which were slatting as the yacht rolled and doing themselves no good, the silence was profound; so noticeable was it after the din of motor horns, church bells and fiesta rockets in our recent Spanish and Portuguese ports, that we sat for a time 'listening' to it, and marvelling at the emptiness of the vast ocean on which our small floating home was such an inconsiderable speck.

For two whole days and nights the calm persisted. We began to lose faith in the pilot charts which, beautifully printed in four colours, show with a wealth of detail the direction and strength of wind and percentages of calms and gales which have been recorded from thousands of observations made by seamen over a period of many years, and which, one there-fore supposes, can be taken as indicating with fair accuracy the weather to be expected. 'This', we said, 'is no way for the trade wind to behave', disregarding for the moment the fact that percentages and averages, though they may be quite correct, can be misleading when applied to weather over short periods of time, and that no efforts of man to reduce nature to a formula are infallible. Our hopes of a swift passage began to fade, and there seemed to be no good reason for expecting the wind ever to return.

But on the third day the wind did return. To start with it was only the faintest whisper of an air, not enough to lift the tired burgee at the masthead or to smooth the wrinkles from the light nylon ghoster which we set the moment the smoke from my pipe began to drift away. But, for such is the property of really light large sails, the ghoster gave us steerage way; a tiny ripple spread from the bow, and the log line, which until then had been hanging vertically with its rotator 80 feet below the surface of the sea, streamed out astern, and as the breeze gathered strength almost imperceptibly, the log wheel began to turn. *Wanderer* was on the move at last. Presently we reset the mainsail, and from then on our daily runs from noon to noon improved, being mostly over 100 miles, though our best on that passage was only 130, for the wind was never strong.

A few days later the wind settled down to blow from dead astern, so we took in the mainsail and set our twin spinnakers for the first time. With these sails set, one each side and forward of the mast, each on a boom of its own, and with the braces leading aft through blocks on each quarter to the tiller, the yacht will steer herself before the wind unattended. (*See p. 32.*) That is what she proceeded to do for the next eleven days.

It was a welcome relief for us to be able to make good progress without having to sit and steer, for with only the two of us aboard we do get very tired when constant steering is necessary. Taking watch and watch, with three hours at the helm and three below, by the time we have cooked and eaten, navigated, and attended to the many little daily tasks, there is not a lot of time left for sleep. But under the self-steering twins, our lives became more leisurely. Susan, often singing in her galley, cooked more elaborate meals and baked cakes which we usually ate ravenously at a sitting, and I was free to navigate and work about the ship to my heart's content, doing some of those many small jobs for which one never seems to find time when in port. I even contrived to develop some films by standing the tank and the bottles of chemicals on the swinging galley stove when Susan was not using it, a necessary precaution because, with no fore-and-aft sails to steady her, the yacht's motion was violent. That was the one big disadvantage of running under the twins. Never for a moment did *Wanderer* cease to roll when under that rig, and every few minutes she would build up a kind of period roll, going over to thirty-two degrees each way and taking only two seconds for the roll, then hurling herself back the other way. The centrifugal action was considerable, and anything which was not securely lashed or chocked off, including ourselves, was thrown violently across the cabin. It is said that the human body will in time accustom itself to anything, but I fancy the motion of a small yacht at sea must be one exception.

However, in spite of that we quite enjoyed ourselves. Each evening we sat together in the cockpit for what we called our twilight hour. Over a drink we discussed the doings of the day, and although those who have not made an ocean voyage under sail may consider it is a dull business, I can assure them it is not, for there is always plenty to do. We admired the wide and empty ocean across which we sailed so effortlessly, and watched the sunset with its usual gathering of cumulus clouds piled up all round the horizon. If the sun set clearly, as he sometimes did, we looked for the vivid, and so far as I know unexplained, green flash which sometimes appeared just as he dropped below the horizon. Then almost at once it was night. The planet Venus could then be seen between the luffs of the twins, chasing the sun to bed, while Mars soon rose astern. Most evenings, shortly after sundown, a black cloud approached from astern bringing with it a shower of rain, then the sky cleared and most of the night was fine, but there was often another small shower of rain at breakfast time. Usually these showers brought with them a shift of wind, but that was only temporary, and within half an hour or so the trade would be blowing from its usual quarter again. While the rain lasted we had to close the hatches and ports, but those were the only occasions during that Atlantic crossing when we did have to close them. Once during the night I heard heavy rain beating on deck. Then, much to Susan's surprise, for I am not normally of a spartan nature, I rose from my bunk, took a cake of soap and had a thorough wash on deck; but all the time I was fearful that the rain might stop before I had rinsed the suds off, for not until we had passed the half way point did we use any of our seventy gallons of fresh water for washing purposes. This does not mean that we were dirty, for although we never bathed at sea because of the risk of sharks, we often used to sluice ourselves down on deck with buckets of sea water; also we discovered that we could get an excellent wash in salt water, using one of the modern soapless shampoos, while for washing clothes and dishes we used a liquid detergent.

After supper we hung the riding light in the rigging and both turned into our bunks. We considered the risk of collision to be negligible, for now that there are no sailing ships, the trade wind routes are empty except for the occasional yacht, and steamships generally keep to regular routes which are shown on certain charts; when crossing those routes we always kept a lookout. So for the most part we slept with easy minds. From our bunks it was possible to see whether *Wanderer* was holding a steady course, for a small telltale compass was fixed to the table leg between us, and we could easily reach to turn on its battery-operated light and read it without getting up. But during the night one or other of us usually had a look round several times to see that all was well. It was fascinating to go on deck and find our little ship forging steadily on her way at five knots, with a tumbling bow-wave and a broad hissing wake alight with pale green phosphorescence. Looking up from the foredeck I could see the twins, ghostly white, bellying out firm and round, pulling with silent power, while aft the tiller was moved, mysteriously, it seemed, a little this way and a little that way as the self-steering gear held the course. Perhaps I would give a touch of grease to the fore-guy and braces where they worked through the stemhead and quarter blocks, a glance at the luminous compass and the star-filled sky, a slow and careful search of the horizon for lights, and then I went back to my comfortable bunk. By daybreak another fifty miles or so would be ticked off by the patent log.

On the passage across the Atlantic we fed simply but adequately. For breakfast we had porridge, Macvita and marmalade, coffee and vitamin pills. During the early part of the trip lunch was always a cold meal, tinned meat or fish or cheese with biscuits and fresh tomatoes (they lasted for sixteen days with some wastage) and Portuguese wine. We abandoned afternoon tea as being a waste of time, for by then the heat of the day was declining and it was possible to work more comfortably on deck or down below. To begin with supper was a hot meal, the meat coming out of a tin, of course, but always with plenty of boiled, mashed, roast or fried potatoes (we had 40 lb. for that trip, and with an occasional picking over they lasted very well) and usually onions, of which we carried 8 lb., carrots, etc. Sometimes we had an egg dish, but we were short of eggs because many of those we had brought from England went bad owing to the lard with which they had been coated melting and running off them in the hot weather. All future supplies of eggs we greased with petroleum jelly, and they kept perfectly for as long as three months. As a sweet we often had a chocolate rice pudding, or mashed bananas with milk and sugar. Oranges and lemons wrapped separately and kept in tins lasted the whole voyage, so we were always able to have a fresh fruit drink during the forenoon. When night watches were kept, the helmsman had chocolate and biscuits within his reach and perhaps a cup of cocoa at the change of watch.

With the fair wind blowing right through the yacht, in at the main hatch and out of the forehatch, she was always fresh below; but in the evening, to prevent the paraffin wick lamps from smoking or blowing out, we had to close the forehatch; then the cooking of supper made the cabin unpleasantly hot and stuffy. So after a time we changed the routine, and had our hot meal in the middle of the day immediately after I had worked out the noon position, and the cold meal in the evening.

Of wild life in the Atlantic we saw very little. Sometimes

storm-petrels came and had a look at us, their tiny feet pattering on the surface of the sea, and one morning we found one staggering about in the cockpit. He seemed dazed, and we think our light may have dazzled him so that he struck the rigging and fell inboard. As the bird would accept no food or drink, the best thing seemed to be to launch him, and Susan did that skilfully—like getting off a moving bus—and he looked content as we left him bobbing in our wake. Twice we saw what we took to be bosun birds, large white creatures with a curious tail consisting of a single long feather. Most mornings there were flying fish on deck, but never enough or of sufficient size to justify dirtying the frying-pan. During our second week out a blue and black striped pilot fish, whose job in life is to swim with sharks, joined company with us. This jolly little chap seemed to like the shade, and during the forenoon he swam along just ahead and a little to starboard of the stem, where he had to work hard to keep station in the foaming bow-wave; at noon, when the sun came round and flooded his station with light, he dropped aft and swam beside the rudder. He remained with us for twelve days in spite of occasional visits by schools of porpoises, and according to my reckoning he covered 1,330 miles in that time.

As day followed day, each seemingly alike, but each presenting some new interest or occupation for us, the row of pencilled crosses, each marking a noon position, strung out farther and farther across the chart towards our destination. The quarter, the half, and the three-quarter way positions were passed. Always our circle of visibility was empty of shipping; there was never so much as a smudge of smoke on the horizon, never the faintest drone of an aircraft's engine overhead; there was not even a floating bottle or grapefruit skin to remind us that there were others beside ourselves alive on this planet. But although we were constantly aware that *Wanderer* was probably the only floating object for hundreds of miles and that we must depend entirely on our own resources for everything, even for medical attention should the need arise, I do not believe either of us was very conscious of a feeling of loneliness or real anxiety. We had each other and our brave little ship for company. We had prepared ourselves and her as carefully as we could; we had made our plans and tried to visualize in advance what a long, short-handed voyage would be like in reality. Now we were putting ourselves to the test and our plan into operation, and trade wind sailing was proving to be much as we had expected. All was going well; we were both perfectly fit, and there was nothing to worry about until the time should come for making a landfall.

Towards the end of the passage the wind became less steady in direction, and at times fell light. As *Wanderer* would then no longer steer herself on the course for Barbados under the twins, we took those sails in and set the mainsail, and then enjoyed the almost forgotten ease of motion which only fore-and-aft sails can give. But of course steering then became necessary, and we did not take to it very kindly after our eleven days of freedom, particularly during the dark night watches.

We got our greatest thrill of the whole passage at noon on our twenty-sixth day at sea, when the low, green island of Barbados lifted over the horizon ahead just about where and when the navigator had said (and secretly prayed) it would appear. Although navigation by observation of celestial bodies is an almost exact science, the small-boat navigator on a passage out of sight of land has little or no opportunity for checking the accuracy of his work; so I, for one, always suffer from a feeling of apprehension as the time for making a landfall approaches, especially when the land is a small or low island. A successful landfall—and in spite of everything most of them are that— is surely the cruising man's greatest moment. The feeling of satisfaction, achievement and elation is immense and, I believe, never stales no matter how often it may be experienced.

The wind then freshened considerably to a strength greater than we had had for many a day, and *Wanderer* stormed along towards the land; but night was upon her before the island's south point came abeam. There at last she ran out of the ocean swell which had been her constant companion for so long, and at eight o'clock that evening she found an anchorage in Carlisle Bay off Bridgetown, the island's capital.

Almost at once we were hailed from the police launch. Out of the darkness came a soft, lilting voice to ask us who we were and where we had come from, and it concluded by wishing us a pleasant stay at the island. Soon the rising moon illuminated the white sand beach that fringed our anchorage, and a magnificent grove of royal palms. Friendly lights shone out, the first we had seen for many a day. In a restaurant white-coated waiters were serving dinner, and there came to us across the water the warm, earthy smell of the land. Slowly, as we moved about the strangely steady deck, stowing the sails and setting the riding light on the forestay, we began to realize that the first part of our adventure was over. The broad but kindly Atlantic lay astern. This was our first tropical island.

ISLANDS TO WINDWARD

T HE day starts early in Barbados. We were awakened at dawn by the cheerful noise of people bathing, and on following their example into the limpid water, we discovered that several of them were accompanied by horses which appeared to be enjoying themselves as much as their owners were. At 6 a.m. an immaculate and smartly handled launch brought the port doctor off to us.

'Welcome to Barbados', was his greeting as he stepped aboard. The granting of pratique took only a few minutes, for the doctor seemed already to know a lot about *Wanderer* and us, and that was the only formality throughout our stay at the island. He was followed in quick succession by several callers, including the Captain of the Port, who kindly came to offer us any help we might need. All this was before 8 a.m.

Wanderer was lying in seven fathoms of the clearest of pale green water over smooth, white sand. Inshore of her lay a number of local boats, and beyond them the remarkable Aquatic Club, a red and white building which stood out in the bay on its own wooden pier. To seaward three merchant ships lay at anchor with lighters plying between them and the careenage, which was packed with inter-island schooners, fine, rakish-looking vessels. (*See p.* 33.) To starboard a low spit of sand jutted seaward; round this the Atlantic rollers curled before breaking on it, the spray from them being blown back by the trade wind, so that they resembled galloping horses with flying manes. To our eyes, accustomed as they were to empty horizons, the scene was full of life and interest, sparkling, vividly coloured, gay.

With mail waiting for us we did not delay our landing, but launched the dinghy and stepped ashore at the Aquatic Club where we were promptly made honorary members. A stranger, who became a friend, gave us a lift by car into town, where the ground seemed to sway a little as we walked with unsteady legs. Even in the deep shade of the arcades with which Broad Street is flanked, the town was very hot, and we were grateful for the long-bladed fans in Barclay's Bank, where we went to collect our mail and to draw island dollars on our letter of credit. We drank frosted chocolate through long straws up on Goddard's balcony; from there, looking diagonally down, we watched the crowds of cheerful, dusky people, and the milling traffic which was controlled by black policemen wearing smart, white tunics and pith helmets, each on a little stand of his own beneath a wide sunshade.

Having bought vegetables and fruit from stalls in the side alleys, we made our way to the terminus and boarded a bus. This was a typical island bus, open-sided, with full-width seats and canvas curtains which could be let down in wet weather; the conductor, something of an acrobat, balanced on the narrow step as he collected the fares. While we waited, a negro, accompanying himself on a tambourine, sang catchy songs of a religious nature to the passengers. 'The beautiful city of God' had a particularly rousing tune, and another song which contained the line: 'I was praying to Jesus and somebody stole my soul', was very popular.

Sugar is the life blood of Barbados, the greater part of the island being given over to the growing of sugar cane. It is a prosperous, happy place, and is known to those who love it as Little England. There is nothing very impressive about it except its golden, sandy beaches, where the swell thunders to a spectacular end; but it is a friendly island, and the day after our arrival the round of hospitality started with a rum punch party on the tree-shaded beach in front of the yacht club. Thereafter, scarcely a day passed without a lunch or dinner engagement, or a drive out into the country. We tried to repay a little of this hospitality aboard *Wanderer*, and that was not difficult to do with excellent West Indies rum selling at 5s. a bottle, and fresh limes and sugar in plenty. But Carlisle Bay is an open anchorage, and although it is a safe one, except during the hurricane season, on the occasions when the trade wind fell light or died away for a little while, *Wanderer*, responding to the slight tidal stream, turned beam on to the swell and rolled heavily. If that happened, as it sometimes did, when we had visitors aboard, it was not long before one or more of them had to be ferried ashore in a hurry.

One day Ian Gale, editor of the *Barbados Advocate*, and his wife came on board, and during their visit a boat arrived with a stranger who introduced himself as a friend of a friend of ours. As he climbed over the rail he suddenly cried out:

'Oh! Oh, my God!'

We looked at him in some surprise, wondering whether he had suddenly been taken ill. Then after a pause he added: 'My watch'.

Instantly Ian in all his clothes dived in, and we could see him swimming down and down in the glass-clear water. He returned to the surface breathless and empty-handed.

'I could see it sinking ahead of me,' he gasped, 'but forty feet's too deep.'

That evening after supper Susan shook the crumbs from the tablecloth over the side, and with them my cigarette lighter. Next day we could see the watch and lighter sparkling in the sunshine side by side on the sand beneath us, and although some of the best divers in the island came off to try their luck, for a large reward was offered for the recovery of the watch which was an expensive and waterproof one, so far as I know both still lie there at the bottom of Carlisle Bay.

It was a great occasion when Sten and Brita Holmdahl arrived in *Viking*, having taken thirty-two days for the Atlantic crossing from La Palma. We invited them aboard for supper which, as was our habit when at anchor in hot places, we ate in the cockpit where it was cool and airy beneath the awning. The meal was barely over when we spied *Moonraker* rounding the sand spit, and at once rowed over to greet her. She also had come from La Palma, and Peter Pye's first words were: 'How many days?' When we told him we had taken twenty-six he seemed a little sad for *Moonraker* had taken twenty-eight. As she had a crew of three, and as both she and *Viking* were longer than *Wanderer* on the waterline, they should in theory be capable of higher speeds. We therefore felt well pleased with *Wanderer*'s performance, but without good reason, for unless vessels start out on a passage together, it is unlikely that they will find identical weather conditions.

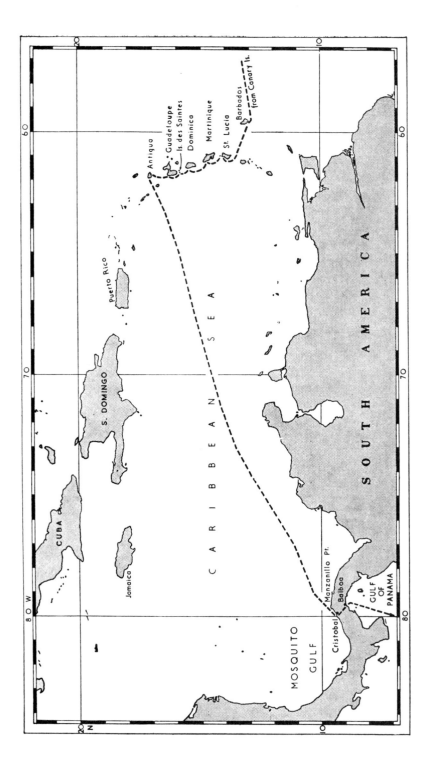

Antigua
Guadeloupe
Is. des Saintes
Dominica
Martinique
St. Lucia
Barbados
from Canary Is.

Puerto Rico

S. DOMINGO

CUBA

Jamaica

C A R I B B E A N   S E A

S O U T H   A M E R I C A

Manzanillo Pt.
Balboa
GULF
OF
PANAMA

Cristobal

MOSQUITO
GULF

N

As Barbados lacks a suitable harbour for yachts, it is not the ideal tropical island. But it was our first, and one of the most colourful, and we left it and its friendly people with many regrets when we sailed away for the neighbouring island of St. Lucia, where we wished to go to find a sheltered anchorage in which I could attend to the darkroom work which had been accumulating.

David Payne, the port doctor, came with us for the sail, which was not a very enjoyable one, as there was little wind and a lot of thundery rain. We arrived at the harbour of Castries in the dark, for *Wanderer* had developed a passion for night arrivals and was making quite a habit of them. We are not fond of them, for although a night arrival adds to the romance, and the pleasure of having one's first view of a strange port from the inside after a night entry is considerable, the business of getting in and finding a berth in the dark can be hazardous, particularly if the port is an artificial or commercial one. However, Castries is easy enough to enter in any conditions, so we got in safely, and after a short sleep were awakened by the port doctor, for even when moving between British islands of the West Indies, health regulations have to be complied with. David left us, and after we had had a quick look at the town, where we were not impressed by the begging habits of the cheeky inhabitants, we moved across to Vigie Cove at the north side of the harbour.

Can you imagine a tiny, landlocked pool from which not so much as a distant glimpse of the sea can be had; so small that you can, and we often did, swim right across it from one grassy bank to the other; surrounded by green foliage, palms, and brilliant flowers, and with hardly a ripple on its surface? That is Vigie Cove, and there we lay for a week in absolute peace. After night had fallen with its accustomed suddenness, the still air was loud with the chirping of countless crickets, and mingled with their harmony was the sweet whistling of tiny frogs. In the darkness the shores of the cove provided an amazing sight; there were thousands of fireflies, in the bushes, on the ground and up the trees, their tiny lights making a fairyland of the place. This was a strange and not unpleasing contrast to the open, wind-swept anchorage at Barbados, but it had three disadvantages—the flies, the rain and the heat. We sprayed with D.D.T. against the flies, but with little success, for an hour or so afterwards they were aboard as thick as ever. We spread our awning against the rain and kept dry; but day by day the awning became blacker and blacker as it was attacked by mildew in the humid atmosphere. Against the heat we could do nothing, for there was no wind; so our canvas windsail, rigged over the forehatch, and which in normal conditions pours a stream of fresh air right through the yacht, hung limply in shapeless folds, growing mildew also.

But in spite of these drawbacks I had to make some photographic enlargements with which to illustrate a story I had recently completed for a magazine. So I blacked out the forepeak, rigged up the enlarger and, almost naked because of the heat, got to work. Susan meanwhile took the opportunity to wash her hair while I was out of the way. Our respective jobs were proceeding normally, when I heard a motor boat come alongside and a little later voices in the cabin. Curiosity overcame me; so placing my last print in the hypo, I pulled back the blackout curtain, unlatched the forepeak door, and on hands and knees and just as I was, crawled out into the cabin from beneath the enlarger bench. There I found Susan, her long wet hair wrapped in a towel done up like a turban, talking to a smart young naval officer in immaculate tropical uniform. In true naval fashion he showed no surprise at our strange get-up and habits, and invited us to a cocktail party aboard his ship, H.M.S. *Bigbury Bay*, that evening. We sat talking for a little while, then he climbed back aboard the boat in which he had come, a high-speed motor launch which was in the hands of an unskilled coxswain. The powerful engine started with a roar; the officer stood rigidly at the salute in the sternsheets, and the coxswain, without slowing his engine, rammed the gear lever into the ahead position, with the inevitable result that our friend was thrown off his balance and collapsed backwards. We scarcely knew whether to laugh or to pretend we had not noticed. Nevertheless the evening's party was a great success.

PLATE 5

Top: We set the twin spinnakers for the first time and (*bottom*) left *Wanderer* to steer herself across the Atlantic, rolling heavily.

The town of Castries, after its third great fire, had just been rebuilt. The work had been done by a British firm, and the English executives were not leaving the island until March—we were there in November. With time on their hands rum punch parties were the vogue, and these often started in the forenoon and continued until midnight; the members of one family we met told us they had been to twenty-eight such parties in twenty-nine days; but perhaps I have got this wrong, for we also attended one or two, and our memories of St. Lucia became rather confused.

Next we called at Pigeon Island where we were met on landing by Miss Josset Legh, late of the D'Oyly Carte opera company. She with her mother rented that tiny island, on which stands the fort where Rodney conducted operations against the French. The Leghs had built some charming houses for themselves and their friends, and on the beach, about 50 yards from where *Wanderer* lay at anchor, had erected an open-fronted building with a kitchen and bar under a high-pitched roof thatched with citronella grass. After exploring the island, we had a luxurious dinner there with Miss Legh, who was a little unusual in her tastes and habits; she wisely wore the minimum of clothes and went barefooted always; her house was partly built in a tree, the great trunk of which passed right through her bedroom, and she relied, so she said, on a parrot pecking her toes to wake her in the morning. But at the time of our visit she was sleeping not in her house but anywhere she fancied on the island: in Rodney's fort, among the undergrowth, or on the sandy beach, according to her fancy; her idea was to intercept the thieves arriving by canoe from St. Lucia who were in the habit of making off with her ducks or garden produce. The setting for our dinner was delightful. The table stood beneath the dark vault of the high-pitched roof almost at the water's edge, where gentle ripples lapped on the sand, and we could look straight out at *Wanderer* riding serenely in the starlight, while we ate stuffed eggs, locally

PLATE 6

Top: The careenage at Bridgetown was packed with inter-island schooners, fine, rakish-looking vessels. *Bottom:* Yachts lie at the old dockyard in English Harbour which Nelson's fleet once used.

A.W.W.—D

caught fish, and guavas. Whistling frogs and chirping crickets formed our orchestra. Next morning, before our early departure, we received a gift of vegetables; most of these looked like privet hedge trimmings, but tasted like excellent spinach.

Our plan was to sail up the chain of Antilles, stopping a night or more at each island, until we reached Antigua, 200 miles to the north. It is difficult to imagine a more pleasant cruising ground. The islands are separated from one another by channels varying in width from fifteen to thirty miles, so unless one is unlucky there is no need for night sailing. It is possible to find a good anchorage on the western side of each island, usually in some gently shelving bay where there are no pilotage difficulties. The inter-island passages are boisterous because the trade wind funnels through them and they are open to the full drift of the Atlantic. Sailing across these passages is exhilarating and wet. But in the lee of the islands, most of which are mountainous, the wind is interfered with and there are calms and squalls to keep one alert whilst admiring the fine scenery; however, the sea there is sometimes short and confused, hampering to a small sailing vessel. Had *Wanderer* possessed a reasonably powerful engine, we would have used it a lot then. But her auxiliary is only a 4-horse-power petrol motor, the chief function of which is to charge the 12-volt battery In a calm and quite smooth water it gives the yacht a speed of three knots, but in a popple or against a slight headwind it scarcely gives her steerage way. So we had to make the best we could of the light and fluky breezes under sail.

A passage across seventeen miles of rough sea brought us under the lee of the French island of Martinique, and that evening we lay at anchor in St. Pierre Bay, close beneath the frowning heights of terrible Mount Pelée, a volcano which in 1902 had destroyed the town and killed its 40,000 inhabitants with a sudden blast of flame and super-heated steam.

Prince Rupert Bay, in the British island of Dominica, was our next stopping place, but we were so delayed by the calms in the island's lee that we made the anchorage in the dark. We remained a day there to buy the finest grapefruit we have ever had at 1½d. each in the little town of Portsmouth, and to have a look at the Indian River where the British fleet used to get fresh water. It did not seem to be a very suitable place as a heavy swell broke right across the entrance. But the more we learn of the remarkable feats of British seamen in the lusty days of sail, the more do we admire their skill and hardihood. By way of contrast, we watched a small amphibious aeroplane land in the bay, taxi in towards the shore and anchor just outside the breakers. After picking up its passengers, it weighed, took off and, after its pilot had waved to us, vanished to the south. An independent little machine.

In the channel between Dominica and Guadeloupe lies a group of small French islands, the Iles des Saintes; they were our next objective. The day was gloomy, and as we drew out from the shelter of Dominica the wind increased to force 7 and there was a downpour of rain. We drove on wetly through a short, steep sea, blinded by the rain. In such vile conditions we did not consider it wise to attempt to make the Saintes, so we steered a course which should take us clear to the west of them. But after a time a temporary clearance showed us the Saintes close at hand, and we decided to go there after all. We had an anxious beat in through the south-west pass dead to windward against squalls which were of gale force, and during the afternoon reached the anchorage off Bourg des Saintes. In response to our 'Q' flag the *gendarme* rowed off to us; he courteously removed his boots before walking on our clean deck (how we wish that all visitors from the shore would do that) and charged us sixty francs for a *passeport des navires étrangers*.

After its brief lapse, the weather next day returned to normal. The sky was blue, the sun shone, and the little islands of the group, which are about the same size as the Scillies, looked clean, fresh and rain-washed, sparkling like jewels in their setting of dark blue sea. We explored the little town which straggles picturesquely along its one concrete street on which the only vehicles are bicycles, and watched stems of bananas being unloaded from open boats on the beach. Strangely, there is no trace of dark blood in the Saintes, the population being entirely white. But the hats, looking like giant mush-rooms, which are worn by the women, lend a unique and foreign air to the place. The islanders' only exports are fish and lobsters. The previous day a disaster had befallen; a *vivier* carrying 400 choice lobsters to neighbouring Guadeloupe had foundered owing to the bad weather with the loss of her entire cargo, but fortunately her crew was saved.

We stopped next at Deshayes Bay near the northern end of Guadeloupe, and after a night there left at daybreak on the crossing to English Harbour, Antigua. That is a forty mile trip, and as Antigua lies to the north-east of the line of islands, which here curves comfortably away to the north-west, we knew we would be jammed hard on the wind all the way. The trade wind was strong, and *Wanderer*, well reefed, was crashing into a head sea, so we wondered whether we would be able to reach port before nightfall. If we failed to do so we would have to spend the night at sea, as English Harbour is not an easy place to find, and for strangers is probably an impossible one to enter in the dark.

Close-hauled we were able to steer for a position seven miles to windward of our destination, and we did that to allow for our leeway and for the west-setting current in the channel. We drove *Wanderer* as hard as we could and she responded gamely, forcing her way steadily out to windward and never letting the steep seas stop her, but she hammered them hard so that fountains of spray shot out each side of her rounded, buoyant bows every time she smashed into one. The spray on the windward side was instantly blown back across the deck and into the sails, and every now and then a heavy dollop of water crashed on to the foredeck, sluiced aft and cascaded out of the scuppers. And we her crew, perched up on the windward side of the cockpit, laughed with the sheer exhilaration of it, as the warm spray deluged us; in the occasional quieter moments the hot sun dried our faces, arms and legs, and left them gritty with caked salt. Such wild, wet sailing, and such a violent lurching motion, we could not have endured for long, and had we been bound for a more distant port we would have snugged the yacht well down and taken things more easily. But this short trip we were determined to make into a day sail only, and with the knowledge that port might be reached before nightfall if only we drove *Wanderer* hard enough, we felt we could put up with almost any discomfort and, what is more, actually enjoy it.

English Harbour is not easily seen from seaward, and, apart

from certain hills, which are difficult for the stranger to identify, there is nothing very conspicuous either on the island or on the chart from which the navigator can get a clue to his position. But in time we recognised Monk's Hill, which is wooded, and the long, flat tableland of Shirley Heights. The entrance to the harbour unfolded itself as we drew near. We spied the huge warping anchor in Freeman Bay, and I had scarcely got forward with the reefing handle, for I thought that in the lee of the land we would be unable to work our way in with so little sail, when Susan at the helm had cunningly weathered Barclay Point. The dockyard then opened up, and the Nicholsons, who live there, came to the edge of the quay to wave us a welcome and direct us to a berth. In a flash, so it seemed, we were lying secure in smooth, green water with scarcely a ripple on it.

English Harbour is the most perfectly sheltered haven that any 8-ton sailors could desire, and it is one of the best of the hurricane shelters in the West Indies. Three overlapping points hide it from the sea and protect it from the swell, while the low, scrub-covered hills tame the roaring trade wind to a gentle breeze, with only an occasional gust to remind one of the boisterous conditions outside. For a part of our visit we lay alongside the old dockyard which Nelson used for three years when he was there in command of H.M.S. *Boreas*. (*See p.* 33.) The stone quays are still in good condition, and so is the admiral's house and the officers' quarters; but most of the rest—the boathouse which once had an immense span of roof, as is shown by the position of the pillars which used to support it, the cordage, sail and clothing stores, the lead cellar and the engineers' workshop—lie in ruins. This is an historic place, indeed, and little imagination is required to visualize it teeming with life as it used to be, loud with the gruff voices of pigtailed seamen and the trill of the bosun's call. There might be a ship of the line moored in little *Wanderer's* berth, and perhaps another hove down by the careening capstans which still stand intact, though the capstan house which used to enclose them has vanished, the craftsmen and sailors busy with the refit, caulking seams and painting. The batteries at the entrance points would be manned against a surprise attack by the French, and over all would hang the aroma of new wood shavings from the working mast-house, and pitch being heated in the giant kettles.

We remained in the harbour until Boxing Day, and did a lot of work. We gave *Wanderer* a refit, painting her sides, deck and spars, dressing her rigging with boiled linseed oil and varnishing her brightwork; when we had finished she looked almost as trim as she did when she left her builder's yard.

There was a gathering of yachts in the harbour with us, and we saw much of their people. *Moonraker* and *Viking* were already there when we arrived, along with the Nicholsons' lovely schooner *Mollyhawk* and their 100-tonner *Maria Catharina*, also the American schooner *Blue Goose*; the last three were used for taking paying guests for cruises among the islands. Then there was the French yacht *Atoll*, recently arrived from Brittany, the 5-ton *Ice Bird* which Dr. Cunningham had sailed single-handed out from Ireland, and *Flo* from Panama, built by her owner. The final one to arrive just before Christmas was *Beyond*, a modern aluminium-alloy cutter in which our friends, Tom and Ann Worth, with Pete and Jane Taylor as crew, were making a two-year voyage round the world. They were greeted on arrival with a bath of disinfectant in which they had to paddle before landing, as they had come from Dominica where there was an outbreak of foot-and-mouth disease.

What fun it was, the day's work done and the cool of the evening spreading sweetly over the dockyard, to stroll along the old stone quays, stopping to chat with the various yachts' crews, or all to gather in the Nicholsons' house which we tended to treat more as a club than as the private dwelling of a kindly family. Sometimes we walked up to the Admiral's house with its four-poster bed and ant-proof larder, to browse among the relics there and to see how Rodney Nicholson was progressing with the making of *Mollyhawk*'s new staysail; for that job he was using the Admiral's study as a sail loft.

At the approach of Christmas the dockyard was invaded by calypso bands which serenaded the yachts. (*See p. 48.*) Mostly the instruments were home-made from biscuit tins and oil drums, tempered to produce excellent music; some of the players even drew melody from broken bottles, and there was one who got a bassoon-like note from a long, bent, iron pipe, a pipe which Commander Nicholson had missed from his workshop several weeks before. The syncopated music from these strange instruments, thrumming in the warm darkness, was exciting, and raised the short hairs on the nape of my neck.

On Christmas evening we all gathered in the Nicholsons' house, each bringing something to eat or drink. While we sat in their upstairs living-room, listening to a steel band which played on the quay outside the open door, the smell of cooking floated up from the kitchen below, and through the chinks in the floor we could see the red glow of the fires on which it was being done.

4

PANAMA

WE sailed round to St. Johns before leaving Antigua to fill our tanks with fresh water, a commodity which is difficult to come by at English Harbour, and to take aboard provisions for the 1,200-mile passage across the Caribbean Sea to Panama. *Moonraker* also came round, and Peter and Anne had a quiet dinner aboard with us. That was the last we saw of them until both yachts were back in England two and a half years later.

In the West Indies we had been told a lot about the winter trade wind, the general opinion being that it always sets in fresh a week before Christmas; so we expected to make a swift passage. For the first three days after leaving St. Johns, however, the wind was so light that the sails did not remain asleep for more than a few moments at a time, and our progress was slow. But during the third afternoon at sea the wind freshened, and from then on we averaged 125 miles a day. We took in the mainsail and set the twins to make *Wanderer* self-steering, but because of the chance of meeting other ships we kept night watches. Unfortunately the wind continued to strengthen until it reached moderate gale force, and naturally it raised a rough sea.

As there was no need for us to steer, Susan took the opportunity to experiment with the baking of bread. She had just got out her flour and yeast when *Wanderer* decided to work up to a particularly violent bout of rolling, throwing herself wildly from side to side. During one of these rolls the flour container was thrown on to the galley floor where it burst open. At once the mischievous wind, which was blowing strongly in through the main hatch, picked up the flour, distributed most of it with a lavish gesture throughout the cabin, on settees, books and bulkheads, and puffed the residue

like a cloud of smoke out through the forehatch. Poor Susan!
She referred to the yacht and her pedigree in anything but
ladylike terms as she cleaned up the mess. But little setbacks
like that never daunt her, and in spite of the upset we had for
lunch a hot, crusty ring loaf, all of which we ate with pleasure
but to the fury of our digestions.

Good baker's bread will keep aboard for ten days or sometimes even longer if the weather is cool and dry, though
naturally the mildewed outsides have to be cut off. But at
many of the places at which we called during our voyage the
only bread obtainable was of poor quality and turned sour
very quickly. So on our longer passages Susan used to bake
two or three times a week, using a ring baking dish (*see p.* 112)
in a small round oven, the dough being placed in a warm and
sheltered corner of the cockpit to rise. But in the tropics
baking was never popular because it raised the cabin temperature too much and made both cook and navigator rather
irritable.

In his mind's eye, the sailor pictures the surface of the world
as being criss-crossed by a great many lines, each one of which
means something definite to him: parallels of latitude, meridians
of longitude, the tropics of Cancer and Capricorn with the
equator midway between them, the boundaries of the time
zones, the lines of equal magnetic variation and the limits of the
trade wind zones—to mention but a few. All our previous
sailing had been done on the eastern side of the Atlantic where
the magnetic variation is westerly, i.e. the north point of the
compass points to the west of true north. As we made westing
the variation grew less until, when half way across the
Caribbean, we crossed one of those invisible lines to which
I have just referred, the line where there is no variation, and
for a short time the compass pointed to true north. Thereafter,
and until we reached the Indian Ocean, we were in an area of
easterly variation, a thing we found strange at first and difficult
to grow accustomed to, something similar to driving on the
right hand side of the road.

Towards the end of the passage the wind increased still
more in strength and several of the seams of the twin spinnakers
began to gape. These sails were of nylon which is a difficult
material to sew, and they had been seamed with thread which

had not the same stretch as the material, for at the time they were made not a lot was known about nylon sails. So we took them in and set the trysail instead. Under that the yacht went just as fast, but of course we then had to steer.

The sky became increasingly overcast with low, black, oily-looking clouds, and we began to worry about our landfall; for if we failed to get observations of sun or stars, we might easily overshoot our objective, and find ourselves approaching a lee shore in the Mosquito Gulf of which we had no large-scale chart. We felt as though we were running up a *cul-de-sac* out of which we might be unable to beat back against the strong wind and heavy sea, should the need arise. We could, of course, have hove-to and waited for better weather, but then we would have drifted in a north-westerly direction where some cays and reefs lay; also we knew that the trade wind can blow hard and the sky remain overcast for many days at a stretch. So we held on and relied on our dead reckoning.

Our fears, the kind to which small-boat voyagers are prone when tired, proved as they so often do to be groundless. The sun did shine on the day we expected to make our landfall, and we obtained some satisfactory observations with which to fix our position. The wind took off enough to permit us to set the reefed mainsail, and at dusk the light on Isola Grande off Manzanillo Point flashed its welcome.

At about the time we made our successful landfall we were circled several times by a pelican, a large bird with great wing span and an immense beak with a capacious pouch suspended from its lower mandible. Presently this pelican landed on the mainsheet close to Susan who was steering. The sheet was sagging and tautening with a jerk each time the yacht rolled, and fearing the bird might get its webbed feet caught in one of the blocks beside which it was standing, Susan boldly grabbed it and threw it up into the air with all her strength. This was not to the bird's liking. Again it circled us several times, grunting, and then once more settled on the sheet, but that time well out of reach near the end of the boom. The inevitable soon happened. *Wanderer* rolled her boom end under and, most discourteous treatment to her first Central American visitor, washed the bird off. It was soon airborne again but made no further attempt to land. We were to see many of these amusing great birds fishing at the south end of the Panama Canal. Each had a smaller bird of the gull family perched on its back, patiently waiting to pick up any scraps of food that might be left over. The pelicans did not seem to resent their passengers, or even to notice their presence.

Thirty miles ahead we could see in the night sky the loom of the lights of Cristobal and Colon, and presently, as we sailed towards them, up over the horizon lifted a bright flashing light.

'That,' I said to Susan, 'must be the eighteen-mile light on the end of the eastern breakwater,' and I left her to steer for it while I had a short rest below. I was tired, deadly tired, and I fell into a deep sleep almost at once, for my mind was at ease. We had made our landfall, there was nothing more to worry about, and ahead lay the port where we would soon be at anchor in smooth water. . . .

'Eric, Eric, come quickly!'

I was awakened from my sleep by Susan's anxious cry which was quite unlike the usual words at the change of the night watches; they usually run something like this: 'Darling, can you give me a spell-O?' followed shortly afterwards, if there is no response from the sleeper, by: 'I can't keep awake any longer.'

As I stuck my sleepy head out of the hatchway into the dark and windy night, Susan said:

'I can see houses between that light and us.'

I looked in the direction in which *Wanderer* was hurrying, and there sure enough saw the black shapes of buildings silhouetted against the flashing light. I hurried forward with fast-beating heart to let the boom guy go, then came aft and hauled in the main- and staysail sheets, while Susan, bringing the yacht on to the wind, steered obliquely out to sea. I then did what I ought to have done much earlier. I went below and examined the chart and checked the lights, and quickly discovered that the one for which I had told Susan to steer was an air beacon at the far side of the town. Another visit to the deck showed me the breakwater light, a feeble thing by comparison, winking solemnly away to the westward.

My idleness had nearly lost us our ship—not at sea, where the dangers are slight and there is plenty of room for mistakes, but close to port and with the passage nearly over. Only Susan's alert lookout and common sense had averted disaster.

An hour later we swept in between the great stone break-waters of the harbour on which the sea was breaking heavily. The booming of the surf was loud, but because of the strength of the wind and the noise of our progress, we did not hear it until we were very close, and I shuddered when I thought how near we had just been to the lee shore. A fast motor launch ranged up alongside, and a voice asked who we were and where from. Apparently satisfied with our answers, she sheered off into the darkness, and left us to grope our way to an anchorage, dazzled and bewildered by the neon advertising signs and bright lights of the town. At 4.30 a.m. we let the anchor go and fell into our bunks exhausted.

Next morning we were boarded from a skilfully handled launch, which was considerably longer than *Wanderer*, by three officials representing the health, immigration and canal authorities.

'Gee!' said one of them as they all crowded down into the cabin, 'and you've come all the way from England in this little thing.' He looked round him with interest, and then opened his briefcase on the table. 'Now, Cap, you won't be much good at the paper work, I guess, so we'd better do it for you.'

They then set to in a brisk, efficient manner, shooting questions at us and writing the answers on form after form, each of which I had to sign. One asked my age, and I told him 'Forty-four '. He wrote that down and said:

'And Mrs. Hiscock's thirty-nine.'

'However did you know?' I asked in some surprise, for that was her age.

Without looking up from his writing he replied: 'No dame is *ever* more than thirty-nine.'

If that was a typical sample of American tact, we felt we were going to like the Yanks.

Meanwhile the admeasurer was busy with his tape and rule, computing the tonnage on which canal dues would have to be paid, for this differs from the registered tonnage shown on the ship's papers.

Within a quarter of an hour all was done, and the launch left, only to return a few minutes later with the day's local paper and the welcome information that the Panama Canal Yacht Club would provide us with a berth if we liked to go along. So we motored a short distance up the old French canal to the club where we were met by the Commodore; he helped us berth with our anchor out ahead and our stern secured to the little wooden jetty so that we could go ashore without having to use the dinghy, and, had we wished for it, electricity and a telephone would have been laid on.

The American-occupied Panama Canal Zone is a strip of territory about ten miles wide with the canal running approximately through the centre of it. But the cities of Colon (at the north end) and Panama (at the south end), belong to the Republic of Panama. The set-up at the north end is a strange one, for the American town of Cristobal, where many of the canal employees live and where the administrative offices are, clings so closely to Colon that strangers, and sometimes even the inhabitants themselves, cannot tell where the one begins and the other ends; in fact it is possible to leave one town and enter the other simply by crossing a street. Yet the contrast is marked. Cristobal has wide, well-laid-out streets and gardens, with tall, modern, deep-eaved buildings, while some of the narrow alleys in Colon, where the shopkeepers, like spiders, try to induce one to enter, are not safe places for the stranger at night.

One does not have to drive far from the towns to see what the countryside is like, and every time we did so we marvelled afresh at the bravery of the French in attempting to drive a canal through it, and at the perseverance of the Americans in succeeding. Much of the land is swampy and covered with dark, silent, sinister and almost impenetrable jungle, an unhealthy place of heavy rain, great humidity and, until the Americans waged war on them, the breeding ground of malaria-carrying mosquitoes and many other insects. It is said that when the forty-seven miles of Colon to Panama railway was built, a life was lost through illness for every sleeper laid. But now the Zone is no longer unhealthy, for frequent spraying of the land and oiling of the swamps has exterminated most of the insects, and keeps under control those which arrive from the country each side of the Zone. We scarcely saw a fly, and never once a mosquito the whole time we were there.

The transit of the canal had been causing us some trepidation, for we had heard of several yachts having been damaged in the up-locks; when these are being filled by water rushing in through huge inlets in the floor, so great a disturbance is caused that small craft can get out of control and may then be thrown with force against the wall. We discussed the matter with members of the club, and various suggestions were made. 'Go through with a banana boat on Thursday and let her take all the bumps,' they said, 'or share the locks with another yacht.' Others told us 'If your pilot knows his job he will place you between the inlets where you will come to no harm'. Or again 'Lie alongside the wall; the danger has been much exaggerated, and more yachts have got through undamaged than you have ever heard of'.

All this was confusing. So Susan and I did what we usually do when local opinions differ—we formed our own plan of campaign. We agreed that the only safe procedure would be to have *Wanderer* held in the centre of each lock by four lines, one from each bow and one from each quarter; then no matter how much she might be tossed about by the inrushing water, she could come to no harm. So I went along to the dispatcher and asked whether this would be permitted.

'Certainly,' he said 'but you must provide your own lines, each at least 120 feet long, and you must have a separate person to handle each of them. When do you want to transit the canal?'

'How about tomorrow?' for I wished to have done with the business as soon as possible. To my relief the dispatcher at once agreed.

'With your little motor you'll take a long time, so I'll send you off for the first locking.'

I then called at the admeasurer's office for the tonnage certificate, paid the bill—the total charge including the services of a pilot (pilotage being compulsory) was $3.75, which certainly is wonderful value—and visited the Assistant Port Captain's office where it was arranged that a pilot would board us at 6 a.m. next day. And so, in a matter of minutes, all the complicated organization, exactly the same as for the largest merchant ship, was put in motion for our tiny vessel.

Viking had arrived a few days earlier, so we asked Sten and

Brita if they would help us by tending two of our lines in the up-locks at Gatun. They agreed readily, for *Viking* was to go through at a later date and they wanted to see what it really was like before making their own plans.

Shortly before dawn next morning we cast off from the jetty, weighed our anchor and went alongside *Viking* to collect our willing crew. Our pilot, Captain George White, came aboard and the searchlight from his launch played on our bows while I cleaned the soft mud from the anchor and washed down the deck. Then we motored out of the creek to take our place in the queue of ships already lining up in the first light of dawn to make the transit, all hands having breakfast of boiled eggs, toast and coffee as we went. There was no breath of wind to help us, and so slowly did our small motor move us along, that we missed the first locking but were in good time for the second. Astern of the freighter *Loch Avon* we crept into the vast lock, the first of a set of three; each in turn was to lift us up twenty-eight feet until we reached the level of Gatun Lake. Everything was ready for us; two heaving lines, with heavy monkeys' fists at their ends, came snaking out and down to us from the towering walls on either side. To these we fastened our bow warps, the strongest ropes we had on board, and they were at once hauled back to the walls and secured there by the steel-helmeted lock hands. The procedure was repeated with the ropes from the quarters, and *Wanderer* then lay securely held in the centre of the lock where she looked an insignificant speck, for the canal locks are 1,000 feet long and are capable of accommodating the largest merchant ships in the world today with the exception of the *Queen Mary* and the *Queen Elizabeth*. Silently the great gates closed behind us, shutting out the Atlantic, and almost at once the water in which we floated began to boil and swirl like a tide race as the level in the lock rose. Sten and I forward, and Brita and Susan aft, hauled in the slack of our lines foot by foot to keep the yacht firmly under control as she lifted with the rising water, rolling and tugging a little, while our pilot stood by the helm keeping an alert eye on everything. (*See p.* 48.) Within eight minutes we had risen up level with the top of the lock, the boiling of the water ceased, the gates ahead of us opened and the protecting chain was dropped. *Loch Avon* gave a kick ahead with her

propeller to help the mules (electric locomotives) to tow her
into the next chamber, sending a tremendous backwash which
caught us off our guard but fortunately did no harm. Then,
almost impudently it seemed, *Wanderer* followed the big ship
in, our lines being carried along by the lock hands. There the
process was repeated, and again in the third and last lock, from
which we were spilt out on to the broad waters of Gatun Lake,
a flooded jungle eighty-five feet above sea level.

We landed Sten and Brita, and then under both sail and
power, for there was very little wind, we set out to cross the
lake by way of the main shipping channel; elsewhere navigation
is dangerous because the trunks of the thousands of trees which
were drowned when the lake was made are still standing.
Sometimes the channel took us close past jungle-clad islands
where, when the motor died as it did once or twice owing to a
choked jet, we could hear the eerie cry of the puma and the
harsh grunting of wild boar. The sun burned down from a
brassy sky, for this was the dry season (January to March),
and it was very hot, but our pilot refused to relinquish the
helm even for a moment. Throughout the day he sat and
steered in the shade of our gaily striped golfing umbrella, and
every time a ship passed he raised the umbrella in salute to his
colleague on her bridge. He was an entertaining companion;
he told us yarns about the ships he had piloted, the anxious
and exciting moments he had experienced, and he drew our
attention to everything of note or interest. I fancy he enjoyed
himself as much as we did, for never before had he seen the
canal from such a low viewpoint.

Lunch was a cheery picnic affair eaten on deck, and was
finished before we arrived at the famous Gaillard Cut—the
'continental divide'—where a mountain was split in two to
make the canal. Then we came to the first of the down-locks
at Pedro Miguel. When going down there is no disturbance,
for the water runs out as from a giant bathtub; nevertheless, I
insisted on having the yacht held in a central position because,

PLATE 7

Top: At the approach of Christmas, calypso bands with home-made instruments
invaded the dockyard to serenade the yachts. *Bottom:* With our pilot at the helm
and Susan and Brita tending the quarter lines, we are lifted twenty-eight feet in
one of the giant locks of the Panama Canal.

if she had lain alongside, the slightest list, such as could be caused by someone moving about on deck, could cause her crosstrees to foul the wall, which is vertical. We felt very important when the Canadian freighter *Angus Glen* was stopped by signal at the lock entrance to let us in first. She was bound for Japan. As the first down-lock is separated from the other pair at Miraflores by the mile-long Miraflores Lake where overtaking is forbidden, we had the unusual experience of regulating the speed of that great ship, and although our little motor ran manfully, its indisposition of the morning long since forgotten, it could not quite achieve three knots.

We got a tremendous thrill when the seaward gate of the last lock slowly opened, and through the widening crack we had our first glimpse of the Pacific in the twilight. This is the greatest of all the oceans, and for the next year and a half we would be sailing among its countless coral reefs and islands if all went well with us. While we were still in the Atlantic there had always been the possibility of abandoning our circumnavigation if we wished to do so, and returning home by way of Bermuda; but, now that we had reached the Pacific, the best but much the longest way home was to keep on sailing to the westward. We felt that adventure lay ahead.

Night had fallen by the time we reached the yacht club at Balboa, but the club launch was standing by to show us to a mooring. There, after fourteen hours of his pleasant company, we said good-bye to George White who had brought us safely through the canal without so much as a scratch on our topsides.

Our berth lay close to the deep water channel where all day an almost constant procession of ships from most ports in the world slipped quietly by, entering or leaving the canal. It was strange, after the almost tideless waters of the Caribbean, to experience a rise and fall of fourteen feet and a stream so strong that it was at times difficult to row the dinghy against it. At this end of the canal there were a number of genuine cruising yachts, as opposed to the motor boats at Cristobal;

PLATE 8

Left: The sunlight sparkles on the water and the bow-wave roars; perfect sailing in the south-east trade wind. *Right:* In the shade of her broad-brimmed Madeira hat Susan peels the potatoes for lunch while she keeps an eye on the compass. With the spinnaker braces hitched to the tiller *Wanderer* steers herself.

A.W.W.—E

these were mostly sturdy ketches, with great beam, powerful motors and stumpy masts. Some of them had made trips out to the Galapagos Islands and back, and their owners took a great interest in our voyage, and helped us in many ways.

Before we had even washed up the breakfast things our first visitors came aboard with offers of hospitality; among them were Buz and June Champion, a delightful couple who were shortly to set out in their ketch *Little Bear* on a long voyage which they hoped in time would take them round the world. With the help of the kind Americans we spent ten busy and enjoyable days provisioning and generally preparing for our voyage out into the Pacific. Cars were always available to carry us into Balboa or Panama to do our shopping, or on sight-seeing expeditions; and many an evening we dined luxuriously in the cool, spacious homes of our friends, while our dirty laundry revolved in the very latest type of electric washing machine.

Nearly everyone asked us 'When are you leaving?' This did not mean that they were anxious to get rid of us, but was just their way of asking us how long we were staying. We told them Saturday 24 January. Early on the morning of that day they started coming out to say good-bye, and each brought a gift. These little offerings of candy, fruit, biscuits, tinned food, tea and tobacco, to mention but a few, piled up in the cabin to such an extent that we decided we could not put to sea with so many things lying about, but had better remain another day and try to get them stowed away in our already bulging lockers. This seemed to please our friends and one of them said:

'Well, that's just fine. Now you can come to the beach-combers' brawl tonight.'

'To what?' we asked, thinking we had not heard correctly.

'The beachcombers' brawl,' he repeated. 'It's nothing to do with dancing. It's a brawl, a party, and you come in your oldest clothes, or no clothes at all if you prefer.'

During the day we discovered that many people were going in fancy dress, and this worried us for we do not carry fancy dress in *Wanderer*. But presently we remembered that we had on board some old very tattered blue ensigns which we had kept with the intention of sewing new flies on them one day. So we put on our oldest and most ragged shirts and shorts, draped two of the tattered flags round our waists so that one hung in front and one behind, and went to the party as 'the impecunious British', which was something we thought the Americans would well understand.

The brawl was held in the American Legion Club, and one reached it by climbing a ladder and sliding down a shiny wooden chute, the idea being that those already present could see the new arrivals properly and one at a time. Each as he or she arrived was applauded, but when we, wearing our tattered ensigns, slid down the chute we were received in stony silence. We felt very embarrassed and as none of our friends had yet arrived we went and sat in a deserted corner. Presently a tough looking customer in ragged shorts and with matted black hair covering much of his bare, bronzed chest, came to our corner and in a threatening manner said:

'See here, you folks. I'd have you know there's a British yacht in port and', pointing to the blue ensigns on which we were sitting, 'that's no way to treat their flag.'

After explanations the party was most enjoyable, and we got aboard late.

5

FOUR THOUSAND MILES
AND NO LAND

NINE hundred miles south-west of Balboa the Galapagos Islands, famous for their zoological rarities, straddle the equator. It had been our intention to call at one or more of them to take aboard water and some fresh provisions for the long passage on to the Marquesas. But the Ecuadoreans, who own the group, charge so highly for the necessary permit, and in American dollars, that we could not afford one. When we learnt about this we said we would go without a permit and chance it: the worst that could happen might be a refusal to let us land, and surely the islanders would not deny us food and water. But Captain Bavistock, a senior canal pilot who knew the islands well and had sailed out to them on several occasions in his yacht *Inca*, warned us not to do so. He said that an Ecuadorean gunboat frequently visited the group, and it was not unknown for fishing boats and even yachts whose papers were not in order to be seized and their crews taken off to Ecuador. That was a risk we were not prepared to run, so when we left the outer buoy of the canal approach astern and headed away to sea, we were starting on what was to be our longest non-stop passage—4,000 miles of Pacific lay between us and Nukuhiva, our destination in the Marquesas group.

In order to reach the region of the south-east trade wind as quickly and directly as possible, and to avoid the area of calm which lies to the north of the Galapagos, we steered a course to leave those islands to starboard. But even by taking that route, which is the one recommended for sailing vessels, we expected the trip as far as the equator to be tedious on account of the calms, squalls, and contrary currents which are usually encountered there. We were, however, undertaking the trip at a favourable time of year when, according to the available information, there should be a fair proportion of north and north-east winds. That proved to be so, and as we dropped the land the fair wind became quite boisterous, calling for a deep reef in the mainsail and a small staysail, and *Wanderer* made a run of 140 miles her first day at sea. That did a lot to cheer us up at a time when we were preoccupied with sober thoughts.

We were not worried that our ship might let us down, for by then we had learnt to have complete faith in her. But 4,000 miles is a long sail, and after we had rounded the Galapagos our course would not pass near any recognized shipping route. Therefore, as we could expect no help from any other source should anything go wrong or one or other of us become ill or get injured, we must depend entirely on our own resources for everything. We had aboard most of the remedies for common ailments or wounds, and our first-aid kit even contained a set of dental tools and some intriguing shiny little instruments presented to us by dentist and doctor friends; but we doubted whether we had the skill or knowledge to use them should the need arise. Of food we should have an adequate supply, probably enough to last for ninety days, but, of course, anything we had forgotten would have to be done without, and we would certainly miss the fresh fruit and vegetables to which we were accustomed. We should also have plenty of water, for we knew from previous experience that even in hot weather five gallons lasted the two of us a week without rationing, and as our seventy gallons were in three separate tanks, we should not lose the lot if one tank were to spring a leak or its contents go bad. We had done everything we could think of to prepare for this passage, which could take forty days or a good deal longer, all depending on how long we took to reach the south-east trade wind. But we could not forget that Pizarro, the first to attempt to sail out of the Gulf of Panama, returned after beating about for seventy days, having been unable to get anywhere, and that most of the yachts which had made this trip before us had powerful motors and a large supply of fuel for them.

So, as we hurried along on our way, we were a little more silent than usual. But when, during our second day at sea, I did say something to Susan to the effect that this was a big undertaking we had embarked upon and that I had some feelings of apprehension about it, she replied:

'Never mind. If you were a daily-breader working in London, you would just now be trying to force your way into the crowded Bakerloo, and a hoarse voice would be shouting, "Mind the doors".'

It was noon with us. The sun, high overhead, was beating down to make the deck too hot for bare feet, even though we had recently painted the deck a lighter shade of green. Susan, in shorts and shirt, with her bare legs and arms tanned a healthy golden-brown, was sitting at the helm in the shade of her broad-brimmed Madeira hat which was gay with bits of sewn-on coloured material intended to represent flowers. All around was the bluest of blue sea over which our trim little floating home carried us swiftly. Yet, away back in London it was five o'clock of a January evening, probably cold, damp and foggy, and it would be rush hour there. Susan's sensible words brought me back to reality. How stupid and how ungrateful of me to worry about some purely imaginary trouble which was unlikely to occur, when we were living such a wonderfully free life—the life of our choice—and, as she reminded me, thousands of pale-faced office workers were at that moment fighting to get back to their homes in the suburbs.

In the evening of our third day at sea we passed close to barren, inaccessible Malpelo Island, towards which gannets were homing. The sea in its neighbourhood was uneasy with overfalls caused by strong currents, and after nightfall the island, which was the last land we were to see for many a day, looked unreal in the strange, thin light shed by the three-quarter eclipsed moon.

A week out from Balboa, during which time we had been fortunate, for the fair wind had never failed us though it had often been light (on one occasion we made a day's run of only forty-four miles) we crossed the equator. There Father Neptune initiated us into the Ancient Order of the Deep and, apparently pleased with his new subjects, ordered the outstretched fingers of the south-east trade wind to caress our sails. They obeyed, and by the tenth day had brought us to a position fifty miles south of Hood Island, which is the south-easternmost of the Galapagos. There we altered course direct for the Marquesas, some three thousand miles away to the westward.

For the first week on the new course the wind had very little east in it and was mostly just abaft the beam. It varied in strength between ten and twenty-five knots, so that sometimes we could carry the big genoa and at others were reduced to the reefed mainsail and working staysail. We moved along well, but we soon found that we could not drive the yacht as hard as we would have wished, for with a lumpy beam sea the motion was so quick and jerky when the speed exceeded six knots, and the roaring of the bow-wave was so loud, that neither of us could sleep properly during our watches below. For two days we carried on under a press of sail, expecting that we would get used to the motion and the noise in time; but as we did not we reluctantly reduced sail, and from then on rarely exceeded five and a half knots, but we did get some sound sleep. Unfortunately *Wanderer* could not be left to look after herself on that point of sailing, and day and night, week after week, for three tiring weeks, we had to steer watch and watch, and that left little time for anything except essentials.

To start with the weather was a little unsettled, perhaps due to the proximity of the Galapagos and the cold Humboldt current; the nights were overcast and there was rain at times. But as we drew away out into the wide ocean, the weather was as we always imagined it should be in the trade wind areas. Day followed day with the sun shining from out of a bright blue sky across which marched battalions of puffy little trade wind clouds; although there were so many of them—quite close-packed above the horizon—they rarely cast a shadow over us. The sea, more than two miles deep out there, was of that indescribably vivid off-soundings blue with a hint of purple in it, a colour impossible to describe, but which some marine artists, such as Charles Pears and P. C. Thurburn, have succeeded in putting on canvas. A long swell rose and fell in easy undulations, and on top of this ran a short sea with flashing whitecaps here and there. We found the Pacific was more uncomfortable than the homely Atlantic. Often there was a cross sea or a swell from some other direction than the wind, and frequently it appeared that there was more sea running than was justified by the weight or duration of the wind.

The nights were just as magnificent as the days. Early in

the evening we would watch two of the planets carve their way down across the western sky to sink ahead of us, and see Orion with all his glorious bodyguard sprawling across the sky above the gyrating masthead. Later our old friend the Plough, upside down of course, appeared to the north of us, and away on the port beam stood the Southern Cross; this, though not a startling constellation, is the best in the southern firmament and is remarkable for the Coal Sack, a patch of starless sky, jet black by comparison with the rest of the heavens, within its bounds. Bow-wave and wake, and breaking crests all round, were usually brilliant with pale green phosphorescent light, and the yacht's passage through the water often kindled mysterious discs of light the size of dinner plates which floated away in her wake. But the moon was our favourite night companion, for although she was of less interest to us than the stars, she shed more light to help keep the drowsy helmsman awake, and when her lovely silver track shone directly astern, it emphasized in the tumbling disturbed water of our wake the sensation of speed. One dark night we sailed through a patch of sea so phosphorescent that it looked as though a large quantity of luminous paint had been spilt there; its boundaries were clearly defined, and we judged it to measure 300 feet by 80.

All this wonder, we liked to think, was laid on specially for our benefit, with some magnificent sunrises and sunsets thrown in; certainly there was no one else to enjoy it out there. Of man and all his works we never saw a sign; no ship passed within our range of vision, and even the ether was almost free of morse when each evening I searched about on the short-wave band of the radio receiver for a time signal with which to check the chronometer.

On most days we had a few storm-petrels with us. Noddies often used us as a centre for their fishing operations; they caught flying fish on the wing when shoals of those beautiful little creatures, chased no doubt by some larger fish, shot out of the sea to become air-borne for fifty yards or so, the birds' movements being almost too quick to be followed by the human eye. The red fly of our masthead burgee was a source of interest and sometimes of annoyance to them; for hours they flew beside it, intently watching it flap, and every now and again made an attempt to peck it, but always at the crucial moment *Wanderer* lurched and snatched it away. On many an evening, shortly after dark, a school of performing dolphin came to give their show. For half an hour or more these playful, friendly, high-speed people gave a fascinating display of swimming close around the bows and under the keel, then, as suddenly as they had come, they vanished. Phosphorescence, caused by their passage through the water, illuminated them clearly, and their criss-crossed radiant wakes wove an intricate pattern in the inky sea. Once two pairs of whales, cruising in the direction of Peru, altered course to examine us at very close quarters, but much to our relief found us of little interest and then continued on their ponderous, unhurried way. Always there was something to entertain or interest us. If there were no birds or fish there was always the ever changing beauty of the sea itself. The ocean on which we sailed was a vast, colourful desert, something so great and indifferent that our tiny vessel, with straining sails and hissing wake which was obliterated a few seconds after she had passed, seemed indeed a puny thing, allowed to continue safely on her way on sufferance.

There is a lot of blank white space on the chart between the Galapagos and Marquesas, and at the beginning of that long passage it seemed almost impossible that our tiny daily steps, each marked by a pencilled cross, could ever reach out far enough to bridge the gap. It was only then that we realized properly the immensity of the ocean and the magnitude of the task we had set ourselves. The drawing of those crosses was a matter of great interest to us, for we hoped at noon each day to find we had bettered the previous day's run, and we looked forward to finding ourselves in the south equatorial current, a west-setting stream which could give us anything up to forty free miles a day in the right direction. The only means of knowing whether in the past twenty-four hours there had been any current, and, if so, in what direction it had been setting and at what speed, was to compare the position obtained by observations of the heavenly bodies with the position obtained by dead reckoning, i.e. having regard to the course steered and the distance sailed as measured by the patent log. On that crossing we experienced remarkably little current; the most we ever had was ten miles a day, and most days there was none.

It seems to me very wonderful that it is possible to find one's position on the surface of a featureless ocean by taking observations of the very distant sun, moon, stars or planets; yet that is not a difficult thing to do. Anyone can learn this kind of navigation in a few hours if he uses one of the modern methods devised for aircraft, for only a little simple addition and subtraction is called for, and although it is an advantage to understand the theory, that is not essential. The only skilled part of the business is the actual taking of the observation with the sextant, especially from the low view-point of the deck of a small yacht which is being thrown violently about by a rough sea. Nothing but practice, and one gets plenty of that on a long voyage, can make one adept at this, for it is only during the brief moment when the yacht is perched on the top of the highest sea running at the time, that the angle between the celestial body and the horizon can be measured accurately.

I found the best position for the taking of sights was in the main hatchway, where I could wedge myself with my hips firmly braced yet leaving the upper part of my body free to swing and remain upright no matter what antics the yacht performed. I focused the sextant telescope and swung the most suitable coloured glass shades into position, for, in common with most sextant boxes, mine is arranged in such a way that the shades have all to be hinged inwards and the telescope unfocused each time the instrument is put away. Then Susan concentrated on holding as steady a course as possible, perhaps a different one from that she had been steering so as to allow me an unobstructed view clear of sails and rigging, and I, looking at the horizon through the telescope, moved the index bar to bring the reflected image of the sun down until it was close to the water. As *Wanderer* rose on a sea and the level horizon became visible, I turned the tangent screw (the fine adjustment) to try to bring the lower limb of the sun into contact with the horizon; but before I had done so down would go the yacht into the trough, and the sun appeared to be buried in the sea. Next time the yacht rose I closed the gap, but she would almost certainly drop again before I was sure of the contact, and perhaps I would have to wait half a minute or so before another good opportu ity offered. In that time the sun had moved a bit, and again adjustment of the tangent screw was needed. This trial-and-error game could go on for quite a time.

Sometimes, just as I thought I was about to get a perfect sight, a cloud moved over the sun, either obscuring or dimming him, so that a change of glass shades was needed. An additional complication is that, to be sure a perfect contact has been made between the reflected sun and the horizon, it is necessary to swing the sextant through a small vertical arc to be certain that it is upright at the time of contact, otherwise a considerable error can creep in. There is not much time to do this before the yacht drops into the trough again. Sometimes, when the wind was fresh and abeam or on the quarter, I had to lower the instrument quickly when I heard the rush of an approaching crest, so that it should be protected by my body or the hatch-way from a shower of spray.

'Right,' I said to Susan when I felt quite satisfied that the observation was a good one, and she immediately started the stopwatch. Going below, I put the sextant gently in a safe place on the lee berth, opened the lid of the chronometer box, and when the minute hand was exactly on a minute and the second hand at zero, I again called to Susan and she stopped the watch. By taking from the chronometer reading the time shown to have elapsed by the stopwatch, and adding or subtracting the amount I knew the chronometer to be slow or fast, I obtained the Greenwich time when the sight was taken. Finally I read the angle in degrees and minutes shown by the sextant before replacing that instrument in its box.

It is sometimes thought that the difficulty of seeing the horizon when the sea is rough, or when taking star sights, which can normally be done only when the horizon is visible at dawn or dusk, can be overcome by using an artificial bubble horizon. Sextants making use of such a device are used in aircraft, and bubble horizons can be fitted to marine sextants, but in my opinion they are of no use in a small vessel where, even in quiet weather, the movement is sufficient to bounce the bubble from side to side of its chamber.

For most forms of navigation by observations of the celestial bodies it is essential to know Greenwich mean time. We got this from a small chronometer watch slung on gimbals in a glass-topped wooden box. As a change of temperature or a

change in the motion of the yacht could affect its rate, we
checked it each day when possible by radio time signals. In the
Pacific the B.B.C. overseas service was difficult to get, so we
used the American station which is known as WWV. This
gives the time in clear language and in morse every five
minutes throughout the twenty-four hours. How relieved I used
to feel when, faintly among the atmospherics in the earphones,
came the measured ' tick-tock ' which is a feature of this
broadcast, and then the well-remembered voice saying 'This is
station WWV. When the tone returns, eastern standard time
will be . . .'

But Greenwich time was used for navigational purposes only.
On board we mostly kept zone time. As one sails away to the
westward the sun rises and sets later and later, an hour later
for every fifteen degrees of longitude. Instead of putting our
wrist watches and the cabin clock back a few minutes each
day to coincide with noon as shown by the sun reaching his
zenith, we did it a whole hour at a time when we entered a
new fifteen-degree time zone, or whenever it seemed convenient. If, for example, there had been a lot of things to do
one forenoon, or the dough had taken a longer time than usual
to rise and it appeared as though lunch was going to be very
late, we altered our clocks then; but we never altered them in
order to conform with the slavish habits of other inhabitants
of our part of the ocean. On the voyage from Panama to
Marquesas we put our clock and watches back a total of four
hours.

And so, day after day the little crosses showing our noon
positions crept out in an almost straight line across the chart,
aiming at the specks of the distant Marquesas, and although
the days were uneventful they were never dull, for there was
always much to be done. This was our usual daily routine.

At midday, as soon as I had taken the noon sight, worked
out the position, discovered what the day's run had been and
written up the log, I took the helm while Susan cooked the
lunch. She ate hers first, then I had mine, washed up and turned
into my bunk for two hours to try to make up some of the sleep
lost during the previous night. Often the cabin was too hot, or
there was too much motion to permit me to sleep readily, and
then I lay tossing from side to side trying to avoid the shafts of

sunlight which came in through the portholes and decklights and went chasing swiftly to and fro as the yacht rolled. At 3.30 p.m., sticky and not much rested, I went on deck and poured buckets of sea water over myself before relieving Susan. She was better at daytime sleeping than I was, and often I had difficulty in waking her.

As we made westing, the wind hauled round towards the east and permitted us to set a spinnaker. This helped to balance the pull of the mainsail and made steering easier, so that when the wind lightened a bit in the afternoon, as it often did, it was sometimes possible for the helmsman to read, *Wanderer* needing only an occasional touch on the tiller to keep her on the course. Once or twice we even managed to get down out of the blazing sunshine and steer from the cabin. A line from the weather side of the tiller was then led through a block and thence to the watchkeeper's foot, so that he could move the tiller up whenever the telltale compass beside him showed that to be necessary, without having to put aside his book.

At sundown I woke Susan and we sat together in the cockpit, talking about all manner of things—that was the only time we really did have for talking—admiring the sunset and enjoying our evening tot, just as we used to do in the Atlantic. All too soon it was supper time. Susan got the meal and ate hers first, while I at the helm steered into absolute blackness if there was no moon, for the cabin lamps shining out through the hatchway blinded me. At 9 p.m. Susan took over on deck while I turned in, and usually I went sound asleep the moment my head touched the pillow.

During most of our long passages we found it necessary to divide the night into four watches, taking two each. But on the Pacific trip we somehow managed to keep awake better and were able to split the night into two equal parts, Susan taking from 9 p.m. until 1.30 a.m., and I from then until 6 a.m. This was certainly the better arrangement, as a four-and-a-half-hour spell below does give one the chance for a real sleep. But, of course, there were many occasions when the watch below had to be roused out to take in or make more sail, for we never ran any risk of damage to the gear by carrying too much sail in a rising wind, though we always tried to keep *Wanderer* going to the best advantage. So we were usually short of sleep. As I always had the last of the night watches I always got the breakfast, and unless the weather conditions were particularly bad, Susan ate hers at the helm.

Throughout the forenoon we kept no regular watches, for that was a period for odd jobs and daily chores. Susan steered while I cleaned out the cabin, trimmed the lamps, filled them and the stove, took the morning sight, worked it out, and attended to any repairs or alteration of the gear. Then I steered while Susan washed up the supper and breakfast things, made a loaf or cake and prepared the lunch; and before it was once again time for the noon sight and for the twenty-four-hour routine to start all over again, we usually managed to get half an hour or so with our feet up and a book to read.

You will see from this that there was no 'poor weak woman' nonsense about Susan. She shared the night watches equally with me, and in the daytime often had more than her fair share of steering because I had so many little jobs to attend to.

Sleep was our one big problem. We never got enough of it. At night the swinging luminous lines of the grid steering compass mesmerized me as I tried to keep them parallel, and with nothing else but the stars to see, and only drowsy thoughts to occupy my mind, I found myself nodding off to sleep again and again. Each time that happened I struggled to my feet, forced myself to look carefully round the horizon, where there was never anything to be seen, and for a few minutes stood with my feet as wide apart as the cockpit floor allowed, flexing first one leg then the other to remain upright as the yacht rolled. Then I settled down again in a new position on the cockpit seat and enjoyed for a time the serene loveliness of the night and our bustling progress through it, while I nibbled chocolate or munched a biscuit. But presently I dozed off again, to wake with a start as my head fell forward, and find *Wanderer* several points off her course. Then I had to repeat the whole process of keeping awake. In this way the hours dragged slowly past until the first faint hint of dawn began to pale the eastern sky and there was only another hour to go before I could call Susan to relieve me. I decided not to look at my wrist watch again for at least fifteen minutes. After waiting what I judged to be that length of time, I held on for another five minutes so as to be quite sure, only to discover on looking at my watch that not more than three or four minutes had passed since I last looked at it. What a wonderful relief it was when eventually the sun lifted above the horizon, Susan took over at the tiller, and soon after I had lit the stove the reviving aroma of hot coffee drifted out of the galley.

Susan, I know, suffered from sleepiness during her night watches just as badly as I did. Sometimes I woke up during my watch below and looked out through the open hatchway to where the outline of her head and shoulders should be visible against the swaying stars—and saw nothing. With a wildly beating heart, for one of my constant fears was that, in spite of lifeline and guardrails, she might fall or be thrown overboard and that I should not hear her cry out, I investigated and found her with her hand still on the tiller holding the yacht on the course, but with her body slumped over sideways so that her sleep-heavy head was resting on the seat beside her.

The sad thing about our lack of sleep was that it left us in no fit condition to enjoy to the full the wonderful experience of making such a voyage. We could not properly appreciate the satisfying sensation of steady progress as the trade wind hummed a tune in the taut rigging, and the bow-wave flashed and chuckled. Neither were we able to get the full value from the magnificence of the days and nights, as the great ocean swell slowly rolled up on the port quarter to lift our tiny vessel up and up until from the summit we had a momentary view of the horizon all round.

But after three weeks of constant steering there came a day when the wind died, and at last we could leave the lifeless helm. Normally a calm is a hateful thing, but this one gave us a much needed rest. When the wind returned next day it came from the east, almost dead astern, so we set the twins and got *Wanderer* to steer herself. What a relief that was, and how we enjoyed the luxury of being able to lie in our bunks, sleeping, reading, or just being lazy, and to be able to eat our meals together and to talk. And later, when we felt more energetic, we attended to some of the long-neglected jobs, such as picking over the potatoes and onions, developing some films, and scrubbing off the weed which had grown on the long-submerged starboard side. It does seem remarkable that in the warm water of the tropics weed can get a hold and flourish on a yacht's smooth side when it is moving fast through the water; but even more remarkable is the industry and stamina of the marine creatures which attach themselves securely to the trailing log-line where, within two weeks, they grow to the size and shape of cloves, for not only is the line moving forward at an average speed of 5 knots but it is spinning fast all the time.

With the sun shining every day navigation presented no problems until the time came when we met the sun coming north. Then for three days, when his declination was much the same as our latitude, he was so nearly overhead at noon that I was unable to get a meridian altitude. I suppose that from the comparatively steady deck of a large vessel there should be no difficulty, but from *Wanderer's* heaving deck I found it to be impossible, for the sun at the crucial moment changed his bearing from east to west too fast for me. However, three star sights each evening gave a perfect fix, and by the time we were approaching our destination, the sun was again available at noon; but it did seem strange to face north instead of south when observing him.

For eight days we continued running under the twins and were then about two days' sail from the Marquesas. Our sleepiness long since forgotten, we took in one of the twins and set the mainsail in its place, and instantly *Wanderer* gathered her skirts about her and settled down to her six-knot stride.

It was at 10.30 p.m. on our thirty-sixth day at sea that the newly-risen moon showed us the silver-grey lump of Ua Huka island fine on the starboard bow. That was the greatest moment of our passage: our chosen landfall island appearing just where it should be and at the right time, too. Mysterious it looked in the moonlight, its mountain peaks part-hidden in a pile of cumulus clouds, and no gleam of light shone from it, so it was hard to believe the island was inhabited, as indeed it is. But as it offers no good anchorage we hurried along close past its southern shore where we could see the swell breaking high, and continued on our way for Nukuhiva, twenty-four miles to the

---

PLATE 9

Top: At dawn Nukuhiva lay close ahead, the first rays of the rising sun dispelling the mist in which it was partly shrouded. *Bottom:* After her 4,000-mile passage from Panama *Wanderer* lies resting in Taiohae Bay, Marquesas, her first South Sea island anchorage.

westward. At dawn Nukuhiva lay close ahead and looked particularly grand as the first rays of the rising sun began to dispel the mist in which it was partly shrouded. (*See p.* 64.) But of our landfall island there was not a sign; it had vanished astern. Were it not for the chart, we might have imagined our sight of it to have been just a dream.

A large party of dolphins convoyed us to Nukuhiva as we sped on past Cape Martin to the Sentinel Rocks. From there we worked our way with some difficulty, because of the calms and fierce puffs of wind, to the head of Taiohae Bay, and at breakfast time let the anchor go in two fathoms close to the little landing beach.

PLATE 10

Top: Those valiant Swedes, Sten and Brita Holmdahl, also made a circumnavigation of the world and took only two years over it. *Centre:* At Tahiti we were delighted to meet Frank McNulty, one of the two Australians who had sailed our previous yacht out to the Pacific, and Tom and Diana Hepworth of the Brixham trawler *Arthur Rogers. Bottom left:* Nerves of steel and searchlights for eyes: Captain Argod of the schooner *Oiseau des Iles. Bottom right:* Trader Bob McKetterick spins a yarn.

A.W.W.——F

6

NUKUHIVA AND TAHITI

O N three sides our anchorage was closely hemmed in by steep mountains, their basaltic summits rugged and barren, but with luxuriant vegetation covering their lower slopes and the valleys. The fourth side was open to the southern ocean; so the swell rolled in to break on the black sand and shingle beaches, and kept *Wanderer* rolling and pitching uneasily in the backwash. Along the narrow strip of flat ground between the sea and the foothills straggled the thatch- and iron-roofed houses of the village of Taiohae, almost hidden among the palms and breadfruit trees. The fragrant scent of frangipani and wood smoke was wafted out to us whenever a puff of wind came from that direction.

In response to our code flag 'Q', a halfcaste medical attendant from the hospital came off to us in a canoe, for the French doctor was away visiting another island, and grumpily gave us pratique. He puffed his cheeks, fanned his overheated body with a highly scented handkerchief, and complained of the heat in the cabin; that certainly was considerable, for the morning was warm and humid and the stove on which we had just cooked breakfast had not yet cooled. We were as glad to get rid of him as he was to go. After we had tidied up on board and washed ourselves, we launched the dinghy and rowed ashore to pay our respects to the young French Administrator. Then we visited the tiny post office which was almost concealed by a grove of brilliantly flowering *flamboyant* trees, their wide spread branches ablaze with scarlet blooms; finding it had regular radio communication with Tahiti, we sent radiograms to our people at home. Next on our list was a visit to trader Bob McKetterick who was the only Briton in the group. Our way led along the shady road which skirts the bay, and as we were about to pass one of the bamboo and thatch houses that stood beside it, a fine, upstanding native came out, and beckoning to us, invited us to sit on the grass in front of it with his wife and family, among the horses, dogs and fowls, while he opened drinking nuts for our refreshment. He gave a few sharp blows with a machete on one end of the nut, and a small hole appeared; through this we drank the milk. Then, after some more judicious blows, the nut was split in half, a sort of spoon was fashioned from part of the husk, and with this we scraped out and ate the meat. It looked so simple that it was not until we had tried our hands at opening coconuts on board and had broken a hacksaw blade, bent two screwdrivers, driven a chisel in beyond recall, and dented the stainless steel galley bench and still failed to get inside the nut, that we began to realize what skill is needed. The more usual method of doing this job is to drive a sharp stake, preferably of steel, into the ground and to bang the fat end of the nut down on it. But we were unable to fit up anything of that kind aboard *Wanderer*.

A little farther along the road we came to the trader's store and house, and found Bob in a white shirt and brilliant red and white *pareu* taking his ease on the verandah and gazing out over his flowering hedge to where *Wanderer* lay in the bay, resting after her 4,000-mile passage from Panama. (*See p. 64.*) He received us kindly, and we soon came to know him well, for each day during our stay we used to stroll along to his house and share a jug of iced lime with him while we listened to his entertaining yarns. We found it hard to believe him when he told us that in his opinion the smiling friendly islanders would quickly revert to cannibalism, which was practised in the Marquesas less than a hundred years ago, if they could only get rid of their French rulers; but as he had been among the islands for the best part of thirty years, he should be in a better position than most people to judge. However, with Bob you never can tell whether he is pulling your leg or not; he is a great spinner of yarns and as he chatters on with an accent oddly reminiscent of France and Liverpool, there is always a twinkle in his eye. (*See p. 65.*) It was at Bob's home, after we had enjoyed a fine lunch with him and his Marquesan wife, that we first made the acquaintance of *Pim*, as *The Pacific Island Monthly* magazine is affectionately known by its many readers. Its fascinating cross-section of island news contains all manner of interesting items for islanders and island travellers. The inside story of why the Mayor of Papeete refused to fight a duel; a stunning exposure of the stamp racket in the Tokelaus; the current prices of copra and shell; news of the little ships, schooners, yachts and mission vessels; a damning account of travel in a New Zealand inter-island ship—these were some of the piquant features of the first issue we picked up. To those who have been to the islands, just to thumb through a copy of this journal is to smell once more the cloying stench of copra and the sweet aroma of vanilla, and to hear once more the shrill scream of pigs protesting their passage aboard some down-at-heel schooner, the soft music of guitars, and the thunder of the swell on a coral reef.

Beautiful though Nukuhiva is, we did not care for it much. European interference, greed and disease, very nearly brought about the extinction of the fine race that belongs there, and we thought it a sad, silent, and much too empty place; everywhere the foundations of houses now deeply buried in undergrowth speak of a depleted population. In 1941 the total population of the group was only 2,400, while in 1880 that was the population of Hiva Oa alone, just one of the islands. But Bob assured us that the birthrate was now increasing rapidly.

We had other reasons for not enjoying the place. The hot, wet weather we experienced during our stay prevented us from making up much of the sleep we had lost on the long sea passage. Every night we had to get up in a hurry to close the ports and hatches against torrential downpours of rain; that made the cabin so airless that we lay restlessly waiting for the rain to stop so that we might open up again, only to have to shut up once more a few minutes later. As a result we felt tired and lethargic. The constant motion of the yacht caused by the swell prevented us from making the enlargements necessary for illustrating the serials I was writing for *Yachting World* and American *Yachting*, and I was anxious to post the latest instalments the moment we arrived at Tahiti, for it was only by selling articles regularly that we could continue to pay for our cruise. So we moved five miles along the coast to a cove called Tai Oa, which we judged from the chart might offer a quieter berth. Harry Pidgeon on his voyage round the world in

Islander called there in 1922, but we had not heard of it being visited by any other yacht.

The entrance to Tai Oa was not easy to find, for it was narrow with overlapping points; the chart was on so small a scale as to be of little help, and the *Pacific Islands Pilot*, abandoning for once its precise information, stated that the eastern point was 'of some elevation'. But we did find it, and most spectacular it looked with a cliff rising almost sheer for 2,000 feet on its western side. There was an awkward, jumpy little sea running and not a breath of wind close in under the lee of the island, so we motored, and when we had rounded the sheltering point we found ourselves in a beautiful pool of green water with a white sand beach at its head. The pool was bounded on three sides by low, scrub-covered hills, and on the fourth by that fantastic cliff. The cliff continued in an inland direction where a mountain torrent poured down a narrow ravine, deep cut in it, to form a swift flowing stream which hastened through a shady, palm-filled valley to the cove. We brought up close to the beach in the farthest corner, and as there was a slight swell even in there, we laid out a second anchor from the stern to keep the yacht end on to the swell so that although she might pitch slightly she could not roll.

We remained four days in that lovely spot while Susan drew sketch charts and dried and glazed the enlargements which I made in the blacked-out forepeak. At night the silence in the cove was eerie; only the muffled rumble of the surf outside, and the occasional splash of some large fish jumping, broke the stillness. But the *nono*, a small black fly peculiar to the Marquesas and having a bite more irritating than that of a mosquito, liable to swell and become septic, was a pest. Hot and humid though the weather was, we were compelled to screen the ports and hatches with mosquito netting in the daytime, though that much restricted the ventilation down below. But fortunately the *nono* does not feed at night, so after sunset we were able to open up and let some fresh air into the cabin and have a bucket bath on deck. We did not bathe over the side while at Nukuhiva because a man-eating shark, said to be as long as the counter in Bob's trading store, was reported to be cruising in the bay and on the coast.

On two occasions we landed. The first time was on the beach,

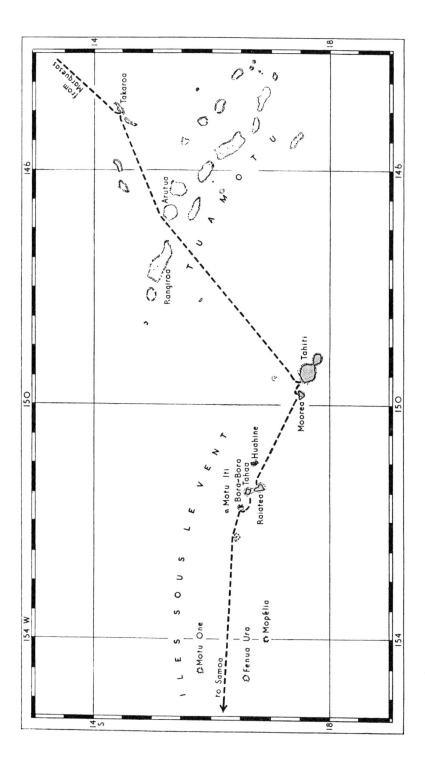

from Marquesas

Takaroa

Arutua

Rangiroa

T U A M O T U

Tahiti

Moorea

I L E S S O U S L E V E N T

Huahine
Tahaa
Bora-Bora
Motu Iti
Raiatea

Motu One

Fenua Ura

Mopélia

to Samoa

14
18
146
146
150
150
154 W
154
14 S
18

from which we made our way through the undergrowth to the summit of one of the hills to admire the view. Then we rowed across the cove and landed at the mouth of the stream, where we found the remains of a large village which had once possessed a broad street; but now the encroaching jungle had buried the ruins and narrowed the street to a mere track. There were only three inhabited houses there. A handsome Marquesan woman invited us into one of them to eat papaya close to a smoky fire over which her husband was crouching to get a respite from the attentions of the flies, mosquitoes and *nonos* with which the room was infested. Then, with the woman as our guide, we forded the stream and made our way through a coconut plantation where the silver light shone diagonally among the palms to lend the place the appearance of a vast cathedral. The palms grew right up to the foot of the great cliff, and there in a cave we were shown the remains of a war canoe, a big dugout measuring forty feet by three and a half; but as the bow and stern had been cut off, we could not tell its original length. On both these expeditions we wore as protection against the insects, and in spite of the intense heat, trousers and long-sleeved shirts buttoned to our chins; but even they did not defeat the *nonos*; on our return from the village we counted ninety-seven bites on one of Susan's legs. We were not sorry, therefore, when, our work completed, we were able to leave Tai Oa, and as we motored out in a calm we were much relieved to see the *nonos* in twos and threes abandoning ship. Within half an hour of leaving the entrance, when we picked up the trade wind clear of the high land, not one remained aboard.

In the Pacific there are three main types of island. One is the high island without a protecting reef, usually of volcanic origin and rising sheer from the sea; the Marquesas are of this type. Then there is the high island, surrounded or partly surrounded by a coral barrier reef, the sheltered water of the lagoon between the reef and the island forming a natural harbour; the Society Islands are of this kind. Finally there is the atoll, a ring of coral, parts of which may rise a few feet above the sea, enclosing a lagoon. The Tuamotu, or Low Islands, among which we had next to find our way, are all of this last type, forming an archipelago of seventy-eight atolls which lies right across the track of vessels bound from the Marquesas to Tahiti. It can only be avoided by making a detour to the north of the direct course, and then for the final 150 miles of the passage in a southerly direction one would be close-hauled, or perhaps even turning to windward. We therefore decided to pass through among the atolls, where there is a choice of several routes. We chose to pass close north of Takaroa. Clumps of trees grow on all sides of that atoll, making it safe to approach, whereas some of the other atolls have large areas of reef which are awash and can be dangerous at night. We intended to stop for a day or two at Takaroa if conditions were suitable. From there our proposed route would take us between Arutua and Rangiroa. These again would be safe to approach, for the former is wooded on its northern side, close to which we would pass, and the other is wooded all round.

For the first three days of the trip we had fine settled weather, though rather light winds, and we used such spare time as we had in looking up all the available information about the Tuamotu, which in truth was not a lot. Though every island was mentioned in the *Pilot*, all are apparently so similar that it would be easy to mistake one for another, and the following note printed on the chart was not encouraging.

'The native name Tuamotu signifies distant islands. The appellation "Dangerous" has been applied to this archipelago by seamen, and deservedly so, for numerous coral islets, all low and some extensive, obstruct the navigation; while unknown currents and strong squalls, and a total want of soundings, add to the risk of sailing, especially at night. Singular interruptions to the trade wind are caused by these low lagoon islands; not only does the customary wind often fail among them, but heavy squalls come from the opposite direction, and more frequently by night than by day. The details have been collected from the voyages of various navigators extending over a long series of years; the relative positions therefore may not, in all cases, be exactly given, while there may be others still undiscovered, rendering extreme caution necessary on the part of the navigator while sailing among these low reefy islands.'

This gloomy little essay did nothing to cheer us up, especially when, at supper time on the night we expected to make our landfall on Takaroa, a barrage of squalls began. Black as soot they were, each bringing with it a tremendous downpour of rain, a thirty-five-knot wind and blinding flashes of lightning with peals of thunder. Other sailing people who plan to go that way will be glad to know that the Tuamotu have recently been re-surveyed by the ketch *Zelée* of the French navy, and that all the islands have now been exactly located and the off-lying reefs of all the big atolls have been triangulated; up-to-date French charts of the group are now available.

By 2.30 a.m. the night looked so threatening and the visibility seemed to be so poor, that although Takaroa still lay twelve miles ahead according to our reckoning, we grew so nervous of approaching it that we hove-to and kept watches on deck until dawn, when the squalls died out and the sky cleared. At 6.30 a.m. in bright sunshine we let draw on the course, and an hour later sighted what we took to be Takaroa fine on the weather bow, just an irregular line of palm fronds lifting momentarily above the tumbling horizon as *Wanderer* climbed to the top of the swell.

Very soon much of the fifteen-mile-long atoll was in view; a white coral beach on which the swell broke to send a fine spray, like smoke, high into the air where the sun made rainbows in it; the beach was backed by a bright green band of thick scrub out of which protruded the heads of many palms. Here and there the line was broken, and through the gaps as we sailed along we got occasional glimpses of the smooth, pale green water of the sheltered lagoon within. Any doubts we may have had about this being Takaroa were dispelled when we sighted the wreck of the sailing ship *County of Roxburgh*, which went ashore there in a hurricane in 1906, and now lies high up on the white beach, a contrasting, rusty red.

There is only one pass into Takaroa's lagoon, and, as is usual on atolls, that lies on the leeward side. We sailed fast and were soon up with it, but to enter was impossible. The wind was funnelling out almost with gale force, and a strong current boiled out through the narrow cut between the jagged coral reefs to rip the long swell outside into choppy white crests. There was no possibility of beating in, and our low-powered motor was useless in such conditions. There was no suitable anchorage outside, while to stand on and off waiting for the wind to moderate might keep us jilling about there for days or even weeks. So, with only a fleeting sight of the village clustered round its red-roofed church in the shade of the palms—their heads, bent by the fierce wind, were glinting in the intense sunlight—and with a regretful glance at the tranquil water of the lagoon, we hurried on our way.

Another vivid atoll, Takapoto, but one without a pass, swept into view ahead and quickly dropped astern, for we were sailing fast and these low islands can only be seen from the low deck of a small yacht for about six miles. Then we settled down to steer most carefully by compass for the channel between Arutua and Rangiroa 100 miles farther on. That evening a check on our position by means of star sights was impossible because of the squalls which started their nightly procession at sundown, and again we had an anxious night. But we continued sailing at high speed, and, experiencing none of the 'unknown currents', made a landfall on Arutua at daybreak. We had our breakfast in comfort under that atoll's lee, and then thankfully headed out into reef-free waters for Tahiti, the Dangerous Archipelago astern of us.

Next day at noon, our sixth day out from Tai Oa, we sighted the 7,000-foot peaks of Tahiti when they were still forty miles away. It seemed impossible that we could reach an anchorage there before dark. But *Wanderer* had her own ideas, and with mainsail and genoa drawing to a fresh beam wind, she sailed faster than she ever had before, and in mid afternoon we suddenly realized that unless the wind died we would be in civilized surroundings after all that day. Kettles of fresh water were heated on the galley stove, and in turn we washed our vile and *nono*-bitten bodies. I had had no time for shaving during the past few days, and now, so that the operation should not be too painful, I first removed some of the stubble from my face with a pair of clippers; the stubble was sticky with salt, and as in my haste I omitted to clean the clippers afterwards, when next I had occasion to use them, some months later, I found them rusted solid. We gave *Wanderer* a clean-up too, washing the caked salt from deck and gear, and polishing the furniture, for ahead lay Tahiti, the glamour isle of the South Seas, or so we had been told, and we wanted to look our best on arrival. Sometimes I think we overdo this business of being ship-proud. We go to a lot of trouble to arrive in port looking much as we did when we left our last one, no matter how great the distance or how rough the weather may have been, instead of turning up with dirty sides, weathered brightwork, and a tangle of rotting rope and rusty jerry-cans cluttering the deck—a condition in which many people who live ashore expect to find an ocean-going yacht. Yet we persist in this time-absorbing procedure and are absurdly proud of our yacht's appearance.

At 4.30 p.m. we were up with Venus Point, the northern extremity of the island, and were soon skirting the reef, which was clearly marked by a line of breakers, though not majestic ones like those of the Tuamotu. The wind fell light, and *Wanderer*, having by then got her arrival well in hand, was gently ghosting. Papeete, the capital of French Polynesia, came into view across the reef; schooners were lying at the quays, and anchored off in the lagoon was a Brixham trawler wearing an enormous red ensign. This, we thought, must be the *Arthur Rogers* of which we had already heard much at Panama and Nukuhiva, and so it proved to be; the trawler's owners, Tom and Diana Hepworth, having recognized *Wanderer* from photographs they had seen, were flying their best and biggest ensign in our honour.

Presently the red-and-white-striped leading beacons came into line. Turning to port we kept them so to enter the pass, and then stole peacefully across the mirror-smooth water of the lagoon towards the town above which the mountain spires were bathed in rosy light from the setting sun. The heady, never-to-be-forgotten perfume of the south sea gardenia, *tiare Tahiti*, floated out on the warm land breeze to envelop us. All was peace and loveliness until a small motor tug, apparently propelled by aeroplane engines without silencers, roared out to meet us as we crept in towards the quay. From this monster the pilot jumped aboard to trample our immaculate deck with his hard shore-going shoes, and to show us to a berth.

With the loudly roaring tug in close company, it was difficult to hear and understand what the pilot said; but he seemed to be very cross about something (we learnt later that his irritation was caused by our arrival at a time when he was just about to enjoy a sundowner). We also felt irritated by the time he had anchored us with too short a scope of cable much too close to a schooner, and had crossed the two lines by which

our stern was secured to the shore. While I was filling in some
of the forms he had brought, Susan asked him politely to have
the lines put right, for pilotage at Papeete is compulsory, and if
you have to pay for a pilot you do not want or need, at least
you have the right to see he does his job efficiently.

'*Demain matin*,' he replied, shortly.

'*Mais non, monsieur*,' insisted Susan, '*tout de suite*.' And it was
done.

A *douanier* and a *gendarme* boarded us with more forms to be
filled in, but as politely as we could we waved them away; it
was our turn to say '*demain*'. They smiled as they went, for
they knew what formalities lay in store for us next day.

While we were mooring up a dinghy came alongside, and in
it we were surprised and delighted to see our friend Frank
McNulty. (*See p.* 65.) He was living for the time being aboard
Arthur Rogers. Since last we had met in England he and Bill
Howell had sailed our previous yacht, the 4½-ton cutter
Wanderer II, out to Tahiti, and there had parted company.
Bill had continued single-handed to Hawaii, and Frank was
trying to get a passage to his home at Sydney. Bill is a dentist,
and apparently he had left a trail of toothless islands half way
round the globe; he had been paying his way by pulling teeth
at a dollar a tooth or three teeth for two dollars. The natives,
set on getting the best value for their money, had the lot extracted
at the cut rate. At least, that was Frank's story; and we heard
much more: how *Wanderer II* had nearly been lost in one of the
locks of the Panama Canal, and later made the amazing average,
for a vessel only 21 feet on the waterline, of 124 miles a day on
the long run from Galapagos to Tahiti. All this he told us
while the three of us had *chow mein* and red wine together in a
Chinese eating-house overlooking the busy main street, and
within earshot of the music welling out in syncopated waves
from Quinn's near-by dancing hall.

The cruising way of life is full of strange contrasts. For five
weeks on the passage out from Panama Susan and I had only
each other for company in the lonely wastes of the ocean; then
we had stopped at the sombre and too silent island of Nukuhiva,
and we had hurried through the clean, wind-whipped, brilliant
Tuamotu. Only the previous night at about this time we had
been roaring along over a rough sea with the stiff curves of our

dark sails straining to half a gale of wind. Now we found ourselves suddenly amidst the noise, dirt and entertaining companionship of civilization, and at Papeete, which of itself is a mass of odd contrasts.

That night, as we lay in our strangely still bunks, the light from a street lamp poured in through the open hatchway, and we listened to two fishermen who sat talking in a strange language on the quay close astern; now and then we heard the noise of traffic, and the high-pitched childlike giggles, which in Polynesia take the place of normal male laughter, of some late revellers.

When we awoke in the morning there lay Papeete looking much as we had expected it to look. Ahead of *Wanderer* the quiet lagoon stretched away to the murmuring reef and, on either side of her, island schooners lay as she did with anchors out ahead and stern lines to the shore. Astern was the deeply shaded waterfront road, alive with pedestrians and traffic, for at Papeete the market starts business at 4.30 a.m. Across the road stood the post office and the pagoda-like building of the Stuart Hotel, together with a row of houses, offices and shops. The Tahitians looked well built, healthy and happy people. The men mostly wore shorts, coloured shirts and soft straw hats, while the *vahines*, now mostly of mixed blood, and famous the world over for their golden-brown skins, their long black hair, and the 'I like you' look in their eye, were dressed in cotton frocks, for the wearing of the *pareu* in the town is forbidden. They appeared to be in no hurry, often stopping to chat in a shady spot, or strolling across the strip of grass which separates the road from the lagoon—the books we had read did not tell us that this grass verge is pock-marked with what in any ordinary place might be rabbit holes, but at Papeete are jointly shared by rats and land crabs—to mount a gangway and sit on the deck of a schooner and sing to the music of a guitar played by a member of the crew. Many of the *vahines* now ride motor cycles, and it is not uncommon to see two of them sharing one machine, the pillion rider languidly combing the driver's long hair as they wobble through the town. Roaming pigs and smart limousines jostle one another on the roads; slant-eyed Chinamen, who are the shopkeepers here, rub shoulders with camera-necklaced tourists; on the pavements under the verandahs of the shops and hotels many islanders nightly spread their mats and sleep, while waiting for some overdue schooner to carry them back to their homes in the Tuamotu or Iles sous le Vent. On the lagoon outrigger canoes crowd round the recently arrived T.E.A.L. flying boat which has just brought the mail from New Zealand, Fiji and Western Samoa.

Our very first morning at Papeete Susan, as is her custom, was sitting in the cockpit brushing her hair, and I was finding it difficult to concentrate on cooking the breakfast, for again and again my eye wandered out of hatch or port to see what went on in the street. Presently a tall, thin man with dark, flashing eyes and a neat, black, pointed beard, approached. Addressing Susan he lifted his pandanus hat with its band of shining shells, and bowing stiffly from the hips, said:

'Madam, will you dine with me tonight?'

For a moment Susan hesitated, and I thought she was going to refuse. But she smiled and said, 'Thank you. I shall be delighted to.'

'And your husband also,' the Frenchman added. 'I will come with a car at six o'clock.'

That was Captain Argod, skipper of the big three-masted schooner *Oiseau des Iles*, and a very good friend to all visiting British yachtsmen. He came that evening with a car as promised, a taxi he had hired to carry us to his near-by home, while he led the way on his motor cycle. And what a delightful evening we had. Madame, who had sailed out from France with her husband and children and others in the little *Fleur de l'Océan*, well understood the tastes of those who had just completed a sea voyage, and the meal she gave us was designed with that in view—all of it was fresh, crisp and cool. We came away with a shell from the Captain's big collection, a fine, black-lip pearl shell which from that day to this has decorated one of *Wanderer*'s bulkheads. Besides kindness and hospitality, we received from Argod much valuable advice about sailing and pilotage among the islands. We are proud to have him as a friend, for a man who can con a big schooner drawing fourteen feet of water through a narrow, twisty pass into a lagoon *by moonlight*, is surely the finest kind of seaman; he must have nerves of steel and searchlights for eyes. (*See p.* 65.)

Our reception by the British Consul was very different. In

English-speaking countries we used to arrange in advance for our mail to be sent care of a bank, and in foreign ports care of the British Consul, if there was one. These arrangements had always worked very well, and had sometimes been the means of making valuable contacts and friends. We were therefore rather shocked on being greeted at the Consulate by the unconsular remark:

'Another bloody yacht. And what trouble are you going to bring me?'

So far as I know we brought no trouble to him or anyone else during our voyage. His odd greeting did not matter in the least to us, but as this man happened to be acting as American Consul also, we were concerned that he might give a wrong impression of the very fine, dignified and helpful consular service to any American who might seek his help or advice.

Normally the business of entering a yacht on arrival in a foreign port, and obtaining a clearance before departure, is simply and quickly done; but not at Papeete where, if only Sullivan could have put it to music, the whole business would have made a highly entertaining Savoy opera. We had to fill in manifests, search lists, provision lists, arms lists, currency lists, and immigration forms, as well as one, the name of which I have forgotten, asking the number of coffins we had on board. Some of the forms, such as the manifests, had to be bought, and most had to be done in duplicate or triplicate; but before we had finished we had written out and signed no fewer than fifteen crew lists. It took us all day to make the rounds of the various offices. The officials were courteous, but they did not help us as much as they could have done. For example, we visited the police headquarters to collect our passports which had been taken there the day before, and to deposit one of the crew lists. The police told us to go next to the port office. On arrival there we were asked for a crew list, but when I gave them one they shook their heads and pointed out that it should have been signed by the police; so back we had to go to get the signature. Finally, we had to deposit our 12-bore shotgun and ammunition with the customs.

But the most entertaining official business was obtaining a permit to remain at Papeete beyond the allowed fourteen days, and to visit the other islands of the group. These permits, in the form of letters, have to be obtained from and signed by the Governor or his representative, and the application is best made by a correctly phrased letter. The writing of such letters for those, like us, whose French is not equal to the task, is one of the many little kindnesses performed for the visiting yachtsman by charming Muriel Gooding, a Tahitian, who runs the *bureau de tourisme*. The letters were written and posted, and a day or so later most of the civil servants, including the people at the post office and the Governor's secretary, went on strike. Muriel, not being a civil servant, closed the *bureau* and became acting secretary to the Governor. He had received the applications for our permits, had dictated his replies to Muriel, and signed them, and she had posted them to herself at the *bureau*, but because of the strike they were not delivered. We visited the Governor's office to see if we could obtain fresh permits, for our time of departure was drawing near, and without them we could not even obtain a clearance. But that could not be allowed; permits had already been issued and no doubt we would get them in time if only we had patience. Deadlock! But a few days before we wished to leave, Commander Faye, who had already helped us in many ways, worked some sort of a miracle, and the permits were delivered by hand.

Obtaining a clearance took even longer than entering the yacht had done. All day we trapsed from office to office. First we went to the port office where we were informed that four more crew lists and two passenger lists were required, as well as another manifest. Having supplied these we called at the hospital for a bill of health, and then went to the police to get a crew list signed for the customs. Then back to the port office for the bill for harbour dues and pilotage (478 island francs) which had to be paid at the treasury. The customs asked us to call again when that had been done, but as someone there was out, we had to wait for an hour and then completed a currency form; but we did not know that the yellow slips from the Banque de l'Indo-Chine, where we had cashed our travellers' cheques, would be needed, and had to return to

---

PLATE 11

We brought up in one of the most beautiful anchorages we had ever seen; Paopao Bay, Moorea.

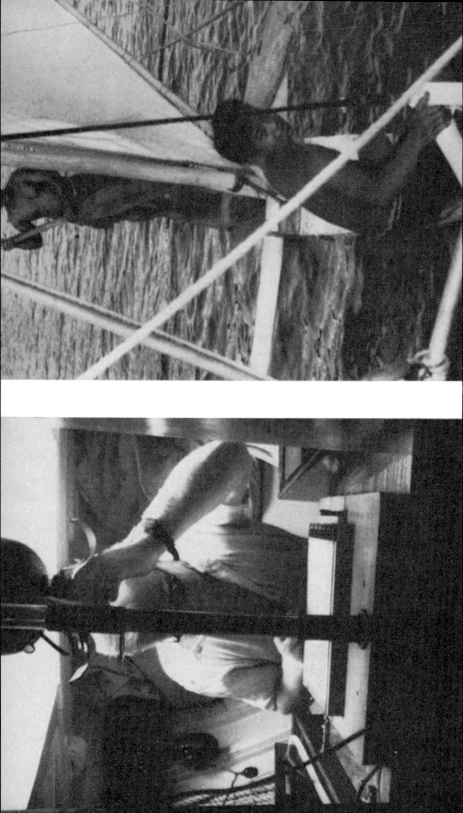

Wanderer to get them. Then we went to another office to collect our gun and ammunition; but the latter had been mislaid, and the officer in charge begged us with tears in his eyes to take the box which belonged to the American yacht *San Miedo*. I refused to do this, and after a tremendous to-do involving most of the customs service, the missing box was discovered in yet another office, and a guard of two policemen was sent to escort us back to the yacht, and to see that we really did go on board instead of shooting up the town. On the way we paid one final visit to the port office, and there at last got our clearance. Thank goodness we were not in any hurry.

But in spite of their petty officialdom, I have the greatest admiration for the way the French run their Pacific islands, and I question whether any other country could so successfully govern these particular native communities without interfering with the happiness of the islanders or their way of life. Among other wise precautions they see to it that beachcombers do not take advantage of the natives, who are traditionally hospitable.

One soon learns that Papeete is not typical of Tahiti. Once the town has been left well behind, the island is in many respects similar to others of the group, friendly, beautiful and strangely enticing. But the town was not without its interests. Mostly it consists of wooden shops and houses, shabby and unpainted. There are several dancing halls, of which Quinn's bamboo hut with its horseshoe bar, and Le Col Bleu, are probably the best known. Normally they only come to life on Saturday and Sunday evenings, when many people invade the town from the countryside, or when a steamer is in port; as on one occasion during our stay there were five ships in the harbour, an unheard-of number, we saw these places in full swing. It was odd to watch the grey-faced, worried-looking Europeans or Americans, garlanded with *heis* which can be bought on the floor, solemnly dancing with the sturdy native girls, so vivacious and full of laughter; and later, when they had drunk plenty of wine, trying clumsily with waggling

PLATE 12

Left: At work making enlargements in my tiny forepeak darkroom. *Right:* The Sanfords sent their *pirogue*, a swift outrigger canoe, for us to sail in.

A.W.W.—G

buttocks to imitate Augustine who had just danced a *hula*. In Papeete's life of drink, dancing and love, I, as an onlooker, would say that the European generally looks dissipated and ill at ease, while the native looks serene and happy. It would appear that missionary teachings have not yet persuaded the Polynesian that indiscriminate sexual intercourse is sinful, and that bearing a child out of wedlock is a misfortune; on the contrary, the more children an unmarried girl has, especially if they are white, the greater is her kudos. I should add that in the Society Islands children are adored; they are well and kindly treated, and if an unmarried woman has more than she can look after, friends or relatives are always happy to adopt them. The result is that the children are delightful, and a cross or squalling child is rare.

As Papeete is the only port of entry in the Society Islands, nearly every yacht cruising in the South Pacific calls there sooner or later; but as we were a little early in the season, there were only two other inhabited yachts there. One of these was the *San Miedo* from Hawaii; aboard of her a party of four were living in great discomfort, for the yacht depended on electricity for most things, even for pumping water from the tanks, and her charging plant had been broken down for several weeks. The other yacht, which I have already mentioned, was the converted trawler *Arthur Rogers*. Tom and Diana Hepworth (*see p.* 65) had spent the best part of five years on the voyage out from England, and doing all manner of interesting jobs on the way to pay for the trip: taking charter parties out to the San Blas Islands and to the Galapagos, for example, and doing a fishery job in British Guiana.

Our old friend *Viking* arrived shortly before we left, and once again we had the pleasure of the company of Sten and Brita at dinner in our cockpit under the awning. They told us of all that had happened to them since last we met. They had taken fifty-one days for the passage from Panama to Nukuhiva, for they had followed their usual practice of spending all night in their bunks no matter whether their vessel was holding her course or heading in some other direction. On arrival they found, poor things, that they could not beat in to an anchorage against the light and fluky airs; after spending the best part of a day in the attempt, they gave it up and went to Ua Pou, where they found an uncomfortable and precarious berth for a short time. Then they took seventeen days to sail the 700 miles to Tahiti. The 'worryment', as they called it, of navigating among the Tuamotu was more than they cared for, and already they felt disillusioned about the Pacific, and were determined to have done with it as soon as might be. We tried hard to persuade them to sail in company with us to some of the other islands of the group, but failed. That was the last we saw of them, but Brita wrote to us from Darwin (Australia), to say they had stopped only at Suva (Fiji), Vila (New Hebrides) and Port Moresby (Papua). So they saw very little of the lovely islands they had come all the way from Sweden to explore. The following extract from her letter gives some idea of the hard conditions they experienced in the central Pacific.

'Ten miles out [from Papeete] instead of the nice light trade we had expected, we got headwind to last us for nine days; 300 miles in those days. But it wasn't finish with that, variables, thunderstorms, pouring rain followed day after day, always worse at nights, as if the nights themselves weren't bad enough, long and terrifying with all those reefs lying in wait. I have no need telling you about the feeling when lightnings strike all around and the poles are the highest things in many miles. The four last days before Suva we hope will not come back. I can't find words to tell you the whole, but you had the same weather, so you know. Our sea-ancor was probably too small for the size of boat; we couldn't keep the stern against the wind but had to run before, bare poles and the sea-ancor dragging after, hoping it would prevent too high speed. Must steer all the time, trying to avoid the enormous breaking waves smashing *Viking* to pieces. Sten couldn't leave the helm for four days and nights as it was too hard for me to manage. With no sleep for none of us, and all the worryment, we were pleased to get in.'

Those valiant Swedes (*see p.* 65) completed their circumnavigation of the world in two years, and for it were justly awarded the Blue Water Medal of the Cruising Club of America. Already they have bought another vessel, this time with a powerful auxiliary engine, and soon, no doubt, they will be off on their travels again.

After three weeks at Papeete, we were ready for a quieter,

cleaner anchorage from which we might see something of the real island life without having to make a journey along a busy road; also our purse was growing empty, for everything at Papeete is expensive. So we decided to sail on to the westward.

Early on the morning fixed for our departure, Commander Faye brought us a breakfast of *croissants* still hot from the bakery. Just as we were letting go our stern lines and hauling out to our anchor, other friends arrived to drop their parting *heis* of sweet-smelling flowers, with the dew still on them, round our shoulders. As *Wanderer* slipped out across the lagoon towards the pass, and we turned to give one final wave to the small knot of figures standing on the waterfront, we were sad, for Tahiti has something I cannot express in words, and always it beckons us back.

7

ILES SOUS LE VENT

OFTEN of an evening while at Papeete we had watched the sun set over Moorea, Tahiti's smaller sister island only twelve miles away, colouring the sky purple, orange and gold, and picking out in black relief the fairy-tale mountain spires of that island. Now we were bound for Moorea, and as *Wanderer* lifted to the first of the rollers running in through Papeete's pass, a fresh east-nor'-east wind pressed her sails into firm curves; instantly she came to life, heeling to port and surging forward, the quiet chuckle of the lazy bow-wave changing to the purposeful rush of swiftly cascading water.

Moorea's north coast is deeply indented by two fjords which strike inland among the mountains. We had no difficulty in identifying Paopao Bay, the first of these inlets; but just as we were looking for the pass through the barrier reef which encircles this island, a strong squall came tearing along the coast to deluge us with rain and obscure the mountain peak by which we had been steering. Susan at once went right forward from where she could make out the pass of smooth water between the breakers and see the pale colour of the water over the shoals. Following her signals I was able to steer safely through the pass, and we were soon slipping up the bay, each side of which the rain-soaked vegetation steamed in the heat of the sun, for the squall by then had passed. Rounding a palm-covered sandy spit, we brought up near the head of the bay on the eastern side in one of the most beautiful anchorages we had ever seen. (*See p.* 80.)

One of the drawbacks of many of the Pacific islands at which we called was the great depth of their lagoons. The greater part of the shore of these islands has a fringing reef with, perhaps, three or four feet of water over it at low tide, and it may extend for twenty yards or so out into the lagoon; from there it slopes down at an angle of forty-five degrees to a depth of anything between ten and twenty fathoms; the bottom of the lagoon is usually composed of mud or sand.

In Paopao Bay we anchored in ten fathoms as close to the fringing reef as we dared to go, near a small hotel which consisted of three separate buildings, the pretty little thatched dining-room standing on stilts in the water. After the constant noise of Papeete, it was pleasant to find absolute peace; *Wanderer* lay gazing at her own reflection in the still water, in which was mirrored the tall, jagged mountain skyline. This was one of the most beautiful places we had ever seen. The sweet smell of drying vanilla, as from some confectioner's shop, is the scent we shall always associate with Moorea.

In the West Indies we had become accustomed to little rise and fall of tide. In the central Pacific it is also very small, the spring rise being only one foot. But the strange thing is that high water always occurs at midday and midnight, instead of changing with the moon as it does in most other parts of the world.

From our anchorage we had an unobstructed view of the barrier reef, and could see the great rollers rising with vertical faces and overhanging crests just before they crashed in a smother of white foam. Often a mirage raised them to absurd heights so that, although they were a mile and a half from us, they looked much closer, and it seemed impossible that the invisible reef could prevent them from invading our lagoon. Always with us in that silent place was the roar of distant surf. Once we watched a waterspout moving to the eastward. It writhed as it moved along and presently grew thin in the middle. Soon it broke in half; a gap appeared and widened as the upper part of the spout was drawn up into the cloud, and the lower part slowly and reluctantly collapsed into the sea from which it had come.

In the central south Pacific the south-east trade wind becomes light and variable and the weather is unsettled for a part of the year; but by April it should have settled down to blow steadily and the weather should be fine. We arrived at Moorea towards the end of that month, and our first week there was fine; but after that the weather became unsettled, with much rain and puffs of wind from various directions, while the diurnal rise and fall of the barometer, which is such a marked feature in the tropics, became slight, the barograph pen drawing an almost straight line.

One night I was awakened by rain blowing in through the open ports on to my face. I got up to close them, and as I did so a fierce gust of wind caught *Wanderer* on the beam and heeled her over sharply. The sudden movement caught me off my balance. I lurched and knocked the glass chimney off one of the lamps on to Susan's head where it shivered into fragments, but fortunately did not cut her. For half an hour the wind blew with strong gale force right into our bay, causing *Wanderer* to pitch and to tail in close to where we knew the fringing reef lay. We had already veered all our chain. We knew it would be impossible to lay out the other anchor, for we could not have made headway against so strong a wind even with a light dinghy, and certainly not when carrying an anchor and warp. To drop the second anchor under foot would be of no use, for if the yacht was going to drag she would strike the reef long before the second anchor had a sufficient scope of warp to have any effect. So we stood miserably in the companionway, cold, frightened and with chattering teeth, for the rain blew in on us, and occasionally we shone the searchlight out through one of the ports to try to see a landmark and judge whether the anchor was holding; but we could see nothing except the myriad silver streaks of the rain which was pouring down in torrents. However, our trusty 35-lb. ploughshare anchor must have dug itself well in, for it held on firmly as it had so often done before, and when the squall was over and the rain stopped, we saw before getting back into our bunks that *Wanderer* still lay in her original position.

Susan and I have become very attached to that anchor, which to us is no inanimate object but a friend with a personality. Unlike the old-fashioned fisherman type, our anchor prefers to have a lot of chain dropped on top of it as soon as it reaches the bottom; then when the strain comes on it the pull is in a horizontal direction, the anchor turns over from whichever side it has been lying on and starts to dig in. Sometimes when weighing from a soft mud bottom after the wind has been blowing strongly, we find the anchor has dug in so far that the whole of it and a fathom or two of chain comes up thickly caked with mud. From a clay bottom it has often been quite a job to make it let go, while from sand it usually comes up fairly easily, clean and burnished, and sometimes with crabs or starfish clinging to it. Although we have great faith in this anchor, we can never ride out a gale without some anxiety, for, unknowingly, we may have anchored on thick kelp through which the anchor is not heavy enough to force a path to the firm ground beneath; or, again unknown to us, the bottom may consist of flat rock with only a thin coating of sand or loose volcanic ash in which the anchor has no chance of getting a grip. Also at the back of our minds lurks the fear that metal fatigue may develop in the chain; such an invisible weakening, produced by a succession of shock loads, could allow the chain to snap without warning if the yacht should snub heavily on it. Throughout our stay in the Society Islands, and again at American Samoa, our anchorages were subject to sudden strong squalls, more especially by night than by day; many an anxious night was spent hoping that the anchor would continue to do its duty and that the chain was still sound.

We remained for nearly three weeks at Moorea, for Susan had strained a muscle in the lower part of her back. This was very painful, and for a time she was unable to lift or pull on anything, so we waited for it to mend. Part of the time we spent in neighbouring Papetoai Bay, where we found a pleasant, well-sheltered berth in Robinson Cove. That is one of the few places where there is no fringing reef and the beach is of sand; so steeply does it shelve that although we were anchored in seven fathoms, we lay close enough to the shore to be in the shade of the palms.

Again we had writing and photographic work to do. The developing of thirty-five millimetre films in a spiral tank loaded in a black satin changing bag, caused us little bother. To our surprise we found that, in spite of the high temperature, there was no need to pre-harden or use special tropical developer. So long as all the chemical solutions and the washing water were at the same temperature, and we shortened the time of development according to the increase of temperature, there was no trouble and the films did not suffer at all from reticulation. Washing was done by hanging the tank spiral, still with the film threaded in it, in the sea on a piece of line, but we had to keep a sharp lookout for fish which were inclined to take too close an interest in it. The final rinse was, of course, in fresh water.

But the making of whole-plate (8½ by 6½ inch) enlargements was much more of an undertaking. (*See p.* 81.) The forepeak had to be cleaned of dust, the enlarger erected there and the place blacked out. While I did that, Susan rigged a temporary awning over the foredeck (our ordinary harbour awning stopped short at the mast) and threw water on the deck to cool it as much as possible. But in spite of this the humidity caused by my sweating body in the tiny airless forepeak was so great that each sheet of bromide paper became as limp as a rag by the time I had removed it from its box and arranged it on the enlarger easel, and when it was there I had to take care that drips from my chin did not fall on it. This was such a handicap to the production of crisp, contrasty pictures that it had to be overcome somehow; this I did by wearing a waterproof suit we happened to have on board made of thin rubber. The enlargements we also washed in salt water with a final rinse in fresh. Drying and glazing was done on a home-made drier over the galley stove.

As Kodachrome cannot be processed by the amateur, all our colour films had to be sent on to the next Kodak processing laboratory and from there to some prearranged address in that country. All the colour films we took in the Pacific we sent to Australia, and the resulting transparencies went to our friends Frank and Muriel Eyre at Melbourne, there to await our arrival. From time to time Frank reported on the quality of the transparencies which reached him, and this was a great help to us when exposing our next films. The following is an extract from one of his letters.

'This is just to report that another batch of your Koda-chromes arrived this morning. They seem quite good, though perhaps with rather less sun in them than the previous batch. I notice the usual preponderance of leaning palms, and you may be interested, therefore, to have for digestion on your next long leg the following masterpiece translated from a French work on the Pacific:

' "The fact that on certain islands some palm trees lean outwards towards the sea is an excellent demonstration of the

theory advanced by some authors in support of this phenomenon." '

We are still trying to puzzle it out, but we did go carefully
with the palms thereafter, though indeed they *do* lean outwards.

In our spare time it was pleasant to stroll ashore and watch
the natives making copra and living their care-free life. We
sometimes wondered, as we made our way through the coconut
plantations, how many people have been maimed or killed by
coconuts falling on their heads, for it is said that a healthy
coconut palm produces a nut a week, and unless these are
picked, which is only done with young nuts wanted for drinking,
they fall to the ground when ripe. The coconut palm is the
most important thing many of the south sea islands grow.
The flesh of the nut is meat, the milk is drink, and even the
fowls, domestic pets and cattle live largely on it. The fibre
from the husk is made into cordage, or the husk is burnt as fuel,
while the dried meat is shipped away as copra, the oil extracted
from it being used in the manufacture of margarine and soap,
among other things. From the fronds thatch is made. In some
islands rats climb the palms and spoil the nuts. To prevent
this happening, collars of aluminium or other smooth metal
are fastened round the trunks of the palms to stop them from
getting a foothold. But the rhinoceros beetle is the worst
scourge of all, destroying palms by the thousand, especially in
Fiji.

As we walked ashore the islanders always greeted us with
a cheerful '*eu ora na*'—'may you live'. Sometimes we met
children going home from school. Each of the little boys
politely raised his straw hat and murmured '*Bonjour monsieur
madame*', which was probably the only French they knew, for
our attempts to talk with them failed completely. When a
shower of rain fell, each child picked a broad banana leaf and
used it as an umbrella.

The Chinese stores along the island's coastal road sold little
except rice, tinned foods and cotton materials, and we would
have been hard put to it to obtain sufficient fresh food had it not
been for the kindness of a French planter, M. Chamelat, for
whom we had been able to perform a small service; he supplied
us with papaya, pamplemousse, bananas, limes, his one and
only pineapple, and some strange-looking things like Chinese

lanterns which Susan cleverly converted into jam. He even persuaded a storekeeper to sell us a few elderly eggs; the value of these useful things does not seem to be properly understood by the islanders; the only use they have for fowls is to eat them.

When Susan's back had recovered we sailed away for Raiatea, one of the Iles sous le Vent, the 'leeward islands' of the Society group about a hundred miles away. But we took two days to reach it, for instead of the expected fair wind, light breezes from ahead were what we mostly got.

Early during our second night at sea there was an almost continuous display of lightning in the western sky until a curtain of rain obscured it. For a time we sailed in darkness so absolute that nothing at all was visible except the luminous grid of the compass. Then with staggering suddenness a vivid streak of lightning split the sky asunder overhead, illuminating for a moment every smallest detail of deck and rigging. Blackness followed, but the flash remained on the retina of my eye, a green zig-zag. Then another streak and another followed in quick succession, each, like the first, with an instantaneous clap of thunder of the sinister, crackling kind which is only heard when it is very close indeed. I thought at once of our tall white mast, the only standing thing in that part of the ocean, and I was frightened, for I doubted whether it could possibly escape destruction with the storm right overhead, even though parts of the rigging were earthed. The rain poured down harder and the wind freshened.

'Time to reef,' I shouted down to Susan, but she being as always alert to the worsening conditions, had already pulled some clothes on and was struggling into her oilskins. She took the tiller from me, and I, with the reefing handle in my hand, started to make my way forward along the slanting deck. Then I noticed that there was a glimmering of light somewhere overhead, for I could dimly make out the shape of the upturned dinghy and other things on deck. Looking up I was startled to see a ball of blurred pale green light apparently perched on the truck—St. Elmo's fire. From what I had read I believed this phenomenon to be harmless, but I could not recollect ever having heard of anyone handling a steel wire halyard with St. Elmo's fire at the masthead. For a moment I hesitated, but reefing was a matter of some urgency as *Wanderer* was becoming more and more pressed by the rapidly increasing wind, and much water was boiling along her lee deck. So I worked my way to the mast, shipped the handle on the reefing gear, and after another thoughtful pause grabbed the halyard. The relief at receiving no electric shock was immense. By the time I had rolled in a deep reef and changed staysails, the fire had vanished as quietly and mysteriously as it had come, and I scrambled back to the cockpit where Susan put an arm round me and said:

'Well done, boy!'

Much to our relief the great electric storm soon moved away to the eastward, and shortly afterwards the rain stopped suddenly, just as though a tap had been shut off, stars appeared, and away on the horizon we could again see the flickering of sheet lightning. By dawn the wind had almost died, and the day became overcast and with indifferent visibility.

Before noon we approached Te-Ava-piti Pass which, on the eastern side, leads into Raiatea's lagoon; but by then the weather looked so threatening that we turned away to see what was going to happen. Susan wisely suggested reefing, and scarcely was that done when a squall, with almost solid rain and a wind so strong that we were compelled to take in all sail, struck us. Had that squall caught us in the pass it might well have put us on the reef alongside a gloomy, rusting wreck which already lay there. With the squall over the wind fell very light, and through the thinning rain we could make out the pass with the leading marks and the *motus* each side of it. We made full sail and headed slowly in towards it. But as we drew near, another squall swooped down upon us and conditions exactly repeated themselves; a gale, a blinding downpour of rain and then a calm. It was not until our third attempt that we succeeded in entering the lagoon.

That lagoon, like most, is a deep one, but the large-scale harbour plan showed a bay close south of the town of Uturoa with depths of from three to six fathoms close to the shore. So, under power, for by then there was again no wind, Susan steered in that direction while I sounded with the lead, for the recent heavy rains had so discoloured the water that it was impossible to pilot by eye. But the sounding lead is never of much use in coral-studded waters. Presently one of my casts found bottom in nine fathoms, and we were just about to anchor when Susan spied a reef on the other side of us; it was only a yard or two away and had no more than a foot of water over it. This near disaster, for a ship ashore on coral is usually a ship lost, so disconcerted us that we gave up any idea of anchoring, cautiously made our way back into deep water and secured alongside the commercial pier off the town, where willing hands took our lines.

We always avoid lying alongside if possible because the yacht gets dirty, we have little privacy, and there is always a risk of theft, though usually only a slight one at small islands, the people of which are generally honest. Being secured to the shore is also the surest way of getting cockroaches and rats on board. It is true that some cockroaches can fly, but only for limited distances; so, by lying at anchor, except on one or two rare occasions such as at Uturoa, by rinsing in the sea all stems of bananas, and by carefully picking over all potatoes and onions before allowing them aboard, we succeeded in keeping almost completely free from cockroaches while we were abroad.

We remained for a day and two nights, borrowing motor tyres to assist our own fenders in keeping our topsides from bumping the pier, for the wind was fresh most of the time and, blowing along the lagoon with a two-mile drift, raised a steep little sea which kept the yacht always on the move. Madame Bonnais and Madame Fixier, the wives of the judge and the clerk of the court respectively, invited us ashore; but as we did not care to leave the yacht in her uncomfortable berth, where she could so easily have damaged herself if a fender got out of place, they came on board instead, bringing with them a bottle of whisky and an enormous cake, which we started on then and there. After we had seen them ashore, we remained on deck for a time, for the night was most extraordinary. Away to the north-east, east and south-east, and particularly over the island of Huahine, there was a display of lightning even more remarkable than we had witnessed during our passage from Moorea. Almost continuously for three hours the lightning flickered. Overhead the sky was clear, but the horizon was topped by a bank of thin cloud, above, below and behind which the eerie light played, sometimes in forks and streaks, but more often in immense unsteady sheets; and every now and again the mountains of Huahine stood out against it in bold black relief. The water near the pier was floodlit by an electric lamp, and from it many small fish were jumping, each making a tiny splash and a widening circle of ripples as it fell back. Fishermen sat on the pier close to *Wanderer*'s bow and stern, each with an enormous rod at least twenty feet in length, to the end of which was secured a short line with a hook. The method of fishing was to cast the hook out over the sea, then draw it back slowly across the surface; as each cast was made the line and tip of the rod produced a strange whistling sound. Away in the distance someone was singing softly to the music of a guitar, and all the time the uncanny lightning danced and flickered on the horizon. Then a mission yacht lying ahead of us—a strange-looking craft with a wishbone schooner rig, engine exhausts leading out from the ends of the crosstrees, turtle deck forward and top-heavy house amidships—started to charge her batteries. The spell was broken, but the fishing, with much laughter, continued far into the night.

The twin islands of Raiatea and Tahaa lie within one common barrier reef which is twenty-two miles long in a north-and-south direction. The greater part of the space enclosed by this huge coral structure is taken up by the two islands, and much of the remaining lagoon is encumbered with coral heads and reefs. When we sailed to Tahaa, therefore, we did not have to go outside, but made the passage entirely in the protected water of the lagoon. Pilotage has to be done there entirely by eye, for the chart is on too small a scale to be of much use, and as coral can grow several inches in a year, one cannot rely implicitly on charts of such places even when the survey was made in great detail, which was not often.

When conditions are just right, that is with the sun shining from some point abaft the beam and the water is ruffled by a breeze, pilotage by eye from aloft is not difficult. The barrier reef may vary in width between fifty yards and something over a mile; it is generally covered with sand and has less than a fathom of water over it, the least depth being at its seaward edge; this shows as a beautiful greenish blue dotted with the brown of coral heads, and is purple at its edges. The deep water inside is dark blue, almost the colour of the ocean itself, but where it shoals the colour becomes lighter. One soon learns to judge the depth of water, or at least to know where there is not enough water for one's vessel, by the colour. But when the sky is overcast, or the sea is glassy calm, all that you can see on looking into the water from aloft is the reflection of the sky staring back mockingly at you. Also, when navigating in a lagoon, it is often necessary to make a considerable alteration of course, which may bring the sun for a time forward of the beam; then you can see nothing in that direction.

We had fitted ratlines to *Wanderer*'s lower shrouds so that it was easy to climb as far as the lower crosstrees, about twenty feet above the sea, for this kind of pilotage. We found that polaroid spectacles were a great help.

The morning we left Uturoa we had a troublesome start, for the lagoon was dead smooth and the sky largely overcast. We proceeded very slowly under power and at times felt quite lost. But later the wind got up and the sky cleared, and we made swift progress under sail, Susan and I taking it in turn to con from the crosstrees. The lagoon colouring was magnificent, and all the dangers showed up well as we wound our way through them towards green Tahaa, where eventually we found a pleasant anchorage on the island's western side at the head of Hurepiti Bay. There, in a little cove behind a sheltering spit and among reefs where we only just had swinging room, we brought up in ten fathoms, an islander who had climbed a palm for the purpose beckoning us in and in. We lay quietly in smooth water out of the wind, and our feeling of cosiness was enhanced by the roar of the surf on the reef a mile away.

Tahaa is quite unspoilt; it has not even a road, only narrow paths winding along the shore beneath the breadfruit trees. We found the islanders particularly friendly. Soon after our arrival two brothers came alongside in a canoe from a village across the bay where some of the buildings stood on stilts in the water, bringing us fifty limes and 150 bananas. They did not want any payment, but when we insisted on giving them a few francs, they were so pleased that while the elder remained aboard to fish for us (he did not catch anything) his brother went off to buy us a loaf, an errand that took him three hours;

but in the islands time means very little, and it is quite sufficient to make a date for 'in the morning' or 'in the afternoon'—provided one has got the day right.

Païpaï Pass, by which we left the lagoon, presented a wonderful spectacle although it lies on the leeward side, for a very heavy swell was running that day from the south-west-ward. That is the usual thing with Pacific islands, the swell which is caused by storms down in the Southern Ocean being much greater than that produced by the trade wind on the windward side. So marked is the difference that if an emergency landing has to be made on an unprotected island or reef, the *Pilot* recommends that it be done on the windward rather than the leeward side. The raft *Kon-Tiki* did this on the reef of Raroia, one of the atolls in the Tuamotu group, and with all her crew survived.

As each great roller began to feel the bottom, increasing in height and getting thinner, it grew paler in colour; then a flash of white appeared on its head, spreading rapidly to left and right to join up with other white flashes, and suddenly the whole thing tumbled over in a great cataract of foam and rushed across the reef. The continuous loud roar at close quarters was awe-inspiring; we had to shout to make ourselves heard, and *Wanderer* seemed an insignificant mite as she stepped daintily through the narrow lane of unbroken water with the great combers thundering on either hand. There is a dangerous shoal spot at one side of that pass, where the swell increases in speed some time before it breaks; but after a few anxious moments we were clear of it and out in the open sea, where the peaks of Bora-Bora fifteen miles away beckoned to us.

Another magnificent spectacle of high-flung surf greeted us as we approached the island and made our way parallel with the reef towards Teavanui Pass. By then we were growing used to passes through coral reefs, but we still continued to treat them with the respect they deserve. A pass is usually only a narrow crack in the reef; we might mistake a blind pass, a *cul-de-sac*, for the real one, or the current, which often runs

PLATE 13

Top: The twin 2,000-foot peaks of Bora-Bora, seen from one of the *motus*, dominate the tranquil lagoon, while outside (*bottom*) the great ocean swell thunders on the protecting reef, some of which is just awash.

out with great force, might set us into danger. The temptation to approach slowly and cautiously is great, but because of the outflowing current—which is caused by the swell breaking on the reef and overflowing it into the lagoon, from which there is probably only the one outlet—and the wind which usually blows out through the pass, it is necessary to carry a press of sail so as to be able to beat in. We always approached with a feeling of apprehension, worked through with our hearts in our mouths and one of us conning from aloft, while the swell burst with unimaginable ferocity on either hand, hurling great clouds of spray high into the air where the trade wind caught it and drove it seaward over the crest of the next advancing roller. When eventually we reached the smooth water within, we felt as though a great weight had been lifted from us and were thankful that one more pass had safely been negotiated.

The sun was dipping low in the western sky by the time we had negotiated Bora-Bora's pass, which is a wide and easy one, and had reached the tranquil water of the lagoon. In the low golden light of evening the island was looking breath-takingly beautiful, but what our eyes fixed on with the greatest delight were the masts and yards of our old friend *Arthur Rogers* which was lying alongside a quay in Faanui Bay. Diana came sailing out in the dinghy to meet us, and very soon *Wanderer* was lying at anchor off the quay and we were aboard the old trawler exchanging news with Tom, Diana and Frank, and meeting for the first time Johnnie and Mary Caldwell, whose ketch, *Tropic Seas*, was lying in the bay. How homely it seemed to have tea with them all on deck under their awning, and to be able to speak our own language for the first time in many weeks —and be understood.

The Caldwells from America were making a leisurely two-year voyage across the Pacific, and they were rearing a family as they went. Their trip was being made on the proceeds from Johnnie's last book, *Desperate Voyage*, in which he described his previous Pacific adventuring, how he sailed towards Australia

---

PLATE 14

Top: The Samoan *fale* is an elaborate building, the framework of its roof as complicated and well fitted as that of any ship. *Bottom:* In Melanesia skins are blacker, faces flatter, lips thicker, and straight hair changes to fuzzy mops; women of Viti Levu, Fiji.

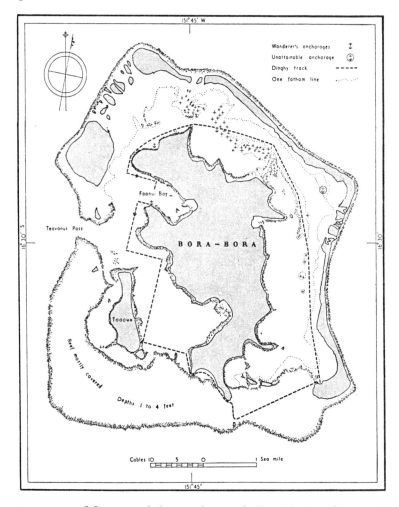

to marry Mary, and how after unbelievable troubles and hardships he finished his trip by getting wrecked on one of the Fiji islands.

During the war Bora-Bora was occupied by 6,000 Americans. Now all that remains to tell of the occupation are one or two quays, some rusting water tanks, and 600 pale-faced children (the total pre-war population was only 500). Yet the island and the islanders are quite unspoilt, which is a fine tribute to both nations. The island measures only five miles by three at its widest, and is much indented by deep bays. Unlike those of the other Society Islands, the reef of this one is largely covered with *motus*, which are low, narrow islands, green with scrub and palms; they form an almost continuous line on the north and east sides, so that Bora-Bora has the appearance of a high island set in the lagoon of an atoll; its twin 2,000-foot mountain spires dominate the tranquil lagoon. (*See p.* 96.) The island has a road but only five motor vehicles, which do not appear except when the *Benecia*, a motor vessel with great beam, clipper bow, immense topheavy superstructure, and row of closets overhanging the stern, calls once a week from Tahiti.

We remained for two enjoyable weeks. Apart from the other cruising folk, our chief friends were Francis and Lisa Sanford; he, a Tahitian, is the schoolmaster and was French agent during the war. In their little house which, strange South Sea island dwelling, consists partly of a Nissen hut, they gave us superb meals of raw fish, lobster and chicken, and they showed us their famous book in which the owners of all vessels calling at their island have written something. They sent their *pirogue* for us to sail in, a swift outrigger canoe (*see p.* 81) about twenty feet in length, a dug-out breadfruit tree with planks stapled on each side to increase the freeboard. This graceful little craft was rigged with a single spritsail and was typical of the now sadly depleted fleet which used often to make the eight-mile trip in the open ocean to Motu-Iti for turtle. What fun it was to sail at high speed among the reefs and coral heads, where the bottom rushes up to meet you without warning—in some-one else's vessel.

The chart of Bora-Bora is on the large scale of three inches to the mile. Having studied it, we decided to sail *Wanderer* round in the lagoon to an anchorage on the windward side close in the lee of one of the *motus*, and there to remain for a few days studying the coral and watching the never-ending swell breaking at close quarters. So, one fine morning we set out, but as we approached the island's northern tip the sky became overcast, and as we could no longer see the dangers then, we anchored temporarily. After a couple of hours had passed the sky began to clear in patches and we started off again, but soon found ourselves among a maze of coral heads through which there appeared to be no passage suitable for our draught.

So we anchored again on a small patch of clear sand and went ahead in the dinghy to prospect, but as we failed to find a way through, we reluctantly had to abandon our attempt and return to Faanui Bay. The chart was based on an American survey made in 1942 with corrections to 1950, and it clearly showed that at the time of the survey there was a least depth of one and a quarter fathoms and a smooth sandy bottom where we found the coral heads.

'That's rather what I thought you would find,' said Tom when that evening over tea we told him and Diana about it. 'We tried to sail round in our dinghy and had to drag her over one part. Why don't you borrow the dinghy for a day?' he went on. 'The lagoon that side of the island is well worth having a look at.'

So we did that, and had the most enjoyable day of our stay at the island. We went round anti-clockwise stopping first at Toopua Island, and, apart from a short stretch at the south end of the island where we had to row through a narrow channel with a strong current against us, managed to sail all the rest of the fifteen-mile circuit. We tried to land on a tiny *motu* at the extreme edge of the southern reef to photograph the breakers there, but were frightened away by the tremendous backwash from them; we did, however, stop at one of the larger *motus* for drinking nuts, and got badly bitten by mosquitoes. The vivid colouring of the lagoon, the island and the *motus* in the brilliant tropical sunshine defies description.

For several months the islanders had been preparing to send a team to Tahiti for the big dancing competition on 14 July, an event they had won on many occasions and were to win again that year. Most evenings after dark the hackle-raising rat-tat-tat of the drums vibrated out across the lagoon. Sometimes we rowed ashore then, and making our way along the track while the throbbing noise grew louder with every step, came to a concrete floor lit by a paraffin pressure lamp. On this the barefooted dancers performed, the men and women, in separate parties of twenty or more, going through the intricate and often swift motions of the dance with the snap and precision of a Guards regiment, their shadows fantastically long and grotesque in the lamplight. Each party had a sort of sergeant-major who with loud words and eloquent gestures encouraged, instructed or just bullied the performers. When the drums suddenly stopped, the dancers appeared as though frozen; there was not a movement among them.

One evening Tom and Diana organized a small party on the grass-grown quay alongside which *Arthur Rogers* lay, and the three yachts contributed food or drink. All of us, and a number of the islanders, sat near a fire of palm fronds and coconut husks, eating spaghetti and drinking rum punch with sliced bananas in it. After the picnic meal was over, Germaine, the most sought-after dancer in the island and, it is said, in the whole of French Oceania, danced a *hula* for us to the music of three guitars. For this she slipped on the traditional white brassière and long grass skirt which, typical of those made in Bora-Bora, had been combed with a needle with such patient care that it was almost as fine as hair; the broad waistband was decorated with intricate designs of shells and sat loosely on her hips. As this attractive young woman, with the long hair and the hibiscus behind her ear, performed the swift but graceful movements of the dance in ever-increasing tempo, the firelight shone in rippling waves on her skirt. The audience exuded a faint perfume of coconut oil and *tiare*; beyond the rumbling reef the sickle of the young moon was setting, drawing a narrow silver path across the lagoon, and overhead the palms rustled in the warm and gentle breeze. Susan and I will never forget that scene or the wistful, haunting music, and now we understand much better than we did what it is that draws people from far away to visit the South Sea Islands.

Arthur Rogers left before us and was bound back for Tahiti where Tom and Diana had a charter job to do. Before they went they kindly filled our fresh water tanks with rain caught on their large awning, for there was no convenient water supply near our anchorage. *Tropic Seas* was due to leave the day after us, and as both she and *Wanderer* were bound for American Samoa we knew we should meet again.

When we weighed our anchor and stood away for the pass, our stern deck was piled with drinking nuts, and stems of bananas, more than a thousand in all, swung in the forepeak and festooned the rigging, while our shoulders were heavy with necklaces of shells—all were gifts from the kindly people of enchanted Bora-Bora.

8

BORA-BORA TO PAGO PAGO

WE had expected to make good time on the 1,100-mile run to American Samoa, but in this we were disappointed, for although the trade wind had at last settled down in the right quarter it was very light for the greater part of the way. This combined with a constant swell made the passage an unpleasant one. Mostly we ran under the mainsail and one of the spinnakers. But the mainsail is necessarily of heavy sailcloth for it has to be strong enough to stand in a gale of wind when well reefed, and is therefore unsuitable for light airs if there is much motion, for then the impetus of its own weight throws it flat aback with a crash each time the yacht is lifted forward on the swell. This is very bad for the sail itself and the rigging, and a few hours of it causes more wear and tear on the gear and the nerves of the crew than a whole gale does. I am sure that a second mainsail of very light material and made without much belly, for use in such conditions as we experienced on that trip, would be worth having; but aboard a small ocean-going yacht where all the available space is already used for stowing something, it would be difficult to find a place for it, and even more difficult to find a place for the heavy, bulky working mainsail when that is not in use. Our nylon spinnakers were very much lighter than the mainsail, and it was noticeable that when we had one of them set at the same time as the mainsail it remained full almost all the time. When we were able to use both the spinnakers on that passage, which was not often because the wind was mostly too far out on the quarter, we got immediate relief from the nerve-rasping slatting, for they remained quiet, drawing almost steadily, and enabled us to get some much-needed sleep.

Our course led close past Maupiti, which is said to be even more beautiful than Bora-Bora, and we had intended to put in there, but the pass into the lagoon is a difficult one, and the swell is reported to break right across it in bad weather. I do not know whether it was breaking the day we passed, for there was so big a swell running and so little wind that we did not dare to go close enough to have a look at it. That was another occasion when we wished we had a more powerful engine. After Maupiti our course passed midway between Motu One on the starboard side and Mopélia and Fenua Ura to port, all low atolls; but as the channel between is forty miles wide they caused us no anxiety. About 800 miles farther on, however, the small atoll of Rose Island, the easternmost outlier of the Samoa group, lay right on our course, and we would have to decide later on which side to pass it.

While we ran slowly on our way, making runs of only between seventy and ninety-five miles a day, our great stock of bananas started to ripen and, for such is the nature of the things, all began to turn yellow at the same time. We did our best to keep pace with them, for it seemed such a waste to throw them away, and for a time we ate fourteen or fifteen a day each. We ate them fried, we turned them into fritters, we had them mashed with sugar and condensed milk, we sliced them and mixed them with tins of fruit salad, and we ate them from out of their skins between meals and during night watches; but they got the better of us in the end. Had they ripened in relays, as we had been assured they would, we would still have had to eat a banana each every other mile throughout the passage if none were to be wasted. Of course we had far too many on board, yet we had not liked to refuse to accept them for fear of hurting the feelings of the generous Bora-Borans. It was a long time before we fancied bananas in any form again.

For the first nine days of the trip the weather was fine and sunny, but on the tenth there were signs of bad weather approaching. The sky looked dirty with much tangled cirrus, and there were low, black, shapeless clouds hurrying from the east; when the sun showed himself he was misty and had a halo; the glass was falling and the wind freshening. Our noon position that day showed that Rose Island lay forty-four miles away, and that by holding our present course we should pass ten miles to the north of it. That was a safe distance, but as usual in such circumstances I wondered whether my observations of the misty sun had been accurate. I therefore took two more sights in the afternoon, and they confirmed the earlier ones. So we held on, running fast under the twin spinnakers, but we bent on the trysail and storm staysail so that they could be set quickly if we had to make a sudden change of course, for there is very little steering latitude when sailing under the twins, which only work properly when the wind is nearly aft.

Just as it was getting dark, and night came early because the sky by then was completely overcast, the wind freshened to thirty-five knots. So without further ado we took in the twins and set the trysail and tiny staysail; an exhausting job because of the wild motion, and by the time it was done night had fallen.

According to my reckoning we should pass north of the atoll at 8 p.m., but to allow for any error, we decided to stand on for another hour after that before altering course for Pago Pago in Tutuila Island, the only harbour in American Samoa. We both remained on deck, one of us keeping a sharp lookout while the other steered, for we did not wish to run any risk of blundering into the atoll if my reckoning was at fault, and we kept the ship darkened so that the lookout should not be dazzled. In almost complete blackness *Wanderer* hurried along; the only light coming from her slightly phosphorescent bow-wave and wake. We felt keyed up, tense, straining our eyes into the blackness ahead, yet knowing there was little chance of seeing a low atoll on such a dark night, while the noise of the wind in the rigging, the roaring of the bow-wave and the hissing of crests all around would mask the thunder of breakers on the reef until, perhaps, we were too close to avoid them. It was no use just then to try to reassure ourselves with the knowledge that my navigation had always been accurate before and our steering good, or that anyway ten miles was a wide margin for error. We knew those things quite well, but nothing except continued vigilance on deck would satisfy us. I did make one quick journey down below to have another look at the chart by the light of an electric torch, and to check once again the time the atoll should bear south. As I leant over the chart table I felt a sharp jolt as *Wanderer* struck something hard. For one dreadful moment of panic I felt certain she had struck Rose Island reef. But Susan at once reassured me.

'It's only a dolphin,' she cried, 'there are lots of them playing round us.'

Presumably the creature had misjudged its distance in the dark, for dolphins and porpoises are usually very careful not to touch a small vessel, no matter how close to her they may be swimming.

Slowly our tension eased, and by 9 p.m. we both felt satisfied that Rose Island was safely past and away on the port quarter. So we altered course for Pago Pago. That should take us close to Tau Island, but as that was sixty miles away we would not be up with it before daybreak.

All through the night we sailed at between five and a half and six knots in spite of our tiny sail area, and at first light could see the grey dome of Tau Island standing up ahead. But it should have been fine on the starboard bow, so no doubt during our periods of steering when in the neighbourhood of Rose Island the previous evening we must have edged to the north of the set course, sub-consciously keeping away from the danger. In the feeble light of dawn I could not judge how far off the island was, so altered course to pass well to the south of it, thus bringing the wind, which by then had increased to forty knots, abeam. The motion was then so bad that for once I found it impossible to get breakfast when Susan relieved me. I was able to keep the kettle on the stove, but the leeward lurches were so violent that the water in it spurted out across the galley, and making porridge was quite out of the question. So we munched a few biscuits and not until 9 a.m. when, well clear of the south of Tau Island, we altered back on to the old course, was it possible to get a meal.

The wind took off a little in the forenoon, but by dusk was blowing as hard as ever again from the east. It did not then seem prudent to continue running for Pago Pago. For one thing we would reach the harbour during the night if we did so, and although it is lighted (except for Papeete it was the only lighted harbour all along our track from Panama) we did not care to enter it in the dark with so strong a wind blowing. But the other reason seemed more important just then. Pago Pago lies on the south-east side of Tutuila Island, a lee shore, and across its approach sprawls a shoal on which the sea breaks in bad weather. By taking the Narragansett Passage it is possible to avoid the shoal, but that is not lit and we did not consider we could find our way through it in the dark. So we hove-to on the starboard tack and drifted in a northerly direction. Every now and again a crest dashed against the weather side sending heavy spray across the deck and into the cockpit, and each time the yacht lurched to windward the whine of the wind in the rigging rose for a moment, then fell; a doleful sound which we had not heard since we were in the Bay of Biscay. We wondered how Johnnie and Mary and their young family were getting on in *Tropic Seas*. Probably still running before it, we supposed, but no doubt they also would heave-to presently and wait for better weather before making port.

Strangely enough we both slept well that night. When I looked out at dawn, conditions were so vile that I quickly went back to my bunk again. I noticed that the barometer had fallen a tenth during the night, which in that part of the world is quite a lot. All through that day we remained hove-to, and we caught a glimpse of Tutuila Island in the afternoon before rain obliterated it. With land not far away to leeward and with visibility so poor, we kept watches during the night; then, the following morning, the wind having taken off considerably, we let draw, closed with the island as the rain stopped and eventually reached the harbour.

Mountain-girt Pago Pago is one of the best harbours in the south Pacific islands for large ships. It is landlocked and almost free from shoals, but for small boats it has the disadvantage of being very deep. Having rounded Goat Island and opened up the town, we were wondering where we would find a safe anchorage in less than seventeen fathoms, when a port official boarded us from a motor launch and directed us to a berth very close to the fringing reef, off a derelict wooden pier. When we had dropped our anchor there in twelve fathoms, he advised us to run out a stern line to the pier to stop the yacht from swinging about too much in the squalls, which he warned us were severe. No doubt it was as good a berth as any in that harbour and was convenient for landing, but whenever the wind outside was between east and south, the squalls which blew across it were indeed violent and caused us many a restless night—the anchor chain rasping on the coral, and the yacht heeling sharply as the squalls caught her first on one side and then on the other. The mountain to the east of the harbour is known as the Rainmaker, and it certainly lived up to that name during our stay; just high enough to interfere with the trade wind clouds, it brought the rain cascading down its sides and over the town and harbour. Between the rain storms the sun shone hotly to make everything steam, and mildew flourished.

To our surprise, for we imagined her still to be astern of us, we saw that *Tropic Seas* was lying alongside a quay close by where she was grinding at her fenders and chafing her warps as the slight scend running in the harbour kept her on the move. As soon as we landed we went to call on the Caldwells and learnt that although they had left Bora-Bora a day after us they had arrived at Pago Pago a few hours before us, for they had kept going right through the bad weather. Johnnie said they had experienced a wind of sixty knots and that both their twin spinnakers had split. When I asked him whether he had not been worried about the shoal outside the harbour entrance in such weather, he replied: 'Waal, Eric, there's not less than thirty feet over that shoal, and I'll say that's plenty of water for us.'

I did not like to ask him if he had seen the little note 'breaks in bad weather' printed across it on the chart, for I thought he might think I was too timid, which is probably true.

The islands we had called at since leaving Tahiti had been unable to supply us with much in the way of fresh food except the inevitable coconuts and bananas, and although the Polynesians appear to thrive on such things, I do not. Apart from our meals with the Sanfords at Bora-Bora, we had had no fresh meat or potatoes, only a few eggs and no butter, for all our tinned butter, together with a large supply of toothpaste, had turned rancid in the heat; neither had we obtained any fresh vegetables except for the starchy and uninteresting root called *taro*. Perhaps as a result of living on tinned food for so long, I had slowly been developing a crop of small boils on legs and arms; each of these turned into a sore which would not heal, and some of them spread over an area two inches in diameter. Such things are common enough in the tropics but they are a nuisance, and one fears infection from the flies. However, Pago Pago has a fine modern hospital, where I was given two injections of penicillin and where each day my sores were dressed by Samoan nurses; but in such a humid climate adhesive plaster does not adhere for long, and usually most of the plaster had fallen off by the time I had walked back to the landing place. Nevertheless the sores healed in a fortnight, but I soon developed a fresh lot when we put to sea, and did not get rid of them until we reached cooler weather in New Zealand; after that they never returned although we again went through the tropics twice. Fortunately Susan had none of these things; the effect of the indifferent diet on her was merely to make her feel weary.

The excellent shops at Pago Pago supplied all our needs. What a pleasure it was to sink our teeth into the tenderest and juiciest of steaks, have real butter out of a refrigerator instead of oily margarine out of a rusty tin (we had almost forgotten there was such wonderful stuff), suck oranges, munch apples and enjoy once more potatoes, eggs, tomatoes and all the other good things of civilization.

Until 1951 Pago Pago had been an American naval base and coaling station. The island, though a beautiful one, is poor, for much of the land is too steep to be cultivated, and all that can be cultivated is already in use, so that only 1,000 tons of copra is exported a year. In navy days that did not matter much, for the Samoans were well cared for, receiving good medical attention, education and a well-ordered pattern of life, while working for the navy provided a large source of income. Now the islanders are finding it difficult to make a living and adjust themselves to a different way of life. In this they have not been helped by the rapid succession of Governors, five in four years, or by the outlook of some of the civil servants who tend to regard their two years on the island as just an uninteresting interlude.

As is only to be expected, the navy has left its mark on Pago Pago; all round the beautiful fjord-like harbour are remains of their installations. But it is not fair to judge any island by its port, which is only the peeling entrance lobby. Away in the country Tutuila, and it is not a large island for it measures only sixteen miles by three, has not been spoilt and the villages are the finest we have ever seen.

Unlike the native house in French Oceania, which can be

built by almost anyone, the Samoan *fale* (*see p.* 97) is an elaborate building requiring a good deal of skill in its construction. It consists of an oval of closely spaced pillars surmounted by a high-pitched thatched roof on a framework as complicated and well fitted as that of any ship, but its members are secured to one another not with nails or screws but with lashings. Woven screens can be lowered from the eaves to provide privacy or protection from the elements, and mats are spread on the coral floor for sitting on. A cluster of such buildings round a larger one, the village hall or meeting place, is most impressive.

The handsome Samoan man looks very tall and dignified in his *lava-lava*, a full length wrap-round skirt belted at the waist. Incidentally, the *lava-lava*, *pareu*, *sulu*, *suvà-suva* or calico are, in the Pacific Islands, much the same type of garment. The women, and we saw several hundred of them one evening at a singing festival in the recreation hall—and how beautifully they did sing—are more portly and less graceful than the Tahitian women; but the bunchy blue or green dresses with tasselled waistbands which they wore on that occasion in no way helped to reveal such charms as they may have possessed.

Several ships, including the *Tofua* from New Zealand, called at the port while we were there. Pacific islanders, no matter how poor they may be, are prodigious travellers, and most of these ships—even the smart *Tofua* herself—carried deck loads of passengers. One evening we watched the small wooden motor vessel *Ada* (she had been held up all day with engine trouble) leave, bound for Niue. She carried a cargo of 200 drums of petrol which smelt strongly, and 127 deck passengers, many of whom were smoking. There was no accommodation below deck or shelter on deck for the passengers, who took their own food with them. There was the inevitable guitar, and bottles of 'coke' were passed aboard by friends on the quay. It seemed to us, and to some of the other white people watching that night, a most hazardous venture, for the trip would take three days if all went well, and during it we felt sure someone would drop a lighted cigarette down in the hold—or were the passengers all too sick to smoke at sea? However, the ship arrived safely at her destination, as we learnt when we met her again later at Suva. But such good fortune does not always attend the voyages of the often ill-found inter-island vessels.

We had arrived at Papeete in April, and already that year four of the local trading schooners had been lost. Recently news has come of the *Joy Ita*. This 25-ton motor vessel left Western Samoa bound for the Tokelau Islands, which lie 280 miles to the north, on 10 October 1955. One month later she was found with nobody on board drifting in a waterlogged condition north of Fiji and some 500 miles to the westward of her direct course.

Also at Pago Pago was the government ship *Manua Tele*; one of her jobs was to make a trip to the Tokelau Islands four times a year. As those islands have no harbours, all communication between the ship and the shore has to be done over the reefs in canoes. Any islander travelling in one of these canoes keeps his small personal belongings in a wooden box of round or oval shape called a *toluma* which has a close-fitting watertight lid. When a canoe gets capsized in the breakers, as frequently happens, the *tolumas* are washed up on the beach and can be retrieved later. They are made from the *taumanave* tree, and used to be made in all sizes from a few inches across to two feet and more. But this tree, which has deep roots, is the only one on the islands to withstand hurricanes, and people lash themselves to it on such occasions; because of this it has now been forbidden to cut them down, so *tolumas* are made from the branches only at present and therefore are of small size. Captain Payne of the *Manua Tele* kindly presented one of them to *Wanderer* for use as a cigarette box.

It had been our intention to call at Apia in Western Samoa, though we could see from the chart that the harbour there was not a good one. But several people who knew the place well persuaded us not to go there for another reason. They said that the thieving habits of the natives were even worse than they used to be—and Apia has always had a bad reputation in that respect. It seems that one native will engage you in conversation from his canoe while his friend the other side of the yacht is cutting off the falls of the halyards and removing anything else he can lay his hands on. Even whole boats have been stolen in recent years. So we agreed to miss out Western Samoa and go direct to the Tonga or Friendly Islands, the last surviving kingdom of the South Seas, which is so capably ruled by Queen Salote, and from there to head for Fiji.

When we went to obtain our clearance at the port office before leaving, we were informed that there would be $9 to pay for harbour dues. This seemed to us unreasonable in a natural harbour where we had lain to our own anchor, and it was contrary to the mutual arrangement between Britain and America whereby yachts are exempt from dues when visiting each other's countries; this was a matter on which we had been advised by the American-organized Seven Seas Cruising Association. Therefore we protested and asked to see the Acting Governor, whom we had met at a dinner party given for us by the Attorney General and his wife. He was much more easy of access than such important people usually are, and received us kindly, but the best he could do for us was to halve the dues. That was not what we were seeking, for it was the principle of the thing rather than the small sum at stake that concerned us, and we had in mind any other yachts that might follow after us. However, there was nothing more we could do except pay what was asked and go. Incidentally, Papeete and Pago Pago were the only ports during our three-year cruise at which we were asked to pay any harbour dues, and we certainly are most grateful to the many port authorities who waived their charges for us. I do wish that foreign yachts visiting England could be treated with similar courtesy.

9

A GALE IN THE SOUTH PACIFIC

WHENEVER Susan and I remain in port for more than a week we lose our sea-legs and on putting to sea have to go through the unpleasant business of finding them again. And so it was when, having worked our way with some difficulty, because of the calms and squalls in the entrance, out of Pago Pago harbour, we found a rough sea kicked up by the strong south-east wind. We are not often sick, but for the first two days we usually feel squeamish, headachy and off our food. Poor Susan suffers in this way more than I do, but she never lets it get the better of her, and will struggle in the galley preparing food which sometimes she is unable to eat, and her feeling of lethargy never makes her late when relieving me on deck.

Our course for Vava'u, the most northerly inhabited island of the Tonga Group, was in a south-westerly direction and the wind was abeam. As *Wanderer* hurried on her way, the spray from the weather bow-wave which she flung high into the air was thrown back by the wind to drench the helmsman, and as each steep sea threw her to leeward he had to hang on tight to avoid being flung away from the tiller. Down below the general discomfort was added to by the fact that the forehatch, which until then we had usually kept partly open on its side flaps, had to be tightly closed, and the ventilators, even those with traps designed to prevent water finding its way below, had to be turned with their backs to the wind. The heat, the humidity and the lack of fresh air made the normally comfortable cabin a wretched place in which to cook, navigate or rest.

PLATE 15

Top: Susan proudly displays her loaf and the ring dish in which it was baked.
Bottom: After the four-day gale our sea-anchor was in a sorry state.

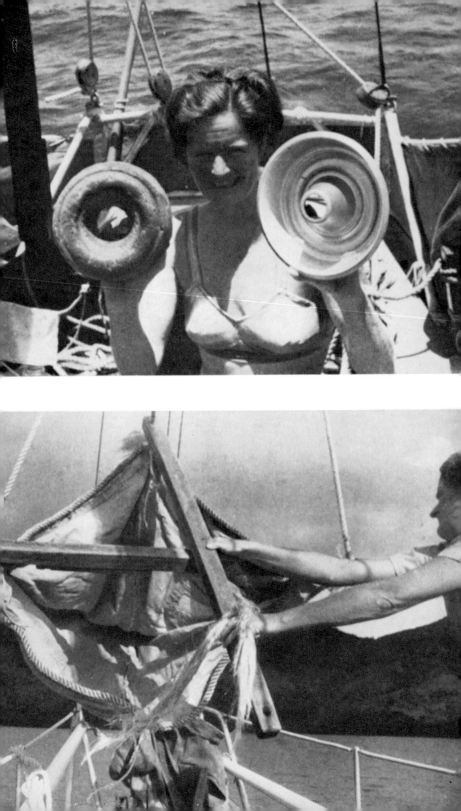

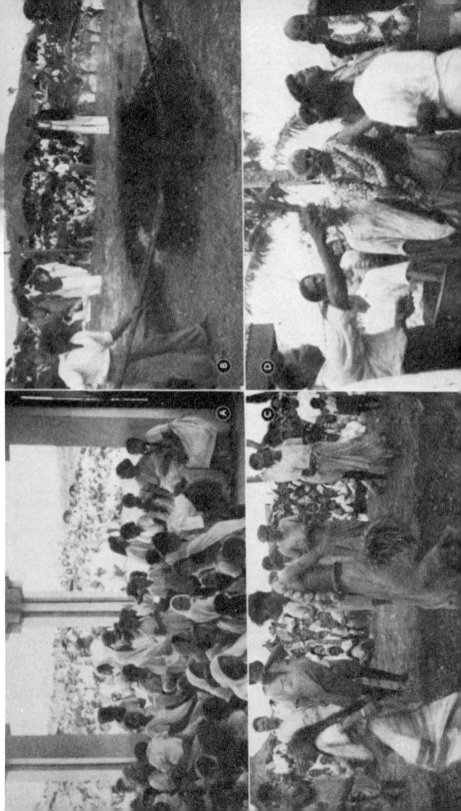

The wind was strong, sometimes reaching moderate gale force in the squalls, and the yacht was under much reduced sail; but even then we could not get the sleep we needed except by backing the staysail to make her sail more slowly; we did that at night on several occasions and for all meals, but even then averaged more than 100 miles a day.

The weather continued to be boisterous and our third night at sea looked thoroughly evil. A smeary sky through which the moon, encircled by a great halo, shone wanly, was partly obscured by low, black, oily-looking clouds of the same type as had been the forerunners of the last gale. But we thought the chance of more bad weather should be slight, for the pilot chart showed in our area winds averaging only force 4, a moderate breeze of fifteen knots, five per cent. of calm, and four per cent. of gales. Nevertheless previous small-boat voyagers, Muhlhauser, Pidgeon, Long and Kaufman, had all found bad weather in the neighbourhood of the Tongas, and the indications were that we would too unless we were able to reach port first, which might be possible as we expected to be in the lee of the island the following morning.

We sailed fast all that night and before dawn saw what might be land ahead, though that should not have been so according to my reckoning. Anxious though we were to get on and find shelter, we did not intend to take unnecessary risks; so we hove-to and waited for daylight, when our land resolved itself into a low cloud bank. At 8 a.m. Susan caught a glimpse of what again might be land, but we were not certain of it until an hour and a half later, by which time I had taken an observation of the brassy, indistinct sun above the black and almost invisible horizon; fortunately I did not have to work out that sight.

At 11.30 a.m. we were up with the land in the vicinity of Houmafakalele Point—what a name for a weary navigator to

---

PLATE 16

The Hindu fire-walking ceremony at Suva. *A* The temple and its surroundings were packed with yellow-robed figures. *B* Attendants with long-handled hoes were spreading the red-hot ash in an even layer. *C* The only woman and one of the thirty-nine men dancing barefoot in the firepit. *D* The majority were dreadfully disfigured. Beneath the pointing hand is a face transfixed with a steel skewer, and immediately to the right one with a toasting fork through both cheeks, its owner wearing yellow wreaths round his shoulders and carrying a whip in his hand.

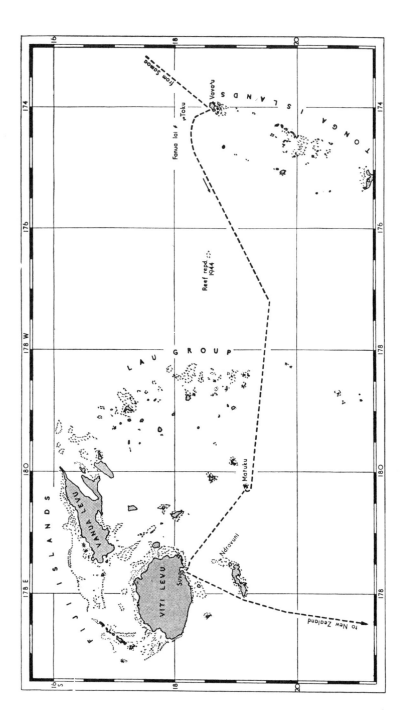

spell. On the port bow the coast, a continuous line of 500-foot cliffs, curved away to form a bay four miles wide; but suddenly the coast was obliterated by a storm of blinding rain. We had by then already taken in the staysail and close-reefed the mainsail, but even so were over-canvased, for the wind increased with the onset of rain to fifty knots, a whole gale. A smother of spume blew low across the grey sea as we roared along, steering by compass for the point at the far end of the bay which came looming out of the rain to meet us when no more than 200 yards distant.

Beyond that point and eight miles to windward up a wide but twisting channel lay Neiafu, the one harbour in Vava'u, and the only place in which we could find shelter and water shallow enough in which to anchor. But we knew it was useless to attempt to beat in, for even under her tiny spread of sail *Wanderer* was heavily pressed, while to try to beat in under the trysail would be dangerous, for in such a strong wind we could not rely on the yacht being under complete control. So we gybed round and stood back across the bay, the shore of which was invisible, undecided what to do. The bay was deep and its bottom of coral, so we could not anchor there. It seemed a pity to run away out to sea when the harbour lay so near and we were both in urgent need of a rest and a good meal, yet we did not care for the idea of standing off and on close to the shore in such poor visibility.

While we were still wondering what we could do and half hoping the weather might improve, the wind decided for us. It blew with such insane, shrieking fury that *Wanderer* staggered under the weight of it, and we, fearful that the mast or boom might carry away, clawed the sail down, muzzled it somehow and got some gaskets round it. Never before, except in short squalls, had we experienced so great a gale at sea, something in excess of sixty-five knots. Then we lashed the helm down and got the yacht to lie beam on to wind and sea. She drifted to leeward and the pressure of the gale on her bare mast and rigging heeled her over to an angle of twenty degrees.

We were both soaked to the skin and our teeth were chattering partly with nervous exhaustion and partly with cold, for the thermometer had fallen lower than it had ever been since we left England. So we went below, changed into dry clothes and had a meal of soup and corned beef fried with onions, quickly prepared and appetizing, but while Susan was getting it she broke a bowl and got a sharp splinter of china in her bare foot.

Apart from its normal diurnal rise and fall the barometer was steady, so we expected the weather to improve soon, and when it did we had every intention of making sail and beating back to the harbour. But no improvement came. The hours went by and the gale continued its high-pitched scream in the rigging. As we blew farther away from the island's lee the sea increased in size and *Wanderer* tended to fore-reach now and then, and by late afternoon heavy crests were beginning to break aboard. We therefore decided to stream the sea-anchor so as to get the yacht more nearly end-on to the seas and at the same time reduce her drift to the minimum.

This was of the pyramidal type, its mouth (two and a half feet square) being kept open by stout crossbars of oak which were held together at the point where they crossed by a brass bolt. It was strongly made, the canvas being a heavy flax, and it was roped throughout with $1\frac{3}{4}$-inch rope the four parts of which, each having passed through a hole at the end of each crossbar, were brought together at a large iron thimble to form the bridle. A lead weight secured to one of the crossbars kept the anchor submerged and prevented it from spinning. Previous experience in another vessel had convinced us that the modern yacht, with her deep heel and shallow forefoot, will not ride head to wind with a sea-anchor streamed from the bow unless she can set a stout riding sail aft. But as *Wanderer* has only one mast we could not do that, so we put the sea-anchor out from the stern on a 30-fathom warp of 2-inch hemp secured to a samson post on the port quarter.

With the tiller lashed amidships the yacht made a course straight down wind at a speed of about one and a half knots and rolled heavily. But we did not wish to continue in that direction because a few miles to leeward of us lay the low island of Toku with a breaking rock a short distance from it, and beyond it lay an active volcano, Fanua lai. Neither was inhabited or lighted. With heavy rain driven horizontally by a gale of such strength that we could show no canvas to it, these were uncomfortable neighbours to have under our lee with night coming on. So we lashed the tiller to starboard, thus bringing the wind well out on the port quarter, and we hoped the yacht would then work across the wind sufficiently to go clear of the dangers. She lay safely like that, only occasionally taking aboard the top of a crest, and there was no strain on the rudder. In my opinion that is the most important advantage of riding by the stern.

Nights in the tropics are always long, and as it was then mid-winter in the southern hemisphere we knew there would be at least twelve hours of darkness. With the cloud pall low and heavy with rain, night came early, and to us lying uneasily in our bunks it seemed interminable. The sea was increasing all the time and it threw the yacht heavily to leeward again and again with a crash which we thought must surely start a seam or butt. On the swift upward lurch after each leeward roll the rigging screamed more shrilly as though in protest at such treatment, and something aloft vibrated furiously, shaking the mast and the whole ship. Several times during the night I looked in the bilge to see if *Wanderer* was making any water, but there was no more than usual there, and I blessed William King's good men who had built the little vessel so honestly and well. I thought of them all in the big black building shop behind the sea wall at Burnham-on-Crouch: Ted Cole, Stanley Jenkins, Rashbrook and the rest, now no doubt at work on someone else's dream-ship under the watchful and sympathetic eye of Herbert Page the manager, for it would be afternoon with them. I imagined I could hear the whirr of the planing machine, the musical rasp of the saw, the hollow sound of a caulking mallet; I could almost smell the sweet scent of sawdust and new wood shavings. It all seemed so peaceful, so ordered and oh, so far away from us just then, enveloped as we were in a howling blackness with dangers under our lee.

In turn Susan and I struggled wearily over our canvas bunkboards, clawed our way to the hatch, slid it back a few inches and had a look round, for the proximity of the unlit islands to leeward caused a constant, nagging anxiety. But there was never anything to see in the darkness except our masthead light, blurred with rain, cutting crazy arcs in the black murk overhead.

Dawn came on leaden feet and it was with a feeling of immense relief that we watched the first faint grey light of day creeping through the ports. A sickly yellow streak in the eastern sky signified sunrise. Having had a good look round, we returned to our bunks and lay late in them for they were the only places aboard where there was some semblance of comfort, and we discussed what we would eat if we could have the breakfasts of our choice. Susan was all for kippers, while I pined for rashers of bacon crisply fried and mounted on fingers of bread fried golden brown; but we both agreed that lots of thin toast with cold, firm butter and Oxford marmalade would be the right thing to follow up with, and coffee, of course, lashings of it with fresh creamy milk. Instead, all I was able to produce after a sordid struggle with sliding crockery and a swinging stove which persisted in leaping right out of its gimbals until I lashed it in with seizing wire, was porridge, coffee essence with tinned milk, and vitamin pills.

During the morning the wind moderated to a strong gale and backed several points, and for a time the rain stopped. Then we were able to see Fanua lai, grey and sinister with jets of smoke belching from its crater to be whipped away by the wind. It was several miles distant and no longer to leeward, so throughout that anxious night *Wanderer* had succeeded in working across the wind and had taken herself clear of the dangers. Of the lower island, Toku, we saw nothing. We could then have lashed the helm amidships and drifted straight down wind had we wished to do so; but such a course would have taken us more quickly from the slight shelter the Tonga reefs and islands still provided and, of course, farther from Neiafu, which port we still hoped to reach when conditions improved. So we left the tiller as it was, crawled once more into our bunks before noon and, except for going on deck periodically to renew the chafing gear on the sea-anchor warp where it passed through the fairlead and round the samson post, remained in them until the next morning.

On the third day the wind dropped to forty knots, a fresh gale, but the rain continued; the sea was larger than before and the motion more violent, but the surface of the ocean was no longer covered with white spume. We were beginning to get worried by then about another danger, a dotted oval line on the chart with the words 'Reef reported 1944' against it. The *Pacific Islands Pilot Vol. II* was published in 1943, so there

could be no mention of this reef in it, but in the latest Supple-
ment we found the following note:

'A reef was reported in 1944 in lat. 18° 33' S., long. 176°
27' W., about 100 miles westward of the northern end of the
Tonga Islands; its western end was reported to be about five
feet above the surface and its eastern end submerged but
marked by breakers.'

I had no precise knowledge of our position, the dead
reckoning being little better than a guess, but the position I
marked on the chart as being ours at noon that day was
barely forty miles to windward of the reef. Assuming that both
our position and that of the reef were correct, we would, with
the helm still lashed to starboard, drift clear of it. But our
position was suspect, and as the reef was marked only with a
dotted line on the chart we must regard it as a vigia. To quote
again from the *Pilot*:

'In no part of the world are there so many known dangerous
coral reefs and small islets rising abruptly from great depths
as in the western part of the South Pacific; in addition a vast
number of vigias, that is, shoals, the locality and even the
existence of which is doubtful, have from time to time been
reported. Many of these have been disproved by laborious
search, but some are still indicated on the charts, and until
they have been clearly disproved must continue a source of
constant anxiety and perplexity to the navigator of this ocean.'

That evening at dusk I slid back the hatch to have one last
look at the dismal scene before night settled in, for that dotted
oval on the chart was much to the forefront of our minds. I
was standing in the hatchway with the upper half of my body
outside in the rain and spray when a crest, heavier than any
we had previously experienced, came aboard over the quarter.
It tore away the canvas dodgers which were lashed to the
guardrails round the after end of the yacht, filled the cockpit
right up and flooded the deck fore-and-aft. It knocked me
down the hatchway and some of it came in after me, where it
ran right through the accommodation into the forepeak,
climbing into my bunk on the way and into the bookshelf
above it; it inundated the chart stowage where 350 Admiralty
charts lay in drawers, and even succeeded in breaking one of
the lamp chimneys which was five feet above the cabin floor.

While Susan upended my mattress to prevent the water from soaking into it, I took a bucket and baled the cockpit, for the cockpit drains were too small to deal quickly with so large a volume of water, and I was fearful lest, held down by the weight of water aft, the yacht might fail to rise sufficiently to the next big sea. Much of that night was spent mopping water from books and charts with towels which had to be wrung out frequently, and in going on deck to look for breakers on the dreaded reef which we knew quite well we could not expect to see more than a few yards off. But we noticed with that strained attention a long-drawn-out gale begets that there were occasional lulls when the wind hummed a lower note in the rigging, and as the night dragged on these lulls were more frequent and longer lasting. The gale was blowing itself out.

Next day the wind dropped to a mere thirty knots; the sun shone fitfully from widening rifts in the clouds, and I was able to get observations of him with which to fix our position. This showed that during the four days we had lain to the sea-anchor we had drifted 120 miles, an average speed of $1\frac{1}{4}$ knots. But, and this is the interesting point for it shows what a sea-anchor can do when streamed over the stern and used in conjunction with the helm, we had made good a course in a west-south-west direction with a wind varying between east and south-east. We were then 100 miles from Vava'u and 150 from the nearest island of the Fiji group. Lack of sleep, worry, and the continuous violent motion had made us so tired that we did not feel equal to attempting the hard beat back to Vava'u against the heavy sea then running, so we reluctantly decided to abandon the Tonga Islands and make a fair wind of it for Fiji.

After lunch we hove in the sea-anchor and found it to be in a sorry state. (*See p.* 112.) One of the four parts of the bridle had parted; the canvas bag was holed in several places; the bolt holding the crossbars together had vanished, and the crossbars themselves were rough and splintered. The state of the warp, an almost new one, was equally bad. It was stranded in six places, and that cannot have been due to chafe, for as we had not used a tripping line there was nothing for it to chafe against. Overloading must have been the cause, and certainly the strain on it had been considerable. I believe that the conical type of sea-anchor might have lasted better. We were given one of these in New Zealand. It was made for a flying boat and had a stainless steel hoop hinged in the middle for convenience when stowing, but throughout the rest of our voyage we had no occasion to use it.

For the first eighteen hours after getting under way from the sea-anchor we ran at five and a half knots under the second staysail only, but after that we were able to make more sail as the weather became really fine at last. We passed south of the Lau Islands, where for a short time we fussed about another vigia until we learnt from the latest *Notices to Mariners* that it had been disproved, and then made a good landfall on the island of Matuku. We chose that island because it had a snug harbour within its reef where we could put in for a rest and a clean-up. The latter was a matter of some urgency, for during the gale a half-pound tin of yeast had burst open and emptied its contents into the bilge where they quickly got together with the bilge water and fermented. In its early stages the fermentation produced the not unpleasant aroma of a brewery, but later the ship smelt like a pigsty. The removal of this mess took the best part of a day and then we slept our fill.

The 722 miles we had covered since leaving Pago Pago took ten days. During that period we were hove-to for thirteen hours, under bare poles for two and a half hours, riding to the sea-anchor for ninety-three and a half hours and running under the second staysail only for eighteen hours. For most of the rest of the time we were more or less reefed.

Just before reaching Matuku we had crossed the 180th meridian, and then in longitude, though not in distance, had sailed half way round the world. We had come some 12,000 miles, but because we intended to sail south to New Zealand, then north round Australia and south once more to round the Cape of Good Hope, we still had 20,000 miles yet to go. As we were sailing from east to west we had to jump a whole day on crossing the meridian, and so had a nice short six-day week. The reason for this is, of course, that zone by zone we had been putting our clocks back an hour at a time until, on reaching the 180th meridian, they were twelve hours slow on Greenwich mean time. As we proceeded to the westward we would have to continue putting them back, so that on arrival in England they would be twenty-four hours or a whole day slow if we did not skip a day. If we had been bound the other way, from west to east, we would have been putting the clocks on instead of back, and so would have had to take in an extra day by having an eight-day week.

We did not land at Matuku, nor did we have any contact with the shore, because we feared there might be trouble with the officials at Suva, the capital of Fiji, if on arrival there it was learnt that we had done so without being granted pratique. At that time Fiji was taking all possible steps to prevent the rhinoceros beetle from getting a stranglehold on the palms in that country. So after resting and eating and drying out all the wet gear, we sailed for Suva. The distance is only 100 miles, but we had some difficulty in finding the entrance to the harbour through the reef, for when we arrived before dawn drizzle obscured everything including the leading lights. So we hove-to and waited for dawn, when we were able to identify two *motus* on the reef and discovered that an easterly current had set us several miles up the coast. We then bore away for the pass, a bearing of which we were able to get when *Tofua* came steaming out of it. Soon afterwards we reached the smooth water of the harbour, where we worked our way up to the town and anchored off the harbourmaster's office. The customs cleared us quickly and without much formality, for this was a British port, but they insisted on sealing our bonded stores locker which then contained only a few cigarettes and two bottles of spirits, all that remained of the stores we had shipped at Antigua, our last British stopping-place.

10

FIJI

THE fine harbour of Suva is formed by a large indentation in the southern coastline of Viti Levu, the biggest of the Fijian islands. To the north and north-west stands a range of mountains with bold peaks and densely wooded slopes; to the south is the protecting reef, parts of which dry, and on the east is the busy town with the red-roofed bungalows of the residential quarter standing amidst the trees behind it and extending over most of Suva Point.

Our berth off the town was an interesting one. Ocean-going ships lay at the quays loading copra and sugar, and there was an almost constant coming and going of small cutters employed in the inter-island trade. But many of these appeared to be under indifferent control and there was some risk of damage being done by collision, so when we had collected our mail and done our shopping, we moved away and found a quieter berth in very shallow and strangely muddy water off the yacht club. On landing at the jetty there we were promptly made honorary members for our stay, and everything possible was done for our comfort and convenience.

The only disadvantage of that berth was its distance from the town, a long walk on the main road where the hurrying traffic splashed us with mud and the buses were always too crowded to be worth consideration. Nevertheless Susan walked into town most days determined to make up for our largely tinned seagoing diet with plenty of fresh food while in port. The market, where she did most of her shopping for fruit and vegetables, was a fascinating place with its strange mixture of burly, cheerful Fijians, thin, colourfully robed Indians and a few immaculate Europeans—a babel of noise and confusion.

I sometimes wonder how the average British housewife would have managed had she suddenly found herself in Susan's shoes. With a purse full of strange-looking banknotes and some chicken feed she would have found herself again and again landed in some place of which she knew absolutely nothing, and where, perhaps, she could not even speak or understand the language. There, after several weeks or even months out of reach of any kind of shop, she would have to buy all the many things she needed. Susan says she does not like shopping, but I know she got much satisfaction from her successful efforts under these unusual conditions, especially when, as at Suva, there was a good market where she could pick and choose and compare the prices asked at one stall with those of another. No matter in what country she might be, she very soon taught herself to count in the strange language and to understand the peculiar money, and the speed with which she learnt the geography of a strange town, which were the best and most courteous shops and which the ones to avoid, always amazed me. At Suva, of course, there were no difficulties about language or money, but the long trudge back to the club in the heat or in the rain, carrying bags filled with heavy fruit, was not a thing that any woman should be expected to do day after day. So when I was not writing or working about the yacht I went with her, but that was not as often as I could have wished.

Many times we have been asked how we managed to keep to our schedule as closely as we did right through the voyage. This was not so difficult as it may at first appear, for in our plans we had allowed ourselves stops of considerable length at the end of each long passage. If we arrived early we made our stop just that much longer, while if we were late we cut our stay so as to leave on the pre-arranged date. As we had failed to call at the Tonga Islands because of the bad weather we had encountered in their neighbourhood, we were able to stay longer in Fiji and were there for seven weeks, as our date of departure on the passage to New Zealand was arranged for 1 September; we had no intention of leaving earlier because we wanted the southern winter to have reached its end before we sailed south out of the tropics.

For most of that time *Wanderer* remained at Suva. This may seem rather unenterprising when one considers that the Fiji archipelago consists of 300 islands of which about 100 are inhabited.

'You simply must go and look at some of our lovely coral

reefs,' several people told us. But there were a number of reasons for our immobility. One of these was that we had already seen quite enough lovely coral reefs to last us for a long time, and there would be plenty more of them when we came to the east coast of Australia. But there were other things to hold us back. Rainfall is heavy on the south-east sides of the Fiji Islands, which are exposed to the trade wind, exceeding 100 inches a year; Suva is a particularly wet spot, with the record fall of twenty-six inches in twenty-four hours, which is more than the average for the whole year in London. It is said that if you can see the mountains from the town it is going to rain,' and if you cannot see them it is raining. For the first month of our stay rain fell every day and often all day; mostly this was a fine drizzle from a low, grey sky, but sometimes for short periods it rained heavily. Also the wind was strong. Ships making the port reported bad weather to the southward, an area of 2,000 square miles of rain and gales which showed no sign of movement for some weeks. A schooner leaving the harbour had all her sails blown away, a yacht from New Zealand had been dismasted, and an inter-island vessel vanished without trace near Numea with the loss of one hundred lives. We were certainly thankful to be in out of it, but even in port such weather was a nuisance, for it hampered us in attending to the many little needs of the yacht. However, the chief reason for our long stay in one place was the large number of friends we made, all of them British and most of them in the administrative or legal services.

Shortly after our arrival the Solicitor General, Gordon Bryce, and his wife Mollie invited us to a cocktail party they were giving for the new Lord Chief Justice who had just been sworn in. The sudden and unexpected appearance of our two new faces in that comparatively small British community came as something out of a conjurer's hat, and quite unintentionally we stole m'lud's thunder; but he was very nice about it. That party started the social ball rolling, and it gathered momentum so that rarely a day passed without someone inviting us out for lunch or dinner or for a drive to see something of the wet but fertile and beautiful island. We were particularly grateful to Kingsley Roth, Secretary for Fijian Affairs, who for twenty-five years had made a study of the Fijian way of life, and his wife Jane, for several expeditions of this sort, and for much valuable and interesting information about the people.

For months we had been cruising among the Polynesian Islands where there is no malaria, and no snakes or dangerous insects, and we had got to know their handsome, brown-skinned, straight-haired people. But on crossing the inter-national date line we had left Polynesia astern and entered Melanesia. Skins there are blacker, faces are flatter, lips thicker, and straight hair changes to fuzzy mops (*see p.* 97), while some of the islands are large land masses where the jungle is loud with the noise of insects, and there is fever. We had grown fond of the Polynesians; but we found the Fijians, with their fine carriage, their ugly but intelligent and kindly faces, their mops of hair standing straight out from the scalp resembling a guardsman's busby, and their clean, communal village life, to be quite lovable. And they commanded our respect, as anyone will understand who has done no more than watch the Suva police in their navy blue tunic-shirts, scalloped white sulus and scarlet cummerbunds, drilling on the parade ground.

But today the majority of the population is not Fijian. In 1879 Indian immigrants were brought to the colony to work on the sugar-cane estates. Finding conditions superior to those of their homeland, most of them elected to remain in the islands, where they multiplied exceedingly and at the time of our visit outnumbered the 124,000 native Fijians by 6,000. There is no love lost between the two races, each considering the other to be inferior and, unlike the Polynesians and Chinese, they do not intermarry. As outsiders taking only a brief look at the colony, we do not know enough to comment intelligently on the situa-tion; but our sympathies are entirely with the cheerful, courteous and friendly Fijian who belongs there, and not with the sour-looking, emaciated invader from India who in time, we fear, will overrun the place.

In August the Hindus were to perform their annual fire-walking ceremony, and although several people had warned us not to watch that sordid spectacle where things do happen which Europeans cannot understand or explain, Susan and I decided to attend, for we were both sceptical of the stories we had heard and wanted to see for ourselves.

It was on a gloomy Sunday afternoon with the usual drizzle falling that we, in company with Ginger Cullen and well fortified by one of Ginger's famous curry lunches, made our way with a straggling crowd of Indians and Fijians up a loose shingle track on a treeless hillside to the Hindu temple outside the town. On two sides the ground rose steeply from the temple, forming a natural grand-stand, and this was tightly packed with a colourful crowd of spectators. As our seats there were too distant to allow us to take any photographs of the ceremony, I asked an usher whether I might go on to the holy ground. He agreed and said I might take any pictures I liked provided I first removed my sandals, took my camera out of its case and left my wallet behind, for nothing made of leather was permitted within the single strand of wire which had been strung on some rickety posts to mark the boundary between common and holy ground. So, barefooted on the slimy, trampled earth, and trying to protect the camera from the drizzle as best I could inside my thin shirt, I entered the temple, which was packed (*see p.* 113), and there had a peep into an inner place where, in the smoky light from oil lamps, I could see the effigies of Nanda Devi (the goddess of healing) and Shiva (the goddess of vengeance). Most of the people in the temple wore yellow robes and some had daubs of yellow paint on forehead and cheeks, while many of the women wore nose ornaments. There were several tin baths containing yellow water, coloured with what appeared to be curry powder lavishly thrown in by the handful. In each bath was a palm frond with which the devout splashed the yellow water over themselves and everyone else within range.

The holy ground extended a little distance to the eastward of the temple's main doorway, and there, grey and sinister in a shallow pit a few inches deep and measuring approximately twenty-five feet by ten, lay a huge heap of ash. For the past two days a great fire of timber had been kept burning in that place, and the heat from the ash, which now and again glowed evilly, almost white, was terrific. When a cigarette carton was thrown on to it by an onlooker it did not burn in the ordinary way; a small jet of flame shot up as though from celluloid and the carton vanished instantly. A strip of charred and trampled grass twenty feet in width separated the pit from the boundary wire, and there I was allowed to remain kneeling so as not to obstruct the view.

While I waited a shower of heavy rain changed the whole appearance of the crowd. Until then it had been a brilliant mosaic, the shirts and dresses and robes being of every rainbow hue; but as the rain came down up went a thousand umbrellas, and the banks of spectators changed from brightness to an almost uniform black.

Presently there was a stir as a roll of drums was heard, and towards the holy ground through a lane which opened in the crowd came a fantastic procession. But for a moment I caught only a glimpse of it, for the spectators started to close in excitedly on the wire guarding the arena. Before they could reach it, however, an Indian attendant near the fire-pit, a tall thin man with sunken cheeks and blazing eyes, produced from somewhere a great whip; cracking this above his head he advanced upon the press, which immediately retreated and thereafter remained at a respectful distance. As the crowd moved away the procession entered the holy ground. Drummers led it and brought up the rear, the fast rattle of the sticks on the taut skins sending a shiver down my spine; between the drummers, jigging fast to the wild tattoo, came a thread of yellow figures, thirty-nine men and one woman. These were the fire-walkers who had been preparing themselves for the ordeal for the past month. Some of the men were bare from the waist up, except for a yellow wreath round the neck, and faces, chests and arms had dabs of yellow on them; others wore shirts. The majority were dreadfully disfigured. Through the softest and tenderest parts of their flesh, in throat and breast and back, were thrust skewers and steel knitting needles, and some —most sickening sight—had such things driven right through their faces, entering one cheek and emerging from the other. One, an elderly man, had a toasting fork through his face, the three prongs protruding from his right cheek and the handle from his left; through his open hanging mouth I could see the steel shaft passing from one cheek to the other. (*See p.* 113.) Some had whips with which they beat themselves. With heads tilted back, and wide, glazed eyes staring unseeingly at the grey heavens, they danced insanely along to the fast beat of the drums, moving past me to the far end of the fire-pit. Meanwhile attendants with long-handled hoes were quickly spreading the red-hot ash in a thick, even layer over the full length and breadth of the pit. (*See p.* 113.)

When the drums stopped beating there was a hush almost as though the entire audience was holding its breath. Susan told me afterwards that she, too, was in a tense state by then, although she was a considerable distance from the scene, which was partly obscured from her by the crowd.

Suddenly one of the fire-walkers stepped off the grass on to the embers and walked right through the pit; he moved fast. Others followed singly or in pairs. Some walked at a normal speed, others plodded slowly, scuffling in the ashes from which wicked little tongues of pale flame licked, while yet others actually danced their way across. The only woman remained a long time on the ashes, swaying from side to side (*see p.* 113), and as she reached the far end and stepped on to the slippery earth she lost her balance; for one awful moment I feared she was going to fall backwards on to the ashes, but mercifully some-one caught and steadied her before that could happen. And so it went on, fanatic after fanatic on bare feet crossing that pit from which the heat, coupled with the drizzle, persisted in fogging my camera lens and making me sweat, though I was twenty feet from it. Each at the end of his walk entered the temple through the main door, there I believe to prostrate himself before Nanda Devi.

It would appear, though few to whom I have spoken seem clear about this, that the fire-walking is done in aid of healing, either for some ailment of the walker's, or his friends or relatives. As each prostrates himself before the effigy his feet are examined by a priest; anyone whose feet are burnt or even blistered is considered to lack faith and must go through the ordeal again some other time; the others get their prayers answered.

While they were in the temple and out of my sight, all the disfiguring instruments, the skewers, needles and toasting forks, were removed; then the fire-walkers emerged and danced in procession five times round the fire-pit following the effigy of Nanda Devi, which was borne on a stretcher shoulder high beneath a large umbrella. I was still kneeling at the side of the pit, and the procession passed so close that the long, damp yellow robes of the people taking part brushed against me.

A.W.W.—K

I could see no injury to any single one of them; no burns or blisters on the feet which had so recently been through the fire and which now were being lifted high and stamped down on the ground as they danced along; and, even more miraculous, there were no visible wounds in the flesh of faces, throats, breasts or backs to show where the disfiguring instruments had passed through, no single drop of blood.

Finally all the procession followed the image into the temple, there perhaps to perform some rite of which I know nothing. The crowd began to disperse and made its way down the hill in the gathering darkness towards the cheerful lights of the town, and Ginger, Susan and I, shocked and silent, went with it.

As we wished to see something more of the Fijians in their natural surroundings and living their proper life than was possible in the neighbourhood of Suva, we made an expedition in *Wanderer* to a small and rarely-visited island in the Great Astrolabe Reef fifty miles to the southward. This was discovered by Captain Bligh, but he made no attempt to enter its lagoon. We left our Suva anchorage at midnight, and as soon as we were clear of the canopy of cloud hanging over Viti Levu, sailed most pleasantly in starlight closehauled to the moderate trade wind. It was an unusual thing for us to make a single night passage, and a brief one at that, and we much enjoyed it. Soon after breakfast the big island of Kandavu stood boldly up ahead and we could make out the smaller and nearer islands within the reef. There was very little swell and therefore not much surf, but from aloft the pale colouring of the reef showed up well. We sailed into the lagoon by way of Usborne Pass, the most northerly entrance. From aloft and with the sun shining brightly from just abaft the beam, I could see the dangers on the port hand side, a cluster of coral heads which gave the pass the appearance of a partly opened door. Avoiding them easily, we were soon slipping across the smooth, sparkling water, which was dark blue except where the shoals showed brown or pale green. Passing close to a small, uninhabited island, we headed for Ndravuni, the island of our choice two miles farther on, but as we came close to it a barrier of brown and purple coral heads lay right athwart our course. Uncertain whether there was enough water over them for us, we anchored and went ahead in the dinghy to prospect.

There proved to be more water in places than we had thought, but along a zig-zag course. So we returned to *Wanderer*, got under way and on the rising tide motored cautiously through into the strip of clear water which skirted the island's north-west shore, and there watched our anchor plunge down to the bottom in three fathoms of bright green water, turn over and dig into the smooth sand. The water there was so transparent, and the light shining up from the bottom was so bright, that *Wanderer* had the appearance of floating in air.

When we landed on the beach of white coral sand, which was pleasantly warm to our bare feet, most of the male population of the island came to meet us. There was one among them who could talk a little English, and saying that the chief wished to speak with us, he went with us to the village. This was a typical Fijian village. All the *bures* (houses) were constructed of thatch, roof and walls alike, on a timber framework. Outside one of these the chief was standing, a tall man with a fine busby of hair; in spite of the ragged shorts he was wearing, he possessed great dignity. In a deep, quiet voice he made a courteous and enthusiastic speech of welcome, which the English-speaking islander did his best to interpret sentence by sentence. I replied, the chief listening attentively, and then he preceded us into the largest *bure* of the village. This had two doors but no windows, and it was cool in there, for the thick thatch of such buildings has great insulating properties, and it was dark after the sun-glare outside. Dimly we made out a circle of sixteen men seated cross-legged on the mat-covered floor. We shook the hand of each in turn and then sat down in the circle facing the chief. In the centre of the circle was a shallow wooden bowl supported on short legs. By then our eyes were growing accustomed to the dim light of the *bure* and we could see that the bowl contained a pale brown liquid. A young native filled a half coconut husk from the bowl, and going down on one knee, presented it to me. As I drank its contents the circle of seated men gave four slow handclaps and all in unison said *a maca*. The ceremony was repeated twice and then the filled husk was presented to every man in turn. Susan also was given the drink, but from a separate husk. This was *yanggona*, a drink made from the pounded *yanggona* root mixed with water; it used to be made by the young maidens of the village masticating the root and was said to be stronger in those days. It has a clean but rather bitter taste and leaves the feeling that the roof of the mouth is coated with something thin that the tongue cannot remove. Taken in excess it is said to weaken the legs, but it is non-alcoholic and has no effect on the brain. Throughout Fiji *yanggona* is prepared with elaborate ceremonial before any event of importance, but people will drink it at any time just as the New Zealanders will drink tea. I understand the Indians in Fiji are now taking to this drink, which they can buy ready-made in bottles, like lemonade.

We had brought with us some tobacco, sweets and old illustrated magazines which we handed to the chief who seemed pleased with them; then the company moved to an adjoining *bure* where a meal of fish and yams was laid out on the mat-covered floor, banana leaves serving as plates. The meal was served by women, but none of them took part in the feast. In a corner of the *bure* was a blazing fire on which part of the meal had been cooked; how this could be safe in a building of thatch was beyond our understanding. Conversation was difficult, for there was only the one English-speaking man among the total population of sixty, and mostly his mouth was full. But many questions were asked about our voyage, and it seemed to be fully understood and greatly appreciated that the Queen of England herself would be visiting Fiji later in the year. Finally we were given weak tea to drink—I imagine this was specially for our benefit, for tea is not much used in the islands—and a bowl of warm water and a cloth was passed round so that all could clean their fingers after the meal. The whole affair was most courteous and dignified.

We spent two days at Ndravuni, and would have remained longer had not the wind changed and sent into the anchorage a teasing little sea to set the yacht rolling heavily. We walked round the 250-acre island, which had the appearance of a rich garden with its profusion of trees, fruit and vegetables, and its well-kept paths. We watched the sailing canoes, the islanders' only means of communication, leave for another and larger island in the reef with cargoes of copra, and we marvelled that anything apparently so unhandy could be made to sail to windward. In Polynesia nobody cares whether the outrigger of a canoe is to windward or to leeward; but the Fijians are very particular to keep the outrigger always to windward. To that end the canoe is made reversible. At the conclusion of a tack, instead of going about in the ordinary way, the canoe's direction of progress is reversed. The helmsman unships his steering paddle at what has been the stern and hurries with it to the other end to use it there to steer with; the sail is swung round the mast so that the positions of sheet and tack are reversed, and away the canoe goes on the other tack, but still with the outrigger to windward. A platform is built on the spars which join the outrigger to the canoe, and the cargo is piled on this.

During the greater part of our cruise we managed to keep *Wanderer*'s copper sheathing free of weed and barnacles, which grow with great speed in the warm water of the tropics, by diving overboard whenever it began to show signs of fouling, and giving it a scrub with a hand brush. For this we wore diving goggles and we rigged a rope beneath the keel with which to pull ourselves down. One of the places where we did this job was in the lovely clear water off Ndravuni, and we greatly enjoyed it, removing all the slime and weed in a morning's work. We took it in turns; the one who was not working stood on deck and kept a lookout for sharks or barracuda. Before I took the first plunge Susan said:

'If I see any large fish while you are under water I shall not be able to make you hear. So I'll dive in and hope my splash will frighten them off.'

Fortunately she did not see any, and neither did I.

We made a day sail back to Suva where we ran out of the sunshine and in under the rain cloud, and as we came up to the town we sighted *Beyond* lying at anchor there. The last time we had met her and her crew, Tom and Ann Worth and Pete and Jane Taylor, was during Christmas the previous year in the West Indies. This was the occasion for a great get-together, which started aboard *Wanderer* the next morning and continued in other places until midnight. Obviously a drink was called for, and as we had none aboard except what was sealed up in the bond locker, I broke the seal and got out one of our two remaining bottles of whisky. My intention was to tell the customs about this before they discovered it for themselves, and to pay the duty. But Tom gave me a rude shock when he said:

'I suppose you know you are liable to a fine of £100 for breaking that seal, plus the duty?'

I did not know that and I was so shaken that I persuaded Susan who, I always maintain, is much better at dealing with officials than I am, to telephone the customs and explain. She did so and was told:

'This is a very serious matter, madam. We will have to look into it and ring you back later.'

For half an hour we sat in the club biting our nails, and then the call came through. Susan took it.

'You may tell Mr. Hiscock,' came the verdict, 'that as he has broken open his bond locker he had better keep it open and consume what still remains in it.'

That was so handsome that I even forgave them when, on leaving Fiji, they compelled me to employ an agent, who naturally required a fee, in order to get back from them duty they had charged on a piece of photographic equipment which, for use aboard a yacht in transit, was not dutiable.

With light hearts we continued our party which then shifted to *Beyond*, and in the evening we all went ashore to feed at a Chinese restaurant. The slant-eyed proprietor was seated behind a little counter in the doorway, and Tom stopped to speak to him.

'Now, see here, John,' he said in his fiercest manner, eyebrows peaked and moustache bristling, 'these are friends of ours and we want a proper meal, none of the hog-wash you dished up for us last time. Muck like that just isn't fit . . .'

'Shush, you idiot,' whispered Ann, nudging him. 'It wasn't here we fed last night, but at the other joint across the street.'

'My God,' said Tom, 'I believe you're right.' And he thereupon climbed up on to the little counter, and to the amazement of the Chinaman, knelt on it, bowed his head and begged pardon.

The meal was good and so was the rest of the party. But Susan and I were not used to that sort of thing, and while we took the best part of the next day to recover, the Worths and the Taylors sailed for New Zealand in the morning.

We were sorry to see them go, for they were a cheerful party and it is not often on such a voyage as ours that one has the pleasure of meeting one's friends in another small vessel which has been along the same route. We followed them a week later.

11

NEW ZEALAND

FOR four days the trade wind sang its merry tune in the rigging, hurrying us south to pass out of the tropics for the first time in eleven months. Almost imperceptibly nights grew shorter, twilight lingered longer and the temperature dropped lower, so that we were glad of sweaters and trousers during our night watches instead of the thin shirts and shorts which had been our seagoing rig for so long.

Then the trade faltered and died. The noise of the bow-wave dropped from a heartening roar to a faint, derisive chuckle; the sails no longer remained asleep pulling steadily, but jerked at their sheets and slammed sullenly as *Wanderer* rolled, and soon we were left without a breath of wind. As the ripples faded from the face of the ocean it changed colour from a dark to a paler blue and became almost glassy, but still heaved silently with a long low swell, like a giant breathing, and we could see down into it for a considerable distance. We had reached the southern limit of the trade wind and had entered the wide belt of variables which separates it from the westerlies of the southern part of the ocean.

All around, becalmed like ourselves, lay countless Portuguese men-of-war, balloon-like rafts from one to ten inches in length, each with a curved sail set and a bunch of long streamers hanging from its under side. They were translucent and of a lovely pale blue colour. Some Portuguese men-of-war are pink, but we saw that kind only in the Atlantic and then never south of the equator. We had often watched them sailing and it appeared that they really could make progress to windward; no doubt this is a necessary ability, otherwise all of them would eventually get blown into the doldrums by the trade winds. They do not seem capable of reefing and on a breezy day it is not uncommon to see whole fleets of them lying on their sides with their sails in the water. They do exist outside the tropics, as many New South Wales bathers have discovered to their cost when stung by the streamers of these creatures, which in Australia are known as 'bluebottles'. Susan managed to capture one and put it in a pudding basin filled with water so that we could photograph it and study it at close quarters.

But there were other strange inhabitants of the deep around us in great numbers that calm and silent day. There were jelly-fish, each of which looked like an orange umbrella with a scalloped skirt draped round the handle, propelling themselves along with slow pulses of the umbrella. These also we were to meet again in Australian waters. But the most remarkable thing of all was the vast number of sea-snakes, if one can call them that. The sea was literally alive with them, and at times it was impossible to plunge the boathook down without touching one. Near the surface there were little snakes, a foot or less in length, but lower down, and just within boathook reach, were snakes as long as *Wanderer* and as thick as my arm. They were of a jelly-like substance, pale brown in colour with dark brown regular markings on them. Our attempts to capture one failed because when we got the boathook under it, which was easy enough to do as the creatures were slow-moving and took no avoiding action, and lifted a part of it above the surface, the snake immediately broke in half and two snakes went wriggling along where one had been before. We have since seen sea-snakes of a more substantial nature, particularly in the Arafura Sea, solid like land snakes and with tough skins; but the jelly snakes we met that calm day in the South Pacific must have been out of the ordinary for we have never seen anything of the kind since, nor have we met anyone familiar with them.

That evening we picked up one of the New Zealand broadcasting stations on our radio set and learnt that Suva and other parts of Fiji had that day suffered from a minor earthquake and tidal wave. The report stated that the wave was fifteen feet high on the north-east side of Kandavu, where a large area was devastated; so we feared that the friendly little village so close to the water's edge at Ndravuni, where we drank *yanggona*, must have been destroyed or badly damaged, for Ndravuni lies within the same reef as Kandavu and is only a few miles from the larger island. The earthquake opened fissures in the streets of Suva; the reef guarding the harbour was raised one foot (that at least should be an improvement) and great boulders were thrown up on it along with the wreck of the *Woodburn*, which was lost near there several years before.

When we left Suva there were two New Zealand yachts lying at anchor there, *White Squall* and *Taurangi*, and we were much worried about them and their people when we heard of the tidal wave. Both survived, and we met them again on arrival at Auckland, but they had a bad time. They were lying in the shallow water off the club, and after the first wave the water level in the harbour dropped so much that they were left lying on their sides; then the next wave came in and poured through their hatches before they could right themselves, depositing mud over everything below and damaging the personal belongings of their crews. The yachts also collided owing to one of them dragging her anchor, but both were later able to sail to their home port without major repairs being necessary.

As we were 400 miles from Fiji at the time it seemed unlikely that we could be within the influence of the earthquake; but if we were, the sea-snakes we saw that day might possibly have been disturbed and forced up to the surface from a great depth by some subterranean upheaval or strong current caused by it.

After dark we shone our searchlight on the sea. In its beam the thousands of Portuguese men-of-war reflected bright silver light like sequins, while the jelly-fish gave off an orange glow which continued for several seconds after the light had been switched off.

When eventually a breeze made it came from ahead, and it remained like that so that we had to beat all the rest of the way, about 700 miles, to New Zealand. Never before or since have we experienced a wind so unsteady in strength; it came in strong gusts, sometimes of moderate gale strength, interspersed with light patches. The gusts raised a small but steep sea against which we were able to make very little progress each time the wind fell light, for we dared not set our masthead genoa, which would then have helped us a lot, because of an accident which had happened a few weeks before.

On one of our short passages among the Fiji Islands, and

when we were turning to windward with the genoa set, both the twin bobstays supporting the bumkin to which the masthead backstay is secured, carried away. These were of bronze rod and were attached to bronze plates on the hull at the water-line by what the builders and ourselves had believed to be bronze bolts. On examination we found that both bolts had been completely destroyed by electrolytic action, so they must have been of common brass. Before leaving Suva we replaced them with monometal bolts which are inert, but we still did not care to use the genoa, which places a heavy load on the backstay, bumkin and bobstays, for we suspected that the fastenings of the bronze plates might also be of brass, and we could not examine them without going on a slip, an expense we were not prepared to face until we reached New Zealand.

Violent motion is bad enough when one is making progress in the right direction, but it is particularly trying when progress is poor and it is impossible to head in the desired direction, and during the rest of that passage we made some very poor runs, the worst being twenty-four miles. Neither of us felt well. The motion put us off our food; Susan had a chill, probably caused by a cold night watch with insufficient clothes on, and I had developed a fresh crop of sores which was particularly unpleasant as all the adhesive dressings we had on board had suffered from the heat of the tropics and, like those from the hospital at Pago Pago, were no longer adhesive.

After five days of unsteady headwinds we had almost worn ourselves out with the frequent sail drill, for we seemed to be for ever changing headsails to make the best use of the wind, and reefing and unreefing the mainsail. Thereafter we usually left the yacht to look after herself during a part of each night under sufficiently reduced sail to be safe in the squalls, while we both turned in to rest our weary bodies. The days' runs suffered accordingly, but we knew it was more important to husband our strength than to drive on and save a day or two at sea.

The heavens changed as we made southing, with the Southern Cross riding higher night after night. By day the watch on deck often had an albatross to entertain him and keep him company. The flight of this, the largest of all sea birds, is a wonderful thing to watch. At high or low speed he soars generally close to the surface so that he is frequently lost behind an intervening sea, and it is rare to see him move even a feather of his great wings except when landing or taking off. But often our speed was too slow for him, and keeping station was such a bother that he would land in our wake and show us that he could paddle himself along with his webbed feet just as fast as we could sail.

During our seventeenth night out from Suva, and a dark and squally night it was, we raised the light on Cape Brett. Dawn revealed the grey line of the New Zealand coast ahead and on the starboard beam, and under short sail, for the wind was strong, we beat up for its lee in the neighbourhood of the Bay of Islands. The sun came out to warm us and dry our sails, and it glistened for a moment on the curved and shapely body of a great blue marlin which, with spear out-thrust, was leap-frogging over the seas. These are big-game-fishing waters, and the Swordfish and Mako Shark Club has its headquarters at Russell. As we sailed into the bay the wind brought off to us the smell of gorse and wood smoke; many birds were fishing in the bay, and on all sides of us lay jolly little islands with cattle grazing in the meadows and patches of vivid blossom here and there, for it was spring in New Zealand. The air had a clean, fresh tang.

By noon we were at anchor in smooth, dark green water off the freshly painted little town of Russell, where the red, green and orange roofs of the houses glowed brightly under the pale blue sky; away on the western side of the harbour stood the tall, white flagstaff marking the place where the treaty between the British and the Maoris was signed not much over a hundred years ago. The first British settlers landed here and Russell was the first capital. We could scarcely imagine a more perfect port of entry, but this part of the Dominion is rich in natural and beautiful harbours. The doctor soon came aboard to grant us pratique and to tell us that there would not be any customs or immigration formalities to bother about until we arrived at Auckland, and not many then. After he had gone we landed to buy in the store on the waterfront the fresh food that we craved for after seventeen days at sea.

We turned in early that evening, and as Susan snuggled down beneath the blankets in her bunk she sighed with content and murmured:

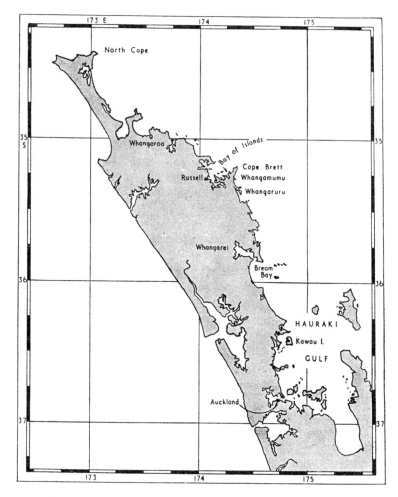

'How still and cool it is. I'm just going to sleep and sleep. No night watches tonight.'

'No,' I replied drowsily as I blew out the lamp, 'and not for many nights.'

In a bay just round the point from Russell, to which we moved a day later to obtain fresh water for our tanks from the crayfish-tail freezing plant there, we found the big topsail-schooner *Fitheach Ban.* She with her New Zealand owner, Captain Watchlin, his niece Laura Webb and a paid crew, had sailed out from the Mediterranean the previous year. She had been wintering at Whangaroa in the north, and was now cruising slowly down the coast to spend the summer in the sounds near Picton. We spent several pleasant evenings in her mahogany-panelled, red-carpeted saloon while Laura, who was a trained nurse and had spent the past twelve years in charge of hospital casualty wards, mixed drinks and cooked tempting meals for us, while Captain Watchlin told us much about his beloved country. With the charts spread out on the big table, he suggested which were the harbours most worth visiting and pointed out the snugger anchorages.

Then we started off on what we intended to be a gentle little cruise in short day hops down the coast for 150 miles to Auckland, where mail awaited us and where we would have *Wanderer* hauled out on a slip for a refit.

We stopped at two of the little islands in the Bay of Islands; first at Motuarohia, where Colonel and Mrs. Browne lived on their own except for their cattle and turkeys, and were busy enlarging their island house. They gave us lunch beneath the trees in their garden, and ointment for my sores. At the top of the steep little shell-and-shingle beach was a notice which read not 'Trespassers will be prosecuted', but 'Afforestation. Please do not light fires'. The eastern hill was planted with young firs, and on the low land wild iris were in bloom. In the afternoon we sailed to Urupukapuka, but grounded at low water on a sand-covered reef just outside Otehei Bay where Zane Grey once had a fishing camp. We soon drifted off on the rising tide, and as there was no wind and we could not get the motor to start, I began towing *Wanderer* into the bay with the dinghy. But almost at once Mr. and Mrs. Baker, who own that 520-acre island and run sheep and cattle on it, came along in their outboard fishing boat and towed us in. They told us that there were no longer any rabbits or rats on the island, all having been killed by the weasels which are believed to swim across the mile-wide strait which separates the island from the mainland. So well do the rocks and islets protect that little anchorage that we lay there through the night without a movement. Before we left we were given a basket of vegetables and home-bottled grapefruit juice.

One could day-sail in the Bay of Islands most pleasantly for several weeks and find a different anchorage each night, but we had to move on. So we rounded Cape Brett and came to Whangamumu, an old whaling station to which, it is said, the great mammals used to come each year to scrape off their parasites on a certain rock; a silent cove where only the ruins of the try-works remain to speak of the busy days long past. Next we stopped at Whangaruru, a good, well sheltered natural harbour where birds with English voices sang to us at sundown. For this harbour we used an historic chart, one of those which Muhlhauser had carried round the world with him in *Amaryllis* in 1921-2. Although this was based on a survey made in 1849, I imagined it would be safe to use as all the dangers are rocks and therefore could not have moved; but it proved to be most misleading. I have since compared it with the new chart, and was surprised to see that there was a considerable difference in the configuration of the coastline. This explains why the crossbearings I took and the transits I used made nonsense, and shows how important it is always to use the most up-to-date charts.

On the way south from Whangaruru the offshore wind freshened to some purpose and towards evening was blowing with gale force. Sailing was exhilarating, but we did not wish to continue thus throughout the night; as we did not care to attempt to beat into Whangarei, the only harbour available, in such weather with the spring ebb running and the light failing, we brought up in Bream Bay, an open roadstead where eleven miles of glistening, sandy beach backed by snow-white, grass-topped sand dunes, described an arc the ends of which vanished in the haze to port and starboard of us, and where there was no single sign of human habitation. The moaning wind some-how emphasized the loneliness of our berth, but it kept most of the swell out of the bay and the night we spent there was not uncomfortable.

In the morning we listened to the weather forecast. It seemed strange after so long without such moral aids to be able to get a forecast several times a day, and already we were getting to know by heart the musical sounding list of districts: North-land, Auckland, Waikato, Waitomo, Taranaki, Bay of Plenty, National Park and Manawatu. But we were also learning that the New Zealand meteorological office, unlike its English counterpart, is chary of giving gale warnings. On several occasions we had listened to forecasts of moderate to fresh winds, and then read in the next day's paper that the wind had reached forty or fifty knots. That morning the wind had moderated and the forecast was favourable, but soon after we had got under way the wind was blowing almost as hard as on the previous day, and it was necessary to roll down more of the mainsail. While I was doing that my left hand slipped off the handle of the reefing gear and I sprained my wrist. I felt so helpless and shaken that rather than attempt to make harbour in so much wind and with my arm disabled, we again anchored for the night off the coast where another wide and lonely bay extended its welcoming arms. But during the hours of darkness a shift of wind, accompanied by the dismal sound of breakers on the shore, compelled us to move. Normally I do the anchor work and deal with the sails while Susan skilfully attends to the steering; but on that occasion, as I was so help-less, we had to exchange jobs. While Susan was forward getting the anchor aboard, she somehow damaged one of her legs, tearing a large, three-cornered piece out of her shin. I bound the copiously bleeding wound up with a sterilized dressing, and then with only three good hands and three good legs between the pair of us, we sailed on to the south, bound for the Island of Kawau, there to seek a sheltered berth in which to recuperate.

In daylight and with a moderating wind we sailed into the deep inlet which cuts Kawau more than half way through. Examining and discarding one cove after another as offering insufficient shelter from all winds, we finally found the sort of anchorage we were looking for in Smelting Cove (locally known as Swansea Bay) on the northern shore. There, tucked well in behind a sheltering point, we shut out the sea and lay snugly out of the wind in perfectly smooth water bounded on three sides by steep, ti-tree-covered slopes. Spanning the clean gravel beach at the point, a pier led to the lawn of a flower-filled garden where a good-looking timber-built house stood. A woman was working in the garden, and Susan, because she could row and I could not, went over to inquire whether it might be possible to buy any bread on the island. I watched her limp up the garden path with the woman and disappear in the house. She returned some time later, not with one loaf but with two, with a fresh baking of hot date scones, a dozen eggs, a jug of milk and a basket of fruit—all of them were gifts— and an invitation to baths and dinner. The house belonged to Roy Lidgard and his wife. That evening as we sat at dinner with them round their satin-smooth kauri table, we could look out through the wide open window to where *Wanderer* lay serenely in the cove beyond the pier. (*See opposite.*)

We soon got to know the Lidgards and their adopted boy and girl from the Cook Islands very well. No one could have been kinder to us than they were; their house was always open to us so that we almost felt it was our home, and never a day passed without them inviting us to a meal, or giving us a cake, a pie or some other delectable thing out of Mum's oven.

A few days after our arrival Susan's injured leg began to swell and became very painful. By then *Fitheach Ban* had arrived at Kawau and anchored half a mile away. Remembering that Laura Webb was a trained nurse, we took an oar each and rowed in our dinghy across to her. By the time we had reached the schooner Susan was in a state of collapse, but kind Laura very soon had her tucked up with hot bottles in the big state-room aft which Captain Watchlin had immediately made available for her. Susan's wound had become septic and by evening her temperature had risen to 102° and her pulse to 118, a dangerous combination. There was no doctor on Kawau, so we tried to get the nearest one over from the mainland. Bob, the Kawau ferryman, took me to Mansion House in another part of the harbour where the post office was specially opened so that I could telephone; an Auckland operator got a distant postmaster out of his bed, and with much help from everyone I eventually got through to the doctor, only to learn that he was not prepared to come over.

'If you want me to see your wife you'll have to bring her to my surgery tomorrow,' he said crossly and rang off.

He was the only person with whom we had contact all the time we were in New Zealand who failed to be helpful, but I could not really blame him.

PLATE 17

Top: We could look out through the wide open window of the Lidgards' house to where *Wanderer* lay serenely in the cove; Swansea Bay, Kawau Island. *Bottom:* Geothermal steam roars across the Geyser Valley at Wairakei, which one day will be New Zealand's power house.

It was late when I got back with that news to *Fitheach Ban,* and Laura was very worried.

'Of course we can't move Susan,' she said. 'The only hope is penicillin.'

There and then Bob set off in his motor launch for the mainland. It was a dark night with a strong wind blowing, but soon after dawn he was back with the urgently needed drug. We never discovered where or how he obtained it, and when I tried to compensate him for all the trouble he had taken, he refused gruffly and said:

'That was the least I could do for you people who come from home.'

Under the influence of penicillin the inflammation subsided and temperature and pulse soon became normal, but for several days Susan was kept aboard the schooner where Laura fussed over her until she was well enough to return to *Wanderer.* I was given most of my meals on board and the Captain took me wherever I wished to go in his motor launch as I was incapable of rowing, and when I happened to be the. other side of the harbour in *Wanderer* the Lidgards insisted on feeding me. All this kindness from strangers surely shows that this troubled world of ours is not such a bad place after all. It is typical of the New Zealanders, and it still brings a lump to my throat when I think about it.

For two weeks we lay at Kawau listening to the thrilling song of the tui, which is often preceded by a clearing of the throat in the form of cackles and chuckles, and the strange laughing cry of the kookaburra, while at dusk, as the 'more pork' owl spoke to his mate across the cove, we could sometimes hear the thump, thump, thump of the wallaby. Kawau has no roads. Each of the harbour's many coves has a house, the front drive to which is always a wooden pier, and everyone's conveyance is a motor launch, or outboard or sailing dinghy. Most of the houses were built by their owners, and each has its own electric generating plant and water pumping

PLATE 18

Top: *Wanderer* and *Ladybird* share a peaceful anchorage at Whangaroa. *Bottom:* Susan cons as we pass inside the Cavalli Islands; ahead and to starboard lies a patch of floating plankton.

A.W.W.—L

or catchment system. Give the New Zealander a few tools and some pieces of timber, or growing trees if you like, and he will build almost anything. First he knocks up a 'bach' in which he and his wife live while they get on with the building of the house. The 'bach' later becomes the garage or, in Kawau, the boathouse. Most of the houses are carefully planned to reduce housework as much as possible, for domestic help is almost unheard of. The only outside services at Kawau are the ferry, which brings mail and necessities from the mainland three times a week, and the telephone; all the houses are on a common line, so everyone knows all about his neighbours' business, but you can tell whose call it is by the number of longs and shorts rung by the bell. Close to the Lidgards' house, and on a piece of ground given by them, members of the Kawau yacht club had just finished building themselves a club house, a four-square timber building which they had completed in four months, There we gave a talk and showed our slides to the members, all of whom, except the Lidgards, had come by boat for the occasion.

Roy Lidgard was a skilled boatbuilder. He had worked up his own thriving yacht yard at Auckland and now had retired to live on Kawau. Hearing that we had been having trouble with our rubber mast wedge, he came aboard one day and made for us a perfectly fitting and absolutely leak-proof set of teak mast wedges. When we asked what we owed him for all his labour, he looked fierce and said:

'I'll go crook at you if you talk like that. But if you'll come ashore and have a drink with me we'll call it all square.' And he rowed away muttering darkly to himself something about 'yachties' and 'cobbers'.

Eventually we felt strong enough to tear ourselves away from that hospitable island and sail the thirty miles to Auckland, which unlike most large towns does provide facilities for the yachtsman; but it is not easy for the stranger to find an anchorage, as the harbour is a large one and the more sheltered berths are occupied by privately owned moorings among which there is not room to anchor. We made for Westhaven, a walled harbour half a mile long, which lies just beyond the commercial quays and is filled to capacity with yacht moorings. At the western end stands a row of yacht club houses and at the eastern end are boatyards and slips. Cyril Hill, the custodian of the haven, met us as we entered at dusk, indicated a vacant mooring which we could use, for it was then early in the season and all the yachts had not yet been launched from their winter quarters, and with his wife Billy came aboard for a yarn. We arrived on a Friday, and as all business people in that country work a five-day week, I happened to mention that we would not be going into town until Monday as we had little money until we had taken our letter of credit to the bank. Cyril said nothing, but early next morning he returned, and handing me a crumpled ball of paper, said:

'You might find a use for this during the weekend.'

He had lent me, a stranger, a £5 note.

A welcome such as that, together with the courtesy of the customs and the complete lack of official fuss, gave us a pleasing first impression of Auckland and this grew stronger as the six weeks of our stay slipped quickly past. It is a place where if you ask a stranger to direct you to some house or shop, he will take you by the arm and lead you to it and in all probability introduce you to the owner. It is a green city, especially when viewed from Mount Eden, one of the steep little hills which rise so unexpectedly in the midst of it, with each house separated from its neighbours by grass and trees.

We had *Wanderer* hauled out on a slip, and that was the first time she had been out of the water since her original launch in March 1952. It would not have been necessary even then except that we wanted to examine the fastenings of the bob-stay plates, and that the copper sheathing had perished along the waterline exposing the bare wood in places, making it essential to effect repairs before the worm got in. We had to put on £20 worth of new copper and refasten the bobstay plates, after which we were able to make use of the genoa once more. While we were on the slip we took the opportunity to paint the topsides, and it is interesting to note that the port side, which was the exposed side most of the way across the Pacific, had to be burnt off, while the paint on the other side was in fair condition. Always it is the sun that causes the damage.

For two weeks we lived aboard on the slip in some discomfort, for the yacht was down a little by the head and her stern was to the prevailing westerly wind, so that the rain, which often fell heavily, blew into the cabin, and soot from the coal-burning ferry boats, which berthed near by, caused us much trouble when painting. But each evening, after the day's work was done and when we were feeling particularly dirty and tired, some kind Aucklander, as likely as not a stranger who had read about us in the paper, would appear with a car and whisk us away to his spotless home for baths and 'tea', a large three-course meal eaten around 6.30, and followed at 10 p.m. by 'supper' of sandwiches and home-made cake. The yard also treated us kindly. Saying that we were 'ambassadors not travellers' it charged us only cost price for materials and labour and the office staff made us honorary lavatorial members during our stay on the slip.

Auckland claims to have the largest yachting fleet in the world, and we were told this so often that once or twice when we thought of the Crouch or the Hamble we could not resist quoting:

'St. Peter's of Rome has a very large dome.
That of St. Paul is not small.'

Most of the yachts were home built. The New Zealander is a good gardener and usually keeps his 'section' as neat and tidy as his wife keeps her home. So as you tour the town or suburbs, if you see a weedy, neglected garden, take a closer look and you will probably see the bow or stern of some partly completed yacht peeping out from behind the garage or house. The workmanship is usually sound and the construction good. Three to five years is the average time an amateur takes to build a 30-foot cruiser to one of the popular Woollacott designs in his spare time.

By English standards the cruising season starts late: not before Christmas (mid-summer down there) do the yachts get away from Auckland in any number; but one has to remember that most people take a fortnight's holiday at Christmas. With some very notable exceptions women do not take an active part in the sport, and even in the ordinary social life of the country there is a sort of voluntary segregation of the sexes. At each of the many parties to which we were invited, the company at once split up, the men congregating at one end of the room and the women at the other, and they remained like that throughout the evening.

Among the many people who motored us about the green and fertile countryside, which is very similar to parts of England, was Jack Brooks, chief of the Department of Scientific and Industrial Research. On one occasion he took us for a 500-mile tour in the North Island, stopping and showing us many things with which his department was directly concerned. He showed us the new paper mill at Kinleath, where the great pine logs, handled by machinery, are tossed about like match-sticks and sawn up in a matter of seconds to be pulped. We saw dams being built on the Waikato River, and a pea-freezing plant which had been designed and built on the assumption that fresh green peas would roll down the chutes from one process to another as readily as dried peas do; the plant was at a standstill until Jack suggested driving the peas through it with streams of water. But to us the most interesting thing, because of its uniqueness, was the thermal region round Rotorua and Wairakei, where steam and boiling water issue from cracks in the earth's crust. One crack had opened in the middle of a metalled road at Rotorua and on the boiling water issuing from it a Maori family was cooking its supper in pots covered with old sacks.

It was growing dark as we approached Wairakei, so we could not see much, but above the brush of our tyres as we drove along to the state-owned hotel we could hear the loud roaring from the bores in the Geyser Valley. These bores are man-made. As the hole, which may be anything between four and eight inches in diameter, is drilled, a pipe is inserted and when eventually the crust is pierced, up through the pipe rushes a great jet of geothermal steam. Some of the bores are more than 3,000 feet deep.

After dining at the hotel we drove to the Geyser Valley, the roar of escaping steam growing louder as we approached. Jack turned off the road where there was a notice 'Danger. Keep out', and there ahead, brilliantly white in the beam from the car's headlamps, a huge jet of steam rushed horizontally from a pipe resting on the ground. The trees in the direction in which the steam issued, though a long way from the pipe, were dead and bleached. As we opened the doors and alighted, the noise was terrific. We felt almost stunned by it, for this particular bore was rated at 10,000 horse power, and the air we breathed and the ground we trod vibrated as the immense jet of geothermal steam roared from its 'silencer'. Conversation was impossible. We felt puny, insignificant mites as we stood beside the pipe watching the steam rush from it.

At the time of our visit the bores were still of an experimental nature. But as they had been working for several years with no apparent sign of diminishing, it was thought that they would remain constant in power perhaps for a thousand years or more. There were then two plans afoot for harnessing the steam. One was to use it for driving a 40,000-kilowatt electricity generating plant which should be in operation by 1958; the eventual target was 500,000 kilowatts. The other plan was to utilize the heat for the making of heavy water for atomic and other nuclear power; for this a great deal of heat is required, and geothermal steam provides that very cheaply. That evening as we stood under the stars in that lovely New Zealand valley which vibrated with the roar of steam, we felt we were standing in what might well prove in a few years' time to be the power house not only for New Zealand but indirectly for parts of Britain also. We had another look at it in daylight. (See p. 144.)

Before leaving Auckland we put *Wanderer* alongside one of the Westhaven jetties so that our friends could come aboard to see her and have a drink; after three days there our visitors' book was the richer by some ninety signatures.

'See you later,' they said as they shook hands and stepped ashore, for in New Zealand that means 'good-bye', and we felt sad as they left, for it seemed unlikely that we should ever see many of them again. But we carried away with us a store of memories of the kindness and help we had experienced at the hands of the people who, whether they have ever been there or not, all refer to England as 'home'. It was with considerable regret that we left Auckland. We had just learnt our way about the city, the names of the streets, where the shops we most needed were and which trolley-buses to catch, and as we had come to know so many of the people, it was like leaving our home town. But leaving places of which we have grown fond and finding new ones was a constant happening to us on our one-way track round the globe, and we knew that very soon we should have to start all over again in another big city, Sydney, of which we knew nothing at all and where we had yet to make some friends.

After leaving Auckland we spent a few days yachting in the Hauraki Gulf, a lovely stretch of sheltered water with many good anchorages. But Christmas was approaching and we were undecided where to spend it until we remembered that a friend had told us of an English family by the name of Oxborrow which farmed somewhere on the east coast of the North Island. He had not got the address, and all he was able to tell us about the position of the farm was its approximate latitude and longitude. We looked this up on the chart and found it was on the north shore of Whangarei Harbour. So we made our way to Whangarei and on Christmas eve anchored in a pretty little bay as close as possible to the spot we had pin-pricked on the chart. We landed on the beach that evening where we met a young man riding a horse and we asked him if he knew anyone of the name of Oxborrow in those parts.

'Yes,' he replied, 'my name is Oxborrow. Who are you?'

So there we spent a happy Christmas with *Wanderer* anchored close to what is reputed to be the largest pohutukawa tree in all New Zealand; it was in glorious crimson full bloom just then.

The Oxborrows had bought their 600-acre farm for £4,500 and ran a herd of eighteen cows and a flock of 750 sheep there. But all the land had not yet been cleared of gorse and ti-tree. They separated the milk, sending the cream to a butter-making factory and the skim milk to a neighbouring pig farm. The fleeces of the Romney Cross sheep averaged five pounds in weight and wool was fetching 5s. a pound, the shearer getting 9d. a sheep. The thing that struck us most about New Zealand farming was the small amount of labour employed. Labour is costly and it is not uncommon to find a dairy herd of fifty cows being run entirely by the farmer himself without any help, for grass there grows nearly all the year round and there is little additional feeding to be done. Milking is usually by machine, the milk being piped direct from the cow to the churn via a cooler, and a floating cock rings a bell when the churn is full. Farming seemed to us to be a good life in that not over-crowded land with friendly and helpful neighbours on every side, but we gained the impression that New Zealand is a country for the man who is prepared to work with his hands and not for the professional man. For example, a stevedore with whom we became friendly was earning about £1,000 a year; he had his own 10-ton yacht and every eighteen months or so took a six-months holiday and went for a cruise 'up the islands', i.e. to Fiji and Polynesia.

Before starting on a long sea passage Susan and I always try to find a quiet and well-sheltered harbour where, untroubled by the swell or the wash from passing craft, we can go carefully over the gear and make our preparations. If the shores of the harbour are sparsely populated, so much the better, for we can then check the contents of the lockers and their stowage, wash our clothes and cut one another's hair without fear of being disturbed by casual visitors. Such a place was not difficult to find on the north-east coast of the North Island, which abounds in good natural harbours.

We chose Whangaroa for our purpose. One sparkling morning at the end of December we were making our way up the coast towards it with a fresh east wind and were passing inside the Cavalli Islands. That passage has only one rock danger, which is easily avoided; but when half way through we were startled to see long streaks of discoloured water and scum extending right across our course. Susan immediately went forward to con (*see p.* 145), and as we sailed into the first patch of scum the water was thick and a strong smell of fish pervaded the air. Each patch of scum was similar and was, presumably, an accumulation of plankton.

A few miles farther on we found the narrow, almost concealed entrance to Whangaroa, and sailed into that perfect, landlocked harbour. It was just the sort of place we needed but it had the one drawback that provisioning facilities were poor. No fresh vegetables were available, the bread was indifferent with black streaks in it, and the fresh water with which we topped up our tanks contained much sediment. But the yacht was well provisioned on arrival, so those things would have mattered little had we been able to sail as soon as we were ready. However, just as we were about to leave on the 1,150-mile passage to Sydney on the Australian coast, we chanced to see a weather map in a daily paper. This showed that a tropical cyclone had formed in the Coral Sea and was heading in a southerly direction. The Tasman Sea, which separates New Zealand from Australia, is notorious as a rough and windy place, and the pilot charts show that there is a risk of encountering a storm there at any time, no month in the year being entirely free. Such storms may be caused either by the depressions which make their way to the eastward off the south coast of Australia, or by cyclones moving down out of the tropics; the latter do not occur in the winter months. The movements of a depression can usually be forecast with some degree of accuracy, but the track of a cyclone, once it has moved out of the tropics, is uncertain; the disturbance may continue south, slowly lessening in intensity, or it may alter course suddenly. Certain rules for the movements of cyclones have been formulated, but the cyclones of the Western Pacific are inclined to ignore them.

So we remained at Whangaroa, watching day by day the progress of the cyclone on the weather maps when we were able to obtain newspapers and, as it came nearer, listened to the radio reports about it. It moved rather slowly and took four days to get down to Lord Howe Island, where it found the 33-foot cutter *Gesture*.

We heard *Gesture*'s story when we got to Sydney. She, with a complement of five including her owner Richard McIlvride and his wife, left Whangarei on Boxing Day and arrived at Lord Howe on 6 January. As neither of the recognized anchorages in South West Bay or off Ned's Beach was possible because of the heavy swell then running, the yacht was anchored off the island's northern shore. Next day the offshore squalls were so strong that during one of them the arms of the anchor were broken off at the crown and the yacht drifted out to sea. An attempt was made to heave-to, but as that was not successful an improvised sea-anchor was made from a pipe cot, coils of rope and the spinnaker boom. This was streamed over the bow and the yacht lay beam to wind and sea. Shortly after noon on the 8th, when the centre of the cyclone was near the island, the yacht was knocked over by a heavy sea. The doghouse windows were broken, the bolts securing the lee coachroof coaming were sheared off and the coaming forced one and a half inches inboard; water flooded the cabin to the level of the tops of the bunks. At the same time the hollow mast was broken in two places, just above the deck and nine feet higher up, though none of the rigging carried away. All the rigging except the topmast stay was then unshackled at the deck and *Gesture* was left riding by the bow to the upper part of the mast which, with the rigging still attached to it, formed an effective sea-anchor. But eventually the cranze iron was pulled off the bowsprit end and then the bobstay rigging screw became unscrewed, so the mast and all the rigging was lost. On 9 January the sixteen-foot spinnaker boom, which had been salvaged, was stepped on deck, the storm staysail was set on it, and ten days later Sydney, 400 miles away, was reached safely.

After leaving Lord Howe Island the cyclone continued south across our proposed course, altered direction as though it was going to attack Sydney, then, having decreased in intensity, it changed its mind, recurved to the south-west and passed through Cook Strait, which separates the North Island from the South Island, and was of no further interest to us.

Our enforced stay in port was enjoyably spent, for Cyril and Billy Hill in *Ladybird* were there, and we, having made our preparations, were free to sail about in the harbour in company with them and make use of several peaceful anchorages. (*See p.* 145.) In the corner of one remote little bay, which for want of a name we christened Wanderbird Cove, we found a clean water-fall and rocky pool where we washed ourselves and our linen.

12

THE TASMAN SEA AND SYDNEY

As soon as the weather reports indicated that the Tasman Sea was temporarily free from cyclones, we left our beautiful haven and sailed north along the coast with a fresh offshore wind. That evening the sky looked stormy; there was a solar halo and a sickly yellowish-green sunset. The temptation to return to the peaceful security of Whangaroa was great; but the barometer was steady, and in those latitudes if we had returned to port for every lurid sunset and each halo we should not have got very far. So we held on our way, rounded North Cape in the night and steered to pass north of the Three Kings, a group of unlit islands which lie twenty-eight miles north-west of the mainland. Our reason for going outside the islands, instead of taking the direct course for Sydney, was to avoid the confused sea which is caused by the irregular soundings in the inside passage and the strong tidal streams which run there. By day we would have gone inside them. At dawn we could see the grey humps of the Three Kings away to port, lifting up now and then above the swell, and we altered course for Sydney 1,000 miles distant.

The passage was an uncomfortable one just as we had expected it to be. Usually there was a heavy swell, and when the wind was light, as it was during the early part and at the half-way point, and when it was abaft the beam, the noise of slatting canvas made it difficult for us to get much sleep. Also, our long stay in New Zealand with only infrequent day sails had temporarily disabled our sea-legs so that although neither of us was sick we had poor appetites and our evening meals often consisted of scrambled eggs and mashed potatoes only.

On the third day the wind improved and with it our sea-legs and our spirits. It backed to east-sou'-east and blew at thirty knots. We double-reefed the mainsail but kept the spinnaker set, and little *Wanderer* hurried on her way rejoicing and was easy on the helm. The sky was overcast so that no sights were possible, but that was of no importance just then for the Tasman Sea is free of dangers and we should not be making a landfall for at least five or six days. Although the moon was nearing the full just then we saw no sign of her. The weather was cold. By day sweaters and trousers were the rig and at night we wore in addition what we affectionately call our eiderdowns, padded, snugly zip-fastened Londonus life-saving jackets, and were glad of them. With the deep hum of the steady wind in her rigging, and so nearly balanced under sail that the helmsman was able to take many a nap without deviating from the course, *Wanderer* flew to the westward with an easy, striding motion, as she was lifted on by each great overtaking swell. It was wonderful sailing and in three con-secutive days under that very small sail area she ran 440 miles, an average speed of just over six knots, which we did not consider at all bad for a deeply laden vessel of her size.

Then came a calm to spoil her average, twenty-four maddening hours of it with never more than a tantalizing air which died the moment we had set and trimmed the ghoster to take advantage of it. The motion was wicked, for by then a second swell from the north was running at right angles to the old one. The glass was dropping, long fingers of wispy cirrus were radiating in the sky from the north, and, with the thought of cyclones still fresh in our minds, we talked ourselves into believing that another was moving towards us. We read again in the *Pilot* the rules for avoiding revolving storms, but having regard to the odd behaviour of such things in the Tasman Sea, we could not decide which would be the dangerous semi-circle. Even if we had been able to do so we could not have taken any avoiding action just then as we had no steerage way. We learnt later that another cyclone had formed in the Coral Sea and started to move south, but fortunately it did not come close to us.

Presently the wind returned and within an hour or so was blowing just as fresh as before, but from the north-east. Once again we rolled in the reefs, gybed, re-set the spinnaker and bustled on our way.

From the navigation point of view we had been fortunate

since leaving England in that the sun or stars nearly always shone when needed for fixing our position; but during the Tasman crossing the sky was mostly overcast, and only when the heavenly bodies peeped out for a moment every third day or so were we able to get hurried snapshots of them with the sextant. The positions so obtained were generally south of the dead-reckoning positions, which was surprising because the pilot chart showed no current flowing in that direction until within a hundred miles or so of the Australian coast, when there should be a south-setting stream of between one and two and a half knots, the speed increasing as the coast is approached. Once we got an excellent check on our latitude when the *Monowai*, one of the regular ships on the Auckland to Sydney run, passed close to us; but we never saw her sister ship bound the other way a day or so later as we should have done if we had been exactly on our course.

For the first half of the passage the weather was cold and we had albatrosses constantly with us. But as we progressed the days and nights grew warmer and the radio told us of temperatures exceeding 100° F. on the Australian coast, and of the worst floods in living memory in Queensland and New South Wales. Then the great albatrosses left us and their place was taken by flying fish larger than any we had seen elsewhere, and there was fried flying fish on the breakfast menu.

One afternoon as we neared the Australian coast, running under full sail with a lighter breeze and smoother sea than usual, and I was dozing below, I was startled by a noise as of a depth-charge exploding. Susan called me immediately, and hurrying on deck I saw astern in our wake and only just clear of the patent log rotator eighty feet away, a sight which I shall never forget. A whale, which we judged to be between twenty and twenty-five feet in length, black and with a blunt head, leapt clear out of the water six feet or more into the air. For the moment it was in the air water cascaded off it, concealing its under parts to some extent. Then it fell back with the same loud explosive noise as I had heard when below, sending a great pillar of spray shooting skyward. That was the second whale to jump, Susan had seen the first one, and then close to port another of the whales came to the surface and blew with a strange, eerie sigh. We knew that sting rays, tunny, flying fish,

squid and swordfish jump into the air at times, but we had no
idea that whales did so also. Later, at Sydney, we were told
that this is quite common, the whales jumping in an attempt to
escape from the sharks which attack them with the intention
of tearing out and eating their tongues. At the time we could
only hope that pod of whales was keeping a proper lookout,
for the idea of one landing on deck was not pleasant.

Shortly after dark on our tenth night out we could see the
loom of Sydney lights some forty miles away, a bright glow
reflected from the low-hanging clouds. We continued to steer
our compass course for a point eighteen miles north of Sydney
to allow for the south-setting current, and our allowance
proved to be correct for we made a good landfall on Sydney
Heads.

Sydney Harbour (Port Jackson was the name given to it by
Captain Cook, and still used on the charts today) is a large
inlet, and without local knowledge the visiting yachtsman
would scarcely know for which part of it to make, with so many
bays and coves to choose from, especially at night. But while
we were in New Zealand we had received a letter from Phil
Davenport, who in 1951 sailed his 46-foot cutter *Waltzing
Matilda* from Sydney to London by way of the Magellan
Straits, and had written an excellent book about it. We had
never met him, but he, hearing of our intention to visit Sydney,
and knowing of the difficulties which might confront the
stranger there, kindly wrote to tell us of the correct procedure.
Among other things he advised us to bring up in Watson Bay,
which is the official boarding station for the customs and health
authorities. He had notified the officials and the secretary of
the Royal Sydney Yacht Squadron of our impending arrival.

The nor'-easter carried us right into the harbour, which is
well lighted, and without any difficulty we found our way into
Watson Bay, where we anchored close to the pilot cutter at
3 a.m., ten and a half days out from Whangaroa, and turned
in for a few hours' sleep.

We had seen many photographs and paintings of Sydney
Harbour bridge and therefore knew its appearance well. It
was, however, a great moment for us when, on looking out at
daybreak, we saw the magnificent arch of the great bridge
rising proudly above the trees of Ashton Park which tried

futilely to hide it from us. We knew then that we really had arrived down under.

The pilot cutter *Captain Cook* made a signal to the port authorities on our behalf and within a short time the customs and health officials boarded us. They were courteous and quick. They did not lock up the stores we had shipped out of bond in New Zealand, but they pointed out that on leaving Australia we should have to pay duty on any of the stores that we consumed while in Australian waters. Scarcely had the officials done with us than a party of press reporters scrambled aboard; with shorthand pads at the ready and pencils poised, they at once started shooting questions at us.

'What was your most desperate situation?'

We said we were sorry but there really had not been any.

'Your mast looks a beaut,' said one of them tapping it with his pencil. 'New, eh? How did you lose the old one?'

We explained that this was the original.

'But surely you have had *some* excitements? A leak? A fire?'

Again we shook our heads.

'Didn't any of your sails split?'

We tried to explain that such things do not usually happen during properly conducted cruises or aboard well-found sailing yachts. But the reporters were losing interest in us rapidly by then and soon took themselves ashore.

After they had gone we sailed up the magnificent harbour, getting an ever better impression of the great bridge which spans it and is in our eyes a thing of beauty, as are most functional works. We made our way to the Yacht Squadron at Kirribilli Point, where Phil Davenport met us with a basket of fruit and an invitation to dinner. It was a great pleasure to us to meet that soft-spoken seaman and his brave little wife. As we were unable to obtain the use of one of the moorings in sheltered water off the Squadron, we had to anchor in a berth which was exposed to the southerly busters, which spring up suddenly and blow with considerable force for an hour or two fairly often at that time of the year; we were also uncomfortably close to the route taken by the numerous ferry boats which serve Sydney's attractive waterside suburbs. So, at the invitation of the Cruising Yacht Club of Australia, we moved over to

Rushcutters Bay on the southern shore and there were lent a sheltered and convenient mooring by Dave Allworth, the secretary, who made us honorary members for our stay of six weeks.

We arrived only a few days before the *Gothic* carrying the Queen and the Duke of Edinburgh on their world tour, and too late to be allotted a berth in the welcoming lines of yachts. But Sverre Berg, who was then Commodore of the club, invited us to join the party aboard his yacht *Horizon*. By seven o'clock on the morning of 3 February 380 yachts were moored side by side in two rows to form a lane, each with her stern towards the lane and every one dressed overall with flags. With the coloured bunting standing out bravely in the brisk breeze against the vivid sky, this great gathering of little vessels was a stirring spectacle. As the gleaming royal barge, with Her Majesty and the Duke aboard, swept through the lane towards the landing-place, each yacht in turn dipped her ensign, the people aboard them cheered and cheered again and a twenty-one gun salute boomed out.

Sydney was the largest town we had seen since London; a busy, crowded, thriving place with some fine, tall, modern buildings in it. But the homely friendliness and courtesy to which we had become accustomed at Auckland was not much in evidence. On our first day there we were looking for the hotel in which we were to meet Vera James, a distant cousin of Susan's who had been taking a great interest in our voyage and had invited us out to lunch. As we were not sure of our whereabouts I said to a passer-by:

'Excuse me, but can you tell me if this is Castlereagh Street?'

He jerked his thumb in the direction of a name board which until then I had not noticed, and said 'Can't yer read, chum?'

Eventually we found the hotel and met Vera, but there was then a setback to the plans for lunch. I was wearing my best shirt and tie and freshly pressed trousers, but as the temperature

---

that day was ninety-five degrees I had no jacket. Because of this I was not allowed into the dining-room, and we then spent an interesting, but not very rewarding, half hour looking for some place where the jacketless are permitted to eat. Of course the fault was mine and I felt that I was, quite unintentionally, being discourteous to our dear little hostess who, bless her, pretended that it did not matter at all. But our last hot place had been Suva, and although during our time there that town was never so hot and humid as Sydney was, nobody ever thought of wearing a jacket for lunch, not even in the palatial Grand Pacific Hotel. I have been told of two ways of getting over this difficulty in Australia. One is to wear your shirt outside your trousers when it at once becomes a tunic. The other method is to wear your shirt in the normal way, but to fit it with shoulder straps bearing some mark of rank or some insignia, such as the badge of a yacht club; the shirt then becomes a uniform. Bob Godsall, a flying man of whom I shall have more to say shortly, devised a nice, cool uniform on those lines for himself, his co-pilot and engineer and, as I have witnessed on several occasions, has the entry to any hotel dining-room without the need of a jacket.

It did seem to us that to enjoy Sydney one needed to be fairly tough. When one of the great clanging trams, in which we had travelled out to Rushcutters from the city, started forward with a jerk when Susan was in the act of getting off, and dragged her along the road with its sparking wheels within inches of her head, the conductor and passengers looked on with indifference; and when I got her disentangled from the tram and we were both left rolling in the road, overtaking traffic swerved just enough to go clear of us but did not stop.

At the time we were in New South Wales all public bars had to close at 6 p.m. The period between 5 and 6 p.m. was known as 'swill hour', for that was when anyone who did a full day's work had to get in all his serious drinking. I found that the

---

PLATE 20

Top: In gold-rush days Cooktown was a busy place; now, with a population of only 500, its shabby buildings drowse beside the main street through the heat of the tropical day. *Bottom:* At Thursday Island which, together with extensive shoals and reefs, lies in Torres Strait off Australia's northern tip, we anchored close to the steamer jetty.

A.W.W.—M

business of buying a schooner of beer during swill hour required a tougher hide and sharper elbows than I possessed. Since then the licensing hours in that state have been extended.

After the quiet life we had been leading we found Sydney rather large, brassy and noisy, but the Australian friends we had the good fortune to make were extremely charming and did a great deal to make our stay in their country an interesting and pleasant one. Thanks to these good people Susan and I were able to see a little of the vast continent from road, rail and air.

One of our friends, Bob Godsall, was the captain of an immaculate D.C.3 plane owned by the Commonwealth Bank of Australia, and he took us flying on several occasions when he was flying the Governor of the Bank, Dr. Coombs, from one place to another. Much of our time in the air Susan and I spent in the co-pilot's seat from which we had an excellent view of the countryside, and Bob often made detours from the direct course to show us things of interest. But when he was unable to fly us anywhere, he and his wife Shirley used to take us for drives. In the boot of their Jaguar was a gridiron and hamper which contained steak and other things. As soon as anyone felt hungry Bob pulled off the road into the bush and there, having well salted four pieces of steak on both sides, he fitted them between the hinged halves of the gridiron and lit a small fire of gum leaves and twigs beneath the grid; the fire melted the fat of the steak so that it dripped on to the fire, and the burning fat then did the rest of the cooking. The barbecued steak eaten on hunks of new bread and butter was delicious. Even for meals eaten in their home out at Broken Bay Bob and Shirley preferred their steak cooked that way, and had built a special barbecue fireplace in their garden for the purpose.

Guy and Margery Ebsworth, strangers just as the Godsalls had been, having heard of our arrival at Sydney very kindly had us out to stay with them on their 1,500-acre sheep farm away inland beyond the Blue Mountains, where their attractive, rambling house forms three sides of a shady square and vines grow over the verandah. Our old friends Frank and Muriel Eyre came by road to Sydney and carried us back to Melbourne to stay with them. On the way we stopped for a night at Canberra, the Federal capital which, ambitiously planned but far from complete, has aptly been described as several suburbs looking for a town. Distances in Australia are great, population is small, and even in the more intensely farmed areas, such as that through which the Hume highway passes, one can drive for many miles without seeing a sign of human habitation. To us the farmland looked parched, grey and poor, but it was considered quite good land capable of carrying one sheep to the acre.

With the Eyres we made an expedition by road to Phillip Island south of Melbourne. We went there to see the evening parade of the fairy penguins, and spent the afternoon watching the koalas, Australia's native bears. These weigh about 30 lb. and may be as many inches high; they are amusing, cuddlesome little bundles of fur which dwell in the trees and live entirely on a diet of eucalyptus leaves and shoots. Much of their time they spend sound asleep comfortably in a crook, and they do not appear to object to visitors. When awake they have a delightfully comical expression of benevolent curiosity and mild bewilderment. The word 'koala' is aboriginal and means 'does not drink'.

After supper in a guest house we made our way down to the beach of Surf Bay on the island's southern shore, which is washed by the stormy waters of Bass Strait. It was a cheerless evening. A slight drizzle was falling and the grey, angry-looking sea was breaking heavily on the sand beach. The day being a Sunday there were about 150 people waiting there to watch the evening miracle, most of them, like ourselves, huddling in the lee of the sandhills. Phillip Island is one of the breeding places of the fairy penguin, which is more correctly, but less frequently, known as the little penguin, *eudyptula minor*. The rookery is a honeycomb of holes scooped out of the sand dunes well above reach of the sea, and there the hen lays her two, or occasionally three, eggs. During the breeding season, which lasts from mid-October to the end of March, the cock penguins leave the rookery at dawn to spend the day fishing. They show great agility and speed in swimming, using their wings as paddles, and sometimes go as many as twenty-five miles offshore in search of fish, cuttle fish and crustaceans. At dusk, heavily laden with the day's catch, they all return to Surf Bay, where they land on one small section only of the long beach exactly opposite the rookery and waddle up to their homes, where they disgorge the fish for the benefit of hens and chicks.

As I sat that evening looking at the heavy swell in the fading light, I could not help but wonder whether we were going to see this much talked-of miracle. For one thing I did not understand how a bird which is incapable of flying could ever find its way back to the home beach after swimming many miles offshore, for with a height of eye of only an inch or two it would be incapable of seeing the land unless it was very close. Even, I argued, supposing the penguin could navigate so accurately by some sixth sense of which we know nothing, it would surely be physically impossible for any bird to make a landing through the surf which was running on the beach that evening. But then as I looked around at the huddled figures waiting expectantly, I felt that surely something remarkable was going to happen and I grew increasingly excited.

And suddenly the amazing thing did happen. A roller broke on the beach, and as its backwash went sucking down the sand to meet the next one coming in, I saw a small dark head and stout beak appear above the white, lacy, foam. Then to left and right of it another and another head popped above the surface of the water and soon thirty or forty little penguins with blue-grey heads and backs and snow-white breasts were struggling to get a foothold. But before they managed to reach the shore the next breaker burst over them, hiding them from my sight. I felt desperately sorry for them, for they would be heavily laden and tired after the day's long swim, but there was nothing I could do to help them. When, however, that breaker receded I was thankful to see that the birds were a little closer than before, and eventually, having been overwhelmed by yet another breaker, they reached the beach, to my great relief. One of their number then advanced and with outstretched wings marshalled the party into a compact formation, and when he was satisfied he went ahead leading the way up the beach. All this was, unfortunately, too much for some of the onlookers who got to their feet and ran about excitedly in front of the birds, shining torches on them and taking flashlight photographs. The bright lights must temporarily have blinded the penguins, whose eyes are accustomed to the dim green light of the sea and the twilight of the burrows. For a moment they

stopped, bewildered; then the leader turned, raised his wings
and herded the entire party back into the cold, grey and
unfriendly sea from which they had only just made their way
with such difficulty. Frank and I, shocked and sickened at such
behaviour, shouted at the hooligans to stay still and leave the
birds alone. This had some effect, for the next time the party
made a landing it was left almost undisturbed to struggle, with
bodies leaning slightly forward, up the beach to the rookery.
From that time on and at irregular intervals more and more
penguins arrived, probably a total of between four and five
hundred; but on several occasions the antics of the onlookers
frightened some of them back into the sea. It was dark by the
time the final landing was made, and by then all the other
onlookers had gone. So we were able to watch the last platoon
plodding undisturbed up the beach close by us, and then we
listened to the bird talk going on in the burrows and heard
occasional angry protests as one of the day's workers entered
someone else's home by mistake.

Then we also made our way up the beach, and the little
Bristol saloon seemed particularly cosy as in her we fled at
high speed back to civilization at Melbourne.

In Australia travelling by air is little more expensive than
travelling by rail, and is, of course, very much more comfortable, quick and convenient. So when we reluctantly parted
from Frank and Muriel we returned to Sydney, which was
sweating and steaming under low, damp cloud, by the swift
Convair air-liner *Thomas Mitchell*.

Soon afterwards we shifted our berth eighteen miles up the
coast to Broken Bay, a place much more to our taste, where
the Godsalls and the Bergs lived; a clean, quiet and unspoilt
estuary at the mouth of the Hawkesbury River. There we went
carefully over all of *Wanderer*'s gear, renewing anything that
showed the slightest sign of wear or weakness, for ahead of us
lay 2,000 miles of Australia's eastern coastline where, especially
among the shoals and islands inside the Great Barrier Reefs, a
failure of any part of the rigging might well prove to be
disastrous. We found an anchorage where we could lie quite
undisturbed while I wrote articles and did some photographic
work, and near to it a small waterfall came tumbling down the
steep, bush-covered hillside to a natural pool where Susan,

13

THREADING THE GREAT BARRIER REEFS

'Look,' said Shirley, as she walked round her living-room bearing on high a great sirloin of beef, 'this will be your supper if you stay. Surely you won't sail now?'

Susan and I cast hungry looks at the magnificent joint.

'There's plenty of beer on the ice,' added Bob. 'Do stop and help us drink it.'

The temptation was great. Only the previous evening we had said good-bye to Sverre and Tui Berg just across the water, wondering, as we closed their garden gate with the familiar click for the last time and made our way down the zig-zag path where the cicadas sang, when, if ever, we would see them again. Then in the morning we had sailed across the harbour to bid farewell to our other Broken Bay friends, the Godsalls, who were apparently as reluctant as we were to say goodbye, and did their utmost to persuade us to stay for just one more night. But our time in Broken Bay was up, *Wanderer* was as ready as we could make her and a fair wind, the first in many days, was blowing. So we felt we must go.

It was then nearly the end of March. The summer with its cyclones was over and farther north along the coast the south-east trade wind, which blows there for nine months of the year, should be well established.

From the sailing man's point of view the east coast of Australia can conveniently be divided into two sections: one lying south and the other north of Sandy Cape. South of that cape there are not many dangers and all of them lie close to the shore, but good harbours are scarce; the coast consists of long sand beaches separated by occasional headlands, and the only real shelter to be had is in the rivers, all of which have shallow bars on which the Pacific swell frequently breaks heavily. Also along this part of the coast, which is 700 miles in length, there is an almost constant current setting south at a rate of between two and three knots, probably running at its hardest along the 100-fathom contour and lessening in strength the farther out to sea one goes. At that time of year the persistent north-easters should have finished and we could expect winds from any direction and of any strength.

North of Sandy Cape conditions are quite different, for there one enters the region of the south-east trade wind and the comparatively sheltered waters which lie within the Great Barrier Reefs, while there is no longer a contrary current. In that section there are several mainland ports, and among the many islands lying between the coast and the Barrier it is usually possible to find an anchorage of some sort each night though it may not always be a cosy one.

Our fair wind carried us eighty miles up the coast and died when we were off Port Stephens. As that was the last of the natural, easy-to-enter harbours for the next 650 miles, we made the most of it, motoring in and spending four quiet and windless days in Salamander Bay, which is not subject to the swell that rolls into the more usual anchorage off the little town of Nelson. Almost immediately we were boarded by a pair of swallows who spent a lot of time on the forward guardrail chattering to each other, and when they started sticking feathers to the rail we feared they had forgotten it was autumn and were going to build a nest.

The southern shore of Port Stephens is a week-end resort for people from near-by Newcastle, and the loose, grey, sand track along which we walked three miles to the primitive little town to post letters and buy some fresh provisions, was lined with dingy, neglected-looking shacks, each standing in a litter of broken bottles and rusting tins, and each with a tall, narrow privy like a sentry box standing near it. One evening we were invited into one of the shacks on the beach. Its interior was most remarkable, for the walls of its two rooms were covered with stuck-on cutouts from papers and magazines, all of them depicting young women in suggestively scanty clothes. The hut was to be let next day to a man with a wife and family, and at the eleventh hour the owner was beginning to feel worried about the probable reactions of the new tenant's wife.

As soon as a fair wind made we sailed away and got as far as Tacking Point, where we fell in with conditions similar to those which had led Captain Cook to give the headland that name. The fair wind died away and after a little while a fresh breeze sprang up from dead ahead. Working in short tacks close along the shore we managed to make a few miles of progress against the current by evening. But after dark we did not dare to hug the coast, where the current has less strength, for the sky was overcast and there was no moon; so we stood out to sea on the port tack for the night. *Wanderer* was just able to carry all plain sail, there was not much sea running and she sailed very well. But eighteen hours later, when we closed with the shore on the other tack, our landfall looked suspiciously familiar. It proved to be Tacking Point again, and we discovered that in those eighteen hours of good sailing we had actually lost four miles. The south-setting current was obviously stronger than we had expected, and the only way of avoiding it appeared to be to go much farther out to sea and keep that offing until we approached the latitude of the next port of our choice. This we did, and I quote from the log:

'1500. Stood away offshore on port tack, course east-nor'-east. Sky looks bad, brassy sun and much scum. Rolled down one reef.

'1515. Wind freshening. Down No. 1, up No. 2 staysail.

'1530. Rolled down second reef and after shipping a heavy crest in the cockpit handed the staysail. Wind north by east, force 8. With helm lashed *Wanderer* steers herself at 2½ knots making considerable leeway. A lumpy sea with heavy deluges of spray and leeward lurches of 35°, when the contents of the galley lockers shift with a crash in spite of careful chocking. Kept steamer watches until 0100 on

'*Wednesday 7 April* when we reckoned we were outside the shipping lane. We both turned in then but the violent motion and the noise prevented sleep.

'0800. A squalid breakfast. Day becoming sunny in patches after an overcast night and wind moderating but sea is still too rough for faster sailing. Returned to our bunks, waiting.

'1145. Noon lat. by observation 31° 48' S. and that is 23 miles south of the dead reckoning although I had allowed for one knot of south-setting current. So the current has averaged

2 knots. Hope there is less out here 50 miles from the shore, otherwise we may be back on the latitude of Port Stephens tomorrow.

'1315. Wind force 6. Set No. 2 staysail and could do with even more sail, but we both feel weary and are going to try to sleep. Yacht self-steering.

'1800. Wind north, force 4. Made all sail and almost at once were becalmed, rolling madly in the left-over sea with sails flogging. A sinister-looking sunset with much scum and small black ball clouds to the south-west. A tremendous lightning display to the south-east.

'1900. A roll of low, black cloud has formed to the south. Very hot and humid. All the portents of a southerly buster are in evidence. May it come soon and last long.

'*Thursday 8 April*, 0000. No buster but instead a terrific thunderstorm, sheets of lightning illuminating the scene for several seconds at a time and at frequent intervals; some heavy rain and St. Elmo at the truck. We sail very slowly nor'-nor'-east.

'0700. Another arched roll of cloud away to the south, same as yesterday.

'1145. All the forenoon we have had calms or light airs with much thunder and rain. So variable were the airs that on one occasion *Wanderer* turned a complete circle without tacking or gybing. Two thick waterspouts passed uncomfortably close an hour ago. Noon latitude by observation 31° 44' S., so we have actually advanced four miles since noon yesterday. There is hope for us yet.

'1230. Wind freshening again from ahead. Rolled in one reef and got moving.'

The cycle then repeated itself: a gale, a thunderstorm and a calm, and there were times when we really thought we would have to visit Port Stephens, or perhaps even Sydney, again. But eventually we did get the longed-for southerly buster and in one twenty-four hour period made good eighty-two miles against the current.

We had decided to make a stop at Ballina on the Richmond River, which is about half way between Port Stephens and Sandy Cape. Through the kindness of Bob Godsall we had seen from the air something of the coast along which we were now sailing (incidentally, that is much the best way of seeing it) and had selected the Richmond as looking a little less difficult and dangerous than the other bar rivers.

Having got nearly to the latitude of the Richmond River entrance, we altered course and headed inshore for a point some distance north of it, to allow for the current which would tend to sweep us sideways down the coast. The night of our approach was squally. Short-handed as we were, squalls always presented something of a problem to the watch on deck. Was it best, on seeing one approaching, to call the watch below and get the reefs rolled in and staysails changed in plenty of time? Or was it better to wait in the hope that either the squall might not arrive until the change of watch, or that when it did arrive it might not be as strong as one had feared? Such decisions certainly helped to keep the helmsman's mind occupied, for it was always his or her wish to leave the one below undisturbed as long as possible; but it was understood between us that when in doubt the safety of the yacht and her gear was always to come first.

When I relieved Susan at midnight there were two evil-looking squall clouds building up and approaching with the wind on the port beam.

'What about a reef?' asked Susan as she lingered in the companionway.

I looked at those two clouds to windward, which because of the rain falling from them appeared to reach right down to the sea. As I was still bemused with sleep I found it more difficult than usual to make up my mind. Then 'No,' I said, 'I'm going to hang on. They may go clear of us, and we want to make what speed we can now we are working across the current, or our reckoning will go to blazes and we shall not know where we are when we close with the land at dawn.'

So Susan went below and turned in, and I at the helm cast my eye to windward again and again. I soon saw that the two clouds out there were joined to one another in the sky by a heavy black arch. As they advanced with a freshening wind, *Wanderer* increased her pace and was soon tearing along at seven knots. It seemed as though some gargantuan trap was closing on her and she, terrified, poor thing, was doing her utmost to escape before it was too late. I should have taken the hint, but I was almost intoxicated with the speed of our passage through the black water; besides I was loath to disturb Susan and I knew that the sails and the gear were good. Then the clouds which until then I had still hoped would pass clear of us, appeared to alter course; one crossed ahead of us and the other astern, and they drew along between them a semi-circular curtain of rain, which obscured the dim horizon to port. Just before the rain enveloped us I could look out to starboard through a tunnel in the clouds and caught a glimpse of the fast-disappearing stars. Then, just as though a jet from a fire-hose had been directed at us, the rain came deluging down, making me gasp for breath; the wind increased still more so that *Wanderer* staggered under the weight of it, burying her lee deck. I bore away and called Susan hurriedly from the bunk into which she had so recently crawled, and went forward to reef and change staysails, all of which I ought to have done much earlier. My judgement had been badly at fault.

But no sooner had I got the yacht snugged down than stars appeared to windward. The squall passed, leaving the heavy, rain-soaked sails to hang stiff and listless with the water dripping from them. So out came the reefs, up went the big staysail and the yacht gathered way; but an hour later we had to reef for another squall, and we repeated the process six times that restless night.

We arrived off the Richmond River bar during the forenoon of our seventh day at sea, having sailed by patent log 495 miles in order to make good only 260 over the ground, thanks to the contrary current and the headwinds we had encountered.

The bar has a charted depth at low water of ten feet, and we reached it at about half flood. The wind, though fresh, was blowing along the shore and there did not appear to be much swell. We got the leading marks in line and headed for the entrance. As we drew near it looked to me as though the breakers at each side of the channel were overlapping one another. But Susan, who was up the rigging and could see better, shouted that there was a clear but narrow way through between them; so we sailed on. But if either of us could have known how frightening were to be the next few minutes, we would have turned away while that was still possible. In a moment it was too late to do so, for *Wanderer* was sinking slowly down into a deep trough of apparently forward-moving water, and the steep, angry sea immediately astern looked unstable and showed every indication that it was about to break on top of her. She hung for what seemed like several minutes on the face of that sea, though in reality it can have been only a matter of seconds, pulling hard on the helm and tearing towards the opening between the stone training walls with which the river mouth was flanked. On either hand in shoaler water that same sea was breaking heavily as it overtook us with increasing speed and collapsed in a cataract of rushing foam. Then suddenly the bar was astern and we were sailing on the placid water of the wind-darkened river where, the day being a Sunday, several small open boats lay at anchor, their people fishing. By an odd chance one of the boats contained Jimmy Gearing Thomas and his wife. We had last met in the West Indies and they were now running the Metropole Hotel in the inland town of Lismore. Jimmy directed us to berth along-side a laid-up coaster, for the ebb runs hard in the river and the anchorage there is not good. On the ebb there was a slight ground swell, but by careful adjustment of her lines we got *Wanderer* to lie to her back spring a couple of feet from her neighbour, and so we had an undisturbed night except for the attention of the mosquitoes. A rat boarded us during the night and without waking us ate a loaf which we had left on the galley bench only a few inches from Susan's head.

Next day Jimmy whisked us away to his hotel—an old timber building which had recently been submerged to a depth of eight feet in the floods—for a night in a still, land-bound bed and to eat meals which Susan did not have to cook. The flood had done much damage in the town, but although such floods are common, we noticed that many of the new houses then being built were on the same low level as the town, instead of being placed on one of the hills close to it.

Largely owing to the frequent strikes of the watersiders (stevedores) and to competition from road transport, few of the ports along the coast of New South Wales now have a regular steamer service. The quays and other facilities are falling into decay and most of the pilots have been withdrawn. Whether or not there was a pilot at Ballina we did not discover, but all the time we were there the bar signal (two balls displayed

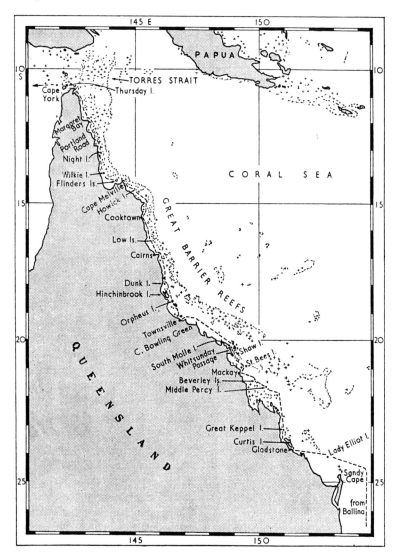

horizontally) read: 'The pilot cannot board you. Stand on and off until morning.' The skipper of one of the prawners lying at the quay assured us that the Richmond bar was one of the worst on that coast and he told us tales of vessels which had recently come to grief while trying to cross it. We were therefore thankful when, on leaving the place after three days there, we found no wind and little swell and were able to creep out under power at high water as a wild-looking crimson dawn coloured the eastern sky.

At sea a light headwind was blowing and the relentless current immediately began to set us south along the coast. So we stood away well offshore before attempting to make northing. Again we had unsettled weather, strong winds and calms. On the second day we made good only twenty-six miles though we sailed ninety-two through the water; on the third day we made good forty, having sailed seventy-three, and on the fourth 100, having sailed 132. But by then we no longer cared much about the current, for the wind was fair, a south-easter and plenty of it, and we felt we had at last reached our old companion the south-east trade wind once more. We remained out of sight of land, and did not alter course to the westward for Gladstone until our observations of the sun showed that we were on the latitude of the lightship marking the end of the long shoal spit which runs to the northward from Sandy Cape. It was a small thing to find, but we were fortunate and in due course it appeared ahead, uninhabited and pitching violently, for it is more of a light float than a proper lightship. There we ran out of the adverse current and entered the waters that lie within the Great Barrier Reefs.

The fresh fair wind hurried us through the night, during which we passed close to our first Australian coral island, Lady Elliot, which looked charming in the moonlight with a ring of white surf round it. In the morning we sailed swiftly for fifteen miles among the sandbanks of Port Curtis, to find a really snug berth at Gladstone, where we moored fore-and-aft between the piles in Auckland Creek. The distance by sea between Ballina and Gladstone is 393 miles, but we had actually sailed 623 through the water as recorded by the patent log.

There were several yachts in port, for the annual race from Brisbane had been sailed a few days previously, and we soon had many visitors from them. On some of the Australian offshore races an army or navy escort vessel goes with the competitors to see to their welfare and to report their positions to the press, for great interest is taken by the public in these events, especially when the weather is bad. Most of the yachts left before we did, bound back to their home port, but a few returned to Gladstone and the others got only a few miles on their way and then sought shelter in Pancake Creek against the strong south-easter which was blowing. And there some of them ran out of food so that the escort vessel, also weather-bound, returned to Gladstone to obtain provisions for them.

The town has wide, straight streets; the main street, which is metalled only in places, climbs laboriously up over a steep hill to the south-east of which spread the shallow, mud-coloured, wind-whipped waters of Port Curtis. Though a draughty street it is not an unpleasing one, except for the inevitable chromium-plated milk bars and chain stores, which today are spoiling the character of so many country towns all over the world. Just then the town was celebrating its centenary, and according to the *Gladstone Observer*, the local one-sheet newspaper, was gay with flags and bright lights; but all we saw were a few rather pathetic strings of wind-torn bunting and some tattered paper streamers in some of the shops.

The sou'-easter was without mercy. Day and night under a hard, clear sky it boomed up the estuary and through the town, and even succeeded in sending fierce little squalls down into the snug creek where *Wanderer* lay. It caused us some worry, for when the time came for us to leave, before we could square away and run up the coast, we should have to beat out to sea the fifteen miles we had run in among the indifferently marked shoals, and because the tidal streams run hard in the estuary we should have to do that on the ebb, thus running the risk of grounding for some hours if we happened to touch one of the shoals. We were therefore very glad when the skipper of the fishing boat *Coral Isle* offered to pilot us out through the back door by way of a narrow, drying, channel to the north, which passes inside Curtis Island, thus saving us many miles as well as the difficult beat seaward. We would not have attempted that channel without local knowledge.

We accepted his offer gladly and, starting off before our pilot, sailed slowly, waiting for him to overtake us. He was late doing so, having made some error regarding the time of high water, and when we reached the narrowest part of the channel among a maze of low, mangrove-covered, mud islands, the ebb was away and there was little time to be lost. So our pilot took us in tow, and almost at once at six knots dragged us high up on to a shoal, having quite understandably mistaken one island for another—they all looked alike—and there we dried out at a most uncomfortable angle. That was the second time in her life that *Wanderer* had accepted the services of a pilot, and it was the first time she had ever run aground. Fortunately at that season the night tide was rising several feet higher than the day tide. Our pilot, who incidentally refused to accept any payment for his time or the fuel he had expended, stood by and took us in tow as soon as we floated at midnight; then at a very sedate pace he towed us through the narrows in the dark and left us only when we had reached water deep enough to float in at any state of tide.

In daylight we found ourselves lying in what appeared to be a broad, smooth river flanked by mangroves, dark green and silent and with no sign of man. We liked it and its peace so much that we remained all day and another night, but after dark we had to screen our bunks against the attacks made by thousands of mosquitoes.

Our river was only shown sketchily and on a very small scale on the chart, so sailing down it to the sea was a small adventure. As we made our way slowly along under the staysail only and taking frequent soundings with the lead, we could see and hear the waders on the banks and in the many muddy creeks which twisted in among the mangroves; several birds as large as the emu, but with black and white wings and very long red legs, flew over us. Eventually we reached the sea, where we made all sail and arrived at an anchorage in the lee of Great Keppel Island for the night.

When I was a small boy I used to imagine the Great Barrier as a wall of rock continuous for its entire length of 1,000 miles, for I did not then understand that it is of coral formation and that coral does not grow above water level. In fact the Barrier is not even a continuous submerged formation, but consists of a great many separate reefs. The Barrier Reefs vary in distance from the coast between 12 and 140 miles, the greater distance being at the southern end and the lesser near the north end. One speaks loosely of the Barrier Reef Islands, but apart from a few sand cays which have formed on the reefs here and there, and some blocks of dead coral which have been lifted above sea level, there are hardly any islands on the reefs, most of which are submerged. Some portions, however, dry a foot or so at low water. The reefs therefore look more spectacular from the air than they do from the sea. The islands are nearly all inside the Barrier Reefs, between them and the mainland, and there are several hundred of them as well as many isolated reefs. South of Cairns most of the islands are high; these, of course, are not of coral formation though they have fringing reefs of coral round their shores. North of Cairns many of the islands are low. This type starts life as a reef, then a sand cay forms at the leeward or north-west end and somehow the industrious mangrove gets a footing and bit by bit reclaims more of the reef.

Many years ago goats were placed on most of the high islands for the benefit of shipwrecked mariners. Having seen the speed and agility of these creatures we wondered how the unarmed castaway was expected to catch them. They have multiplied exceedingly except on Whitsunday Island. There used to be a saw-mill there and when it was abandoned some dogs were left behind; these thrived, ate the goats, and now that island is over-run with wild dogs. Also coconut palms were planted, but on the low islands few of them have survived the cyclones which are common in that part of the world during the summer months.

From Great Keppel we had a wild sail through a grey and windy day and a black and stormy night to Middle Island, Percy Group, where we arrived and anchored in a little bay where there is no coral. On the beach stood a shack with the word TELEPHONE painted on it in bold letters. Feeling a little mystified, for that island is at least forty miles from the mainland, we landed to investigate. I took off the earpiece, wound the handle and got an electric shock, for it was that sort of telephone. A man's voice answered. I said who I was and the voice replied:

'Delighted to know you, Mr. Hiscock. I am one of the White brothers; we own this island and live on the top of it with our sister. Why don't you and Mrs. Hiscock come up and have lunch with us?'

Of course we went. Three miles we trudged in the heat along a winding horse track through the jungle to a plateau 800 feet up. There, where the air was cooler and the jungle did not encroach, the Whites, a Canadian family and the only people on the island, had built their home and lived there for thirty-three years. They had a thousand sheep, horses, bullocks and fowls, and apart from flour, paraffin and a few other needs, which the lighthouse tender on her trips up and down the coast brought them at regular intervals, were self-supporting. We spent a happy day with them, Susan looking quite remarkable in shorts, gay shirt and wide-brimmed sun-hat riding one of their draught horses bareback. When we returned to the beach we were laden with two sugar bags filled with pineapples, bananas and limes, all of which with much else grow in profusion on that fertile island.

After calling at one of the uninhabited Beverley Islands, we made our way to Mackay, an artificial harbour on the mainland, where spring tides rise twenty feet, and there did some shopping most inconveniently in the town, which is several miles from the harbour. A small, disreputable-looking motor vessel came in and anchored close to windward of us. Her crew were black and on a platform projecting over her stern stood a vertical boiler. They soon had a fire going under the boiler and within a few minutes the stench of rotten fish coming from it was so overpowering that we had to shift our berth. This was one of the trochus boats of which we were to see many farther north. The trochus is a free-moving conical-shaped shellfish which normally lives among the tree coral, but comes closer to the surface, usually on the windward side of the reefs, at certain phases of the moon to feed on plankton. On these occasions the lugger, as the vessel engaged in the business is called no matter whether she sets any sails or not, anchors to leeward of the reef; open rowing boats are launched and in these the divers cross to the windward side of the reef where they skin-dive for the shellfish in a fathom or two of water. The shell is exported for the making of mother-of-pearl buttons, and to remove the fish from the shell it is boiled, making the dreadful smell we experienced at Mackay.

We had intended calling at the island of St. Bees, as the Whites of Middle Percy had asked us to deliver a letter and some magazines there; but on the chart the anchorage looked so poor, with a depth of ten fathoms right up to the fringing reef, and the wind, blowing that day not from off the island but along it, was so strong, that we did not consider it wise to stop. We therefore continued to the north and in the afternoon found good shelter from the booming wind in the lee of Shaw Island, but too far from the shore to be able to row to it in our dinghy against so strong a wind. Across from us lay Linderman Island, one of the best known of the holiday resorts of which there are several in the Whitsunday area, a place where people go to fossick, i.e. to gather shells and coral at low water on the reef. But that day the Linderman anchorage was a dangerously rough lee shore.

The colour of the water in the Whitsunday Passage was most remarkable as we hurried through it next day. Although the sky was vivid blue the water was apple-green because of the silt in it caused by the recent floods and the strong winds. The whole neighbourhood, with its many islands and high main-land coastline, looked most attractive, and as we wished to have a look at it from the land we stopped after sailing only twenty-one miles at the island of South Molle and went ashore. We soon wished we had not done so; it would have been better to have retained our memory of the Whitsunday Passage as viewed from the sea where every prospect pleased. The fringing reef on which we had to land was flat, rough and dirty and ashore we found a double row of grey asbestos huts, a dance hall and a shop, for this was a holiday camp with a population of 125 bored-looking people.

We left as soon as the tide served in the morning and enjoyed the only quiet and anxiety-free passage we were to have the whole time we were in Barrier Reef waters. For once the wind was light and we ran pleasantly to the north-west with the spinnaker set for 140 miles to the port of Townsville. On the way we passed Cape Bowling Green, a low, sandy peninsula with shifting banks extending a long way from it. The *Australian Pilot*, Vol. IV, warned us that as all the creeks in the neighbour-hood swarm with crocodiles, great caution must be used when navigating them in boats. Obviously this was no place to make an error in navigation and as it was dark we gave the cape a wide berth.

Townsville is an artificial harbour and the approach to it is by way of a long, dredged channel. We were sailing through this in the wake of a small steamer when she suddenly stopped and the water round her became churned up and muddy. For a moment we thought she had run aground and we wondered on which side we ought to pass her as she seemed to be in the centre of the channel; then it dawned on us that she was a suction dredger at work.

In the harbour we had some difficulty in finding a berth in which it was possible to lie afloat without being in the way of the large ships using the port. As soon as we had done our shopping we left and spent a rolly night in the lee of Magnetic Island, then groped our way through heavy rain to Great Palm Island, which is an aboriginal settlement. We anchored a long way from the shore, the reason being that the chart showed a line of coral heads outside the fringing reef, and the water was so thick with silt that pilotage by eye was impossible, while the leadline is, of course, of no help in avoiding coral heads. The sea was too rough and the distance too great to permit us to land.

The following day, however, the weather improved; the sun shone, the islands of the small group looked very pleasing as we sailed among them and one in particular, Orpheus, took our fancy. With the sun high in the sky and the water clearer than it had been for many days, I was able to con from the crosstrees while Susan worked the yacht into a bay on the island's eastern side. We had scarcely anchored and made all snug when Nan Taylor came out in a launch to welcome us and invite us ashore for showers and dinner that evening. She and her husband Colin—both are New Zealanders and he was a barrister—own the island and run a small and exclusive guest house on it. The fact that they had recently won £15,000 in a State lottery had not weaned them from the simple life one bit. Most of their windfall was being used to improve the island and its amenities; they were buying a new launch in which to ferry off their guests, and a more powerful electric generating set so that an electric washing machine could be used.

The evening was quiet when we landed, and the sunset beautiful. (See p. 160.) Before dinner of tender island goat, which was cooked and served by smiling aboriginal servants with skins so black that they looked almost blue in the lamplight, we were introduced to bush showers. I wonder if, salt and sticky from days of hard sailing in a hot and humid climate, you have ever enjoyed the luxury of one of these? First you take a bucket and fill it with hot water from a copper heated by a wood fire in the open. This you empty into a special container which has a perforated bottom and a plug and is installed in the corrugated-iron shower-house. You add cold water until the temperature is to your liking and then hoist the filled container up to the roof with a tackle. Standing beneath it you pull out the plug and a refreshing shower of warm, wood-smoke-scented water sluices all the stickiness away.

Late that evening the Taylors and their guests escorted us down the beach to our dinghy, and as we pulled out across the star-patterned water towards *Wanderer*'s riding light, they called to us to return next day, for there was to be roast duck and Rhinegold wine for dinner and we must share it with them. How glad we would have been to do so, but our slow passages up the coast of New South Wales had made us late on our schedule, and as there was again a fair wind in the morning we reluctantly sailed on.

Passing large, mountainous, uninhabited Hinchinbrook Island, in the dense jungle of which twenty-foot pythons live, we averaged six knots for the fifty-mile run to Dunk Island. The day was grey with mist and rain and the wind was strong. At Dunk we brought up in the bay on the north-west side where a sand spit fringed with wind-blown casuarina trees formed one horn and the steep side of the island the other. In company with some trochus luggers we sheltered from the fierce wind there for two days. How we wished we had remained at Orpheus, for this island was not welcoming, and although on the third day the weather showed no improvement, we felt we had stayed long enough, and, leaving before dawn, had an exhilarating sail to Cairns, eighty miles away. Again the sky was overcast and there were occasional rain storms. Each of these brought a strengthening of the wind which temporarily shifted to east; then after the rain there was a slight lull before the wind shot back to south-east and blew as hard as ever. H.M.A.S. *Australia*, on her last cruise before being broken up, and with the Governor-General and his lady aboard, overtook us at high speed. We learnt from the news broadcast that evening that she was on her way to the assistance of a tank landing craft

which, because of the continued bad weather, was in difficulties
farther up the coast.

All the way from Dunk Island to Cape Grafton *Wanderer*
averaged seven knots, and it was only as she entered the
dredged approach channel to Cairns, where the wind was
drawing out and moderating, that she eased her mad pace and
beat sedately into harbour. We saw a few small craft clinging
to the edge of the bank on the starboard hand just outside the
entrance, and inshore of them several more lying on their sides.
We did not fancy such a berth as it was our intention to remain
at Cairns for several days; so we sailed on in, past the line
of quays at which three ships were berthed, and came to an
anchorage beyond them close to the shore but in deep water.

At once we were invaded by many mosquitoes which were,
apparently, even hungrier than we were. After a restless night
loud with the high-pitched whine of them, and realizing that
the anchorage we had chosen was an impossibly long way from
the town, we sailed down the harbour and found a cramped but
not too uncomfortable berth free from mosquitoes among the
small craft we had noticed the previous evening on our way in.

There was no proper landing and the foreshore was a
wilderness of sand overrun with convolvulus. But the town
itself, a tourist resort and centre for the sugar-cane country,
which is the most fertile part of Queensland, was a clean,
thriving place with streets unusually wide even for an Australian
town and many shops selling refrigerators, shoes and clothes.
But the kind of shops we needed, grocers, fruiterers and iron-
mongers, were difficult to find and a long way from the harbour.
So we spent most of our five days there shopping and carrying
loads of stores back to *Wanderer*. Cairns was to be our last large
town until we reached Port Louis in Mauritius, which we did
not expect to do until five months had passed; we therefore
had to provision in a bigger way than usual and lay in a good
supply of paraffin for the galley stove. Prices here were higher
than in Sydney, for the farther north one goes in Australia the
more expensive does everything become.

North of Cairns the main line of reefs draws closer to the
coast, and in the water between it and the shore lie many small
islands and isolated reefs. We had spent a considerable time
studying the charts and reading the *Pilot*; because of the currents

and tidal streams, which tend to be uncertain in strength and direction, and the distance apart of the lights marking the main shipping route, we made up our minds to sail in these waters (which appeared to be a navigator's nightmare) only by day, so far as that was possible. The problem was to decide in advance where to spend the next night and then to leave the anchorage in time to reach the next one while it was still light enough to see. The charts, as usual, were mines of accurate information, but it is not always possible to judge from them whether a certain anchorage will be a snug one for a little ship, and of course the *Pilot* was written for very much larger vessels than ours. The recommended route is indicated on the charts by a dotted line, and we decided to adhere to this most of the way, because to deviate from it in such coral-encumbered waters would be asking for trouble unless the sea were less clouded with silt than it had been so far. But naturally we should have to leave the recommended route to find an anchorage each evening, and perhaps to cut corners when racing against the onset of night. In the event of any disaster befalling, the possibility of obtaining assistance on a coast where crocodiles, mosquitoes and snakes abound, where the aboriginals are not always friendly or to be trusted, and where the mission stations are few and far between, is remote indeed.

It was therefore with a feeling of excitement that we set out from Cairns on 18 May 1954 to make our way through those difficult waters to Thursday Island, which lay 500 miles to the nor'-nor'-west. We were determined that we would never relax our vigilance for a moment. Vigilance is desirable if any seamanlike adventure is to be brought to a successful conclusion, but among coral reefs it is absolutely essential; each island, cay or reef must be identified as it is approached, and no opportunity must be missed of fixing the vessel's position, either by cross bearings, transits, vertical sextant angles or observations of the celestial bodies. I do not wish to overstress these points, but they are of vital importance, as has been learnt too late by some small-boat adventurers whose craft have struck the coral in these waters and left their bones to rot there.

The inside route is marked with beacons and lights, nearly all of them unwatched, at some turning points or narrow places. Our first stop after Cairns was at the Low Islets, where one of the very few watched lights is situated. The lighthouse stands on the western islet, which is a tiny patch of coral sand and shingle, and clustered round the tower are the outbuildings and keepers' houses. The eastern islet is long, low and mangrove-covered. The two islets are joined by a reef and the lagoon thus formed, in which we spent a night at anchor, is shallow and alive with sharks, which are sometimes a danger to the keepers and their families when fossicking.

Sharks appear to vary in voracity. On the Australian coast they are regarded as being highly dangerous and bathing is usually done only in fenced enclosures or from surfing beaches where a lookout is kept; if a shark is seen a bell is rung or some other signal is made and then all bathers hurry for the beach. The lagoon of Rangiroa, one of the Tuamotu atolls, is so infested with sharks that the mother-of-pearl diving industry there has had to be abandoned; yet in the lagoon of a neigh-bouring atoll a friend of ours has done commercial shark fishing, and he told us that the sharks are so harmless that he and his companions often swam with them and had been rubbed by their rough bodies, but no one was ever harmed.

All the way from Sydney we had been following in the track of Captain Cook, whose log was a constant inspiration to us, rounding the headlands he had rounded and named, and experiencing much the same weather as he had done, for the time of year was the same. But the passage we made north from the Low Islets had a fuller historical meaning for us, as we passed Endeavour Reef, on which his vessel had struck in 1770. For twenty-four hours she was held fast there, the sharp coral tearing the wooden sheathing from her hull and holing her bilge, and not until she had been lightened by the jettisoning of her guns and many other things did she float off. The hole was fothered with a sail covered with oakum and wool, and search was made for a suitable place in which to beach the ship. The tone of the place names on the chart changes here: Cape Tribulation, Mount Sorrow and Weary Bay following one another in quick succession. Then we came to Endeavour River at Cooktown, where the great navigator brought his ship for repairs, and it was found that a piece of coral, which had remained wedged in the hole it had made in her bilge, had saved her from foundering. Dakin in his book *Great Barrier*

Reef, comments that Cook left Australia 'without realizing the existence of the greatest coral reef development in the world's seas'. To me this is not at all surprising, for we in *Wanderer* on the same track had seen practically nothing of the reefs among which we had been sailing, owing to the mud and sand held in suspension by the water.

In gold-rush days Cooktown was a busy place with a population of 30,000. Now only 500 people live there, and all that remains of the town are a few rusty iron hotels and cobwebby shops, which drowse through the heat of the day beside the wide and dusty main street (*see p.* 161); elsewhere the white ant has destroyed the wooden buildings and tropical growths conceal the mouldering foundations. The memorial to Cook still stands in its little flower garden beside the river.

The town, which in its sleepy way is rather charming, was in the news at the time of our visit. A carpet snake had hidden itself in the innards of the harbour-master's cuckoo clock and had eaten the bird when it came out to announce the time.

As I had an aching tooth I thought I would go down to Cairns to have it attended to as there was no dentist at Cooktown. I knew there was an air service between the two towns, but on inquiry learnt that the plane left on Friday evening and returned early Saturday morning, and anyway all the seats were booked. The distance by road is 300 miles and there was no bus or rail service. The weekly boat left on Thursday and would not return until the following Tuesday. Certainly we had reached an isolated place, and it seemed best to press on for Thursday Island and hope to find a dentist there.

As our next stop was to be at Howick Island seventy-two miles away, we left Cooktown a couple of hours before dawn in the moonlight and had a rousing run before the trade wind, which continued to blow strongly. The day was fine as with flashing whitecaps all around we tore through the channel between Wooded and Three Islands and passed outside Decapolis Reef and between the Turtle and Partridge Groups. We frequently checked our position, and the watch below did what we call homework, studying the charts and reading the *Pilot* so as to have a grasp of the next situation before it was reached. Much of the coast, particularly south of Cape Flattery, consists of white sand hills and white sand cliffs with patches of scrub on them. From the offing it looked like a large seaside town, hotels and all, and we even imagined we could make out streets leading up from the beach to the suburbs behind. In mid afternoon, having averaged six and a half knots, we brought up in the lee of uninhabited Howick Island; all the islands between Cooktown and Torres Strait are uninhabited, and apart from the occasional mission or cattle station and a few aboriginals, the mainland coast has no people either. It is a desolate part of the world where we felt much more alone than we ever did out in the empty oceans.

All through the night the wind roared in the rigging just as it had done day and night with scarcely a pause since the morning we left friendly Orpheus Island. The pilot chart shows that no gales blow here in May or June; but that was not our experience, nor was it Slocum's. In *Sailing Alone Around the World* he says: 'On this parallel of latitude is the high ridge and backbone of the trade wind which about Cooktown often amounts to a hard gale.' We noticed in those parts that the harder the wind blew the poorer became the visibility, which south of Cairns had been remarkably good except during rain.

Again we left our anchorage before dawn and had a furiously fast sail to Cape Melville, which is the eastern point of a fifty-mile-wide bay, frequently checking our position with bearings and sextant angles. The cape is a fantastic affair with immense blocks of granite strewn over it. Here the outside edge of the Barrier Reefs comes closer to the land than it does in any other place and is only twelve miles distant. Having rounded the cape, where in 1899 a cyclone drove ashore the pearling fleet and drowned between 300 and 400 men, our course was for a short time actually south of west, and we felt we were making nothing towards our goal; but it was a pleasant sail in smooth water to the Flinders Group, where in the afternoon we anchored in the lee of Blackwood Island. The squalls off the island were savage but they never lasted long enough to straighten out our chain, and as the holding ground is of clay we were not disturbed by the rasping noise the chain makes when it moves on coral.

Night Island, our next intended anchorage, lay eighty-six miles away, so once again we started early; but we had not gone far when the wind fell so light that obviously it was not going to be possible to reach our objective before dark. We therefore headed for nearer Hannah Island and were just about to anchor there in mid afternoon, when the wind piped up again and we thankfully bore away for Wilkie Island a little farther on, for the Hannah anchorage offered only indifferent shelter from the swell in eight fathoms. We reached Wilkie at dusk, and brought up close to the sand beach at its north-west corner, where we got cover, but only just, from the rising wind and sea.

Not having so far to go next day we did not leave until dawn, which was late coming as the sky was overcast. Two hours later the wind was of gale force and *Wanderer*, under double-reefed mainsail only, was running at seven knots. As usual with the rising wind visibility became very poor, and only the nearest part of the coast and the closer islands were visible, all the rest being hidden in a luminous mist. At lunch-time we tore in behind Night Island, just a mangrove-fringed reef with a sand cay, and there thankfully found smooth water with only a slight swell setting in; and the north-running current held us head on to the swell so that the yacht pitched quietly but did not roll.

For four days we lay weather-bound there. We took the opportunity to catch up with our letter-writing, but the tapping of the typewriter did not drown the doleful whine of the gale. To port of us lay the low green line of the island and to starboard, three miles away and only occasionally visible through the mist, stood the barren, uninhabited coast. The humidity was great, everything on board being damp and sticky to the touch, and the cabin temperature was between eighty-five and ninety degrees. Our nearest human neighbours were probably at Portland Road, forty miles away.

Each morning a large number of small black birds flew from the island to the mainland in arrowhead formations, crying shrilly to one another, and at dusk they returned; they reminded us of city workers living in a suburb. We both felt depressed by the bad weather and the thought of the difficult passages that lay ahead, while the recent days of almost breathless navigation among the reefs had tired us. But we cheered up when during the afternoon of our fourth day at anchor the wind moderated sufficiently to allow us to launch the dinghy and land on the island, where we stretched our legs on the steep sand beach which formed the north-west corner. We saw how the mangroves with root and bough were marching out into the shallow water on the reef, which they seemed to have every intention of reclaiming. On the reef we found among other creatures many clams. The two hinged shells in which the clam lives lie on the reef with their open mouth upward ready to seize their prey. With a stick cut from the undergrowth we poked into the clam's open mouth, and nothing happened until we touched the living creature inside; then the shells immediately snapped together with great force, their sharp, serrated edges cutting the stick in two. The shells of these clams were only a foot long, but they do grow as long as four feet, as we had seen in the shell collection on Orpheus Island.

Though the wind was still strong the weather had much improved when we sailed to Portland Road. On the way the *Wewak* passed us. She was one of the cattle ships plying on that coast, and had recently been in trouble for carrying cattle for forty-eight hours without food or water. From the same broadcast we learnt that the Queensland dingo fence had just been completed. Three thousand five hundred miles long, it had been built in an attempt to prevent the annual loss of half a million sheep which hitherto had been taken yearly by wild dogs. Once again we were impressed by the size of this huge country.

At Portland we had difficulty in landing, for the beach consists of boulders and dead coral with deep cracks on which walking is dangerous and manhandling the dinghy impossible, while the sturdy wooden pier at which the monthly steamer berths had no ladder or other means of access. So we had to wait until high water. Ashore we found some aboriginals and two young Australians; they gave us tea and offered us the use of their water and sink so that we could wash our clothes. The sink consisted of a galvanized steel oil drum sawn lengthways; the two halves, one for washing and the other for rinsing, were supported on wooden trestles in the open. The young men did not tell us what their occupation was, but we gained the impression that they hated the very sight of one another, which was, perhaps, the result of living such an isolated life.

Portland is in the centre of crocodile country. In that neighbourhood the reptiles may be met with almost anywhere on or near the water, even out on the reefs where they go to clean their skins of grass and barnacles. The skin of a fourteen-footer, which is a normal size, was worth about £7 at that time. But crocodiles were becoming scarce, for there had been a great slaughter of them; 1,000 were taken in 1953 and 2,000 the year before.

Margaret Bay, also on the mainland and about fifty miles from Portland, was the next anchorage at which we stopped, after yet another windy day spent threading our way among the isolated reefs. Our berth was a sheltered and attractive one, the bay having a long white beach backed by low country where the occasional thin thread of smoke from some aboriginal's cooking fire was the only sign of life. Close by was tiny Sunday Island, where Captain Bligh landed to gather oysters during his heroic open-boat voyage after he had been set adrift by the mutineers of the *Bounty*.

The final passage inside the reefs to Cape York, Australia's northern tip, was a distance of over ninety miles and more than we could hope to cover in daylight. The only possible anchorage along the route is at the Cairncross Islands, and this, the *Pilot* informed us, is uncomfortable because of the swell which runs round both sides of the island and meets there, and the holding ground is bad.

We left in the late afternoon so as to round the Bird Islands while there was still light enough for us to see them by. Then we steered to leave the light on Hannibal Island to port and passed through the one-mile-wide channel between that island and another that has no light. Four hours later we passed through another channel between Cairncross and Bushy Islands, only one of which has a light. The night was so dark that we saw nothing of the islands, and from a small boat it is very difficult to judge the distance one is from a light; the only possible methods, the four-point bearing or doubling the angle on the bow, being worthless in a slow-moving craft when, as there, a current or tidal stream of unknown strength and direction is running. These were the dangerous moments of that night passage, for had we passed too close to either of the lights we would have struck the reefs of their islands, yet if we had left them too far away we would have struck the dangers at the far sides of the channels. So we were thankful when both were safely past.

As usual we had been sailing fast, and fearing we would be up with unlit Shortland Reef before daylight, we hove-to for an hour and continued on our way at dawn. The sky was then overcast and the water discoloured, so there was not much likelihood of seeing any sunken dangers. However, we got cross-bearings of the beacon on Wyburn Reef and a conspicuous red patch on the cliff of the mainland which was marked on the chart, thus fixing our position, and were then able to set a course to take us safely past Shortland Reef. A few minutes later a shaft of low, yellow, sunlight pierced the clouds and showed us the pale brown colour of a submerged reef close ahead. We just had time to alter course to clear the danger and then realized that we must have mistaken one red patch on the shore for another, and indeed there proved to be several of them; but how very fortunate we were that the sun chose to shine when he did and show us the reef before it was too late. Other reefs for which we then looked failed to show, so instead of taking the short cut through Albany Pass we went the long way round outside Albany Island, where there were heavy tidal overfalls and a rough sea, and at lunchtime came to anchor in Evans Bay hard by Cape York.

Quite unreasonably I always expect a headland which is geographically important, such as the termination of a continent, to be bold and impressive. So I was disappointed with Cape York, which is wooded and rises gently to a height of only 372 feet. But the surroundings, seen in sunshine, were pretty, the giant pinnacle anthills were remarkable and the horses strolling about on the beach gave life to the picture.

The following day we sailed across to Thursday Island, one of the many little islands which, together with extensive shoals and reefs, lie in Torres Strait. (*See p.* 161.) The strait separates Australia from Papua and it is there that the waters of the Pacific and Indian Oceans mingle. It is a place for exciting pilotage as there are many dangers and in some parts the tidal streams attain a speed of eight knots. As the anchorage at Thursday Island is on the windward side, it is not a comfortable one for vessels as small as ours, but neighbouring Horn Island prevents the sea from becoming dangerously large. There we brought up close to and inside of the steamer jetty.

At last we had reached the objective which had been in our minds for so long. Two thousand miles of Australia's eastern coastline with its countless reefs and islands, together with the whole of the vast Pacific, were now safely astern.

14

INDIAN OCEAN ISLANDS

THURSDAY Island, a pearl-shell and trochus diving centre, is a hilly, dried-up little place, and although it is only one and a half miles long and three-quarters of a mile wide, it has a population of 2,000 of which 500 are white. Port Kennedy, its town, with wide, sandy streets and large upstanding custom-house, gives the impression of once having been a busy, thriving place; but now it is shabby and neglected, and even the main jetty is in such a state of decay that when I was coming alongside it in the dinghy and happened to knock one of its rotten piles with an oar, the blade of the oar cut clean through it.

At the time of our visit there were fifty luggers working from the island, most of them ketches with auxiliary motors. Diving is done for two kinds of shell, the conical trochus, which I have already mentioned, and pearl shell, which is flat and sometimes as large as a dinner plate. The latter is obtained in depths often exceeding twenty fathoms by skin divers wearing helmets. Usually there are three pearl divers to each lugger; attached to her by their lines and air hoses, they walk along the sea-bed picking up the oysters as the lugger drifts to leeward, the stream of air bubbles from their helmets scaring away the sharks—so they say. To reduce drift as much as possible, the luggers are of deep draught and have very low freeboard. (*See p.* 196.) The oysters each diver sends up are kept in separate heaps and at the end of the day's diving each diver opens his own oysters; any pearls that he may find belong to him and not to the owner of the lugger, who pays the wages, provides the gear and supplies the food. The owner gets only the shell, which is used, as is trochus shell, for making mother-of-pearl buttons, the handles of knives and forks, etc. Owing to the bad weather that year and the inability of the native

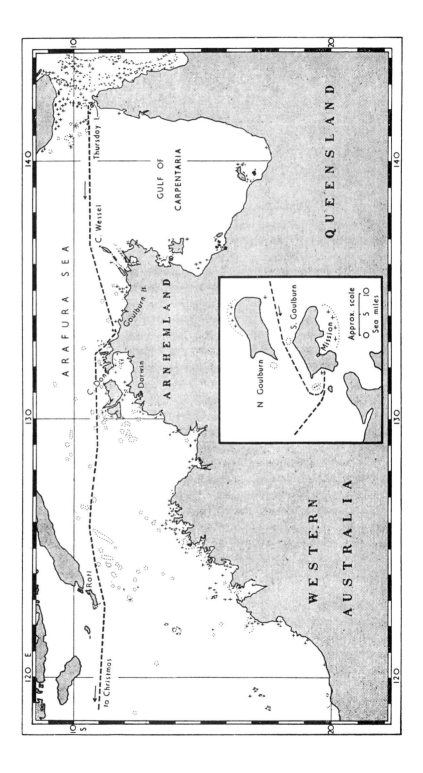

divers to work satisfactorily in a depth exceeding ten fathoms
(before the war most of the deep diving was done by Japanese
divers, but they are at present not permitted to work in the
Thursday Island grounds) the demand had been greater than
the supply; trochus was fetching £250 a ton (if she is fortunate
a lugger can bring in from three to five tons at the end of three
weeks' work), and pearl shell £800 a ton.

Although pearls are rare there are some wealthy divers
living on Thursday Island, and some have so little idea of the
value of money that rather than walk a hundred yards down the
street to buy a can of milk or a tin of bulumakau (corned beef),
they will hire a taxi. In this tiny island with its 2,000 inhabitants
there are twenty-two taxis, four private cars, two buses with
seats for thirty people, four hotels, fifteen stores, two planes a
week and one passenger/cargo ship a month, the old *Elsanna*
from Brisbane.

John Witts, a lugger owner and storekeeper, and his wife
very kindly had us up to their home for dinner one evening.
John told us a lot about pearling and he showed us a perfectly
matched pair of rare gold-lip pearl shells, which he said were
the best he had ever come across. We asked him whether it
might be possible to buy a single gold-lip shell to mount on
Wanderer's cabin bulkhead alongside the black-lip which
Captain Argod had given us at Tahiti. He said he would see
what he could do, but we heard nothing more until the morning
of our departure when he and his wife came aboard to say
good-bye and, much to our embarrassment, insisted on presenting us with the very pair we had so much admired, saying
he could easily replace them, which indeed we doubted.

The dentist I had hoped to find was away and not expected
back for several weeks, and as my aching tooth had quietened
down it seemed best to move on. So we took aboard such fresh
provisions as were obtainable and had to pay highly for them;
bread of poor quality was 2s. a loaf, bananas were 6d. and
oranges 1s. 6d. each. We visited the custom-house and there,
although the officer in charge was as kind to us as his position
permitted him to be, we had to pay duty on some of the stores
we had bought out of bond in New Zealand and had consumed
while in Australian waters. Having concluded that business I
said:

'We are leaving Australia for good tomorrow, so I wish to ship some spirits and tobacco out of bond.'

'I'm very sorry,' he replied, 'but there are two reasons why you can't do that. There is no bond store on this island and even if there was, stores are only granted to vessels exceeding forty tons.'

The forty-ton rule is common and is in force in England as well as in other countries, but except in Australia is nearly always ignored when a yacht is about to sail in foreign waters, unless her cruise is going to be only a short one.

In early June *Wanderer* left Thursday Island by way of Normanby Sound, and dropping Torres Strait with all its little islands astern, headed once more to the westward with 7,000 miles of Indian Ocean before her.

When planning our world voyage we decided to make our way homeward from Australia via the southern Indian Ocean and the Cape of Good Hope, rather than attempt the passage up the Red Sea against the northerly wind which prevails in the northern part. Also we had decided it would be unwise to visit the Indonesian Islands because of the unsettled political situation there, a decision which had been strengthened by reports we had received while in Australia of piracy among those islands and of the chicanery of the port officials. So when we left Thursday Island we hoped to make Christmas Island, 2,100 miles distant, our next stop.

The Arafura Sea, which is that part of the Indian Ocean lying between the northern coast of Australia and the southern Indonesian Islands, is of no great depth. The soundings are irregular and in the western portion there are many shoal patches over which there is a heavy tumbling sea during strong winds, as well as several islets, reefs and drying sandbanks. To quote from the *Australian Pilot*, Part V:

'This sea being little known beyond the routes generally taken by vessels from Torres Strait towards Timor and Darwin, it is probable that shoals exist in addition to those marked on

PLATE 21

Top: A party of aboriginals, the self-made scars showing on their upper arms, cook a meal of fish on Goulburn Island. *Bottom*: A typical Thursday Island pearling lugger, ketch rigged and with low freeboard and deep draught to reduce drift as much as possible.

the Admiralty charts; as the position and even the existence of some of the charted shoals are doubtful, a vigilant lookout should be kept with a view of removing these doubts, as well as for the safety of the vessel.'

As soon as we drew clear of the islands the south-east trade wind, or monsoon as it is sometimes called here, worked up to force 7; for the next three days while we sailed across the wide mouth of the Gulf of Carpentaria, where we saw several turtles and some bright yellow sea-snakes, we had such a wet and uncomfortable time that we decided to put in for a rest at one of the small islands lying off the coast between Cape Wessel and Cape Don. That part of Australia, known as Arnhemland, has not been properly surveyed; so one has to use the charts— on which soundings are scanty and parts of the shore are shown by dotted lines only—with some caution. We selected South Goulburn Island because it has a bay on its western side which we gathered from the *Pilot* is free from dangers. Our course on the chart having taken us close past two shoals reported in 1937 and 1941, with 'P.A.' (position approximate) written against each, our noon position by observation on our fifth day at sea placed us only six miles east of the channel between North and South Goulburn. Approaching these islands of which we knew so little was quite exciting, for we had no idea how high they were or what they looked like. But I had only just finished working out our position when Susan sighted them; both were about fifty feet high and absolutely flat. The *Pilot* suggested that the channel between them was probably free from dangers, but stated that it had not been properly surveyed; so we kept a careful lookout, though it is doubtful whether we would have seen any shoals if such existed, because of the discoloured water which there was of the same muddy hue as one finds in a tidal river. We passed through safely and in the afternoon entered Walla Bay on the west side of South Goulburn. There, close to a sandy beach on which a pearling lugger was being repaired by her crew—a Thursday Island halfcaste skipper, a German, an Italian and a couple of Torres

---

PLATE 22

On one never-to-be-forgotten occasion in the Indian Ocean *Wanderer*, with six rolls in the mainsail and boom guy rove, made a day's run of 157 miles.

Strait islanders—we found a good anchorage in perfectly smooth water.

The island is L-shaped, seven miles by five, is bounded by low red and white cliffs of sand and clay and is covered with thin scrub, gums and huge anthills several feet high. As it is said to be inhabited by venomous snakes, we always beat the undergrowth ahead of us with sticks when walking, a precaution which is said to be effective except where the death adder is concerned, for he being deaf or, more correctly, incapable of sensing vibration, is not aware that one is approaching until, perhaps, he gets trodden on.

Over on the windward side of the island we found a Methodist mission run by a Fijian superintendant and several Australians. It had an air-strip for the use of the flying doctor and a well-tended garden which supplied us with bananas, drinking nuts and paw-paws.

Arnhemland is an aboriginal reserve and I believe one is not allowed to go there without a permit; but the people at the mission seemed pleased to see us and did not ask for our credentials. The aboriginals, many of whom have self-made scars in patterns on their shiny, blue-black skins (*see p.* 196), live a strange, wandering life. They have no built villages or other community centres, and in ones or twos they move about from place to place, sleeping at night in the open or beneath a rude shelter of branches, and living on what they can kill or pick— 'walkabout' they aptly call it. Some with firearms hunt the crocodile and buffalo, and Goulburn mission was one of the places at which they could trade the skins and hides for tobacco, rice and other necessities. It appeared to us that the mission was making a very good thing out of this.

For several days we rested. I attended to a few rigging jobs while Susan did the laundry in a near-by billabong—a shallow, swampy pool of stagnant green water alive with flies and mosquitoes. Then once more we headed to the westward for Christmas Island.

Again it was a rough passage for most of the way with a great shouting wind from east-sou'-east. For the first five days there were unsurveyed shoals to be avoided, for although there may have been ample water over them for us, we did not care to approach them closely as the seas in their neighbourhood might be dangerously steep or even breaking. Not until we sighted the island of Roti (that was the only glimpse we had of the great continent of Asia) on our fifth day out, did we come into deep, shoal-free water and were able to steer direct for our destination without further worry.

On one never-to-be-forgotten day *Wanderer* made a run of 157 miles (*see p.* 197), the best she had ever achieved; the following day she covered 144 miles and then 149. But by that time the sea had risen to such proportions that we did not consider it safe to continue at high speed. As the mainsail was already close-reefed it was necessary to hand it and set the trysail in its place. While I was attending to that job we were as nearly pooped as we have ever been in deep water. I had got the mainsail partly down when Susan shouted at me to hold tight. Looking aft I saw a huge sea rearing up astern. Its crest was breaking heavily, and as *Wanderer* lifted to it, it picked her up bodily and in a great cataract of roaring water carried her along with it. Scarcely had it released her when a second sea of similar character had her in its grip, and then a third. As I clung to the rigging I noticed with dismay that the main hatch was wide open. Meanwhile Susan, with the understanding born of long acquaintance with little ships, concentrated on keeping the yacht dead straight before those seas. That we rode over them safely with no more than a few bucketfuls of water on deck was entirely due to her skill. Obviously we had run quite long enough; so, having set the trysail, we remained hove-to under it alone for the next three days until the wind moderated. Had it not been for that delay we should have made a very fast passage, for we never lacked wind until within a day's sail of our goal, and once the gale had blown itself out we had several days of perfect trade wind sailing: a force 4 wind, a blue sky dappled with small, puffy, white clouds, and the yacht with spinnaker so nearly balancing the mainsail that the helmsman could relax under the sun-shade and read. It was flying-fish weather and at night the helmsman felt as though he was under fire, as the fast-moving fish shot past his head to smack into the cockpit or fall on deck where they flapped for a moment in the scuppers. Some-times by morning the deck was dangerously slippery with their scales and oil. On many a night a party of performing dolphin came to entertain us with a fine display of intricate and luminous swimming.

During our long voyages in the tropics we have sometimes witnessed strange and inexplicable phenomena: the green flash at sunset, the milk-white patches of phosphorescence on a dark night, and St. Elmo's fire, for example. But the strangest thing of all occurred on this trip during Susan's first watch on the night of 24-25 June in approximately latitude 11° 11′ S. and longitude 122° 05′ E. I was awakened by it but I cannot do better than quote Susan's entry in the log book.

'At about 2230 I was startled by an intense light which suddenly illuminated the scene vividly. Turning to look astern I saw two balls of bright green light, one close above the other and each about one third the size of the sun. These were approximately 15° above the horizon. Without appearing to move or fade they went out. The whole incident probably took less than five seconds. It was a clear, starlit night.'

Since then I have read in Philip Davenport's book, *The Voyage of Waltzing Matilda*, an account of a similar phenomenon witnessed when his yacht was running her easting down in the south Pacific.

At sunrise on our fourteenth day at sea, when the wind had fallen light and an enormous swell from south-east was causing the sails to slam mercilessly, we sighted Christmas Island ahead. But so feeble was the wind that we did not enter Flying Fish Cove until dusk. There Captain Rendell, one of the island's three pilots, came out in a launch to show us to a steamer's mooring. The water there is so deep (three cables offshore there is a depth of 150 fathoms) and the bottom so foul with coral, that anchorage is not advisable. The doctor cleared us quickly, there were no customs formalities, and then McLaren Reed, the District Officer who administers the island, which is British and part of the Colony of Singapore, invited us to baths and dinner in his house on the point near-by and to live with him and Mrs. Reed for as long as we wished to stay. We began to realize that we had found the first of the Isles of Hospitality, as the late A. G. H. Macpherson named the small widely-spaced islands which lie along the sailing route across the southern Indian Ocean. A few minutes later, after a short journey along the coast road in a Land Rover, we found ourselves in the Reeds' cool and spacious home sipping iced beer and feeling extraordinarily still and strangely light-headed.

But we did not accept their pressing invitation to sleep ashore, for Flying Fish Cove is open from west through north to north-east. On occasions and without any warning a heavy swell sets in, and then all vessels which cannot be lifted by crane on to the cliffs have to put to sea until the swell subsides, sometimes remaining there for two weeks or more. Several times during our stay we feared we might have to clear out in a hurry, when the booming of the surf on the steep coral beach of the cove and along the cliffs sounded a more ominous note, and Captain Rendell warned us to watch it and to leave if it grew any worse, saying that we must not rely on any help as all the local boats were then being lifted ashore by crane. But fortunately on each occasion the noisy swell subsided as quickly and as mysteriously as it had arisen.

The island is shaped like a roughly drawn and very thick capital T lying on its side with its top to the east, and the cove is just inside the end of the upper arm. The greater part of the coast is formed of steep, often undercut, cliffs from thirty to seventy feet high. (*See p.* 204). Above these is a terrace of varying width which runs almost completely round the island, and behind the terrace is another cliff which rises sometimes sheerly to a height of 500 feet, but in many places is replaced by a steep slope. The upper plateau, which covers the greater part of the island, is between 600 and 800 feet above the sea and from it rise some hills exceeding 1,000 feet. The whole island is densely wooded except where clearings have been made at Flying Fish Cove and near South Point and along the connecting railway line.

Phosphate of lime, which is the only export, is quarried by grabs at South Point, is transported by rail across the island to the heights above Flying Fish Cove from where the laden trucks on a cable run down an incline and haul up the empties. After the phosphate has been dried it is loaded into ships, an average of one every ten days, by means of a cantilever con-veyor, for no ships ever lie alongside the jetty because of the swell. (*See p.* 204.)

In 1954 the population consisted of 80 Europeans, 1,500 Chinese and 500 Malays, all except the District Officer and his staff being employed by the British Phosphate Commission. It was strange to us to see much of the manual work being done by Chinese women, all of them wearing conical straw hats and short-legged black pyjamas. The British Phosphate Commission has an excellent store where everything except alcohol is sold duty and purchase-tax free; there is an abundance of fresh food and some of the basic foods, such as rice and sugar, are subsidized. The islanders also enjoy other advantages such as free medical treatment in a model hospital and free schooling for the children, and my log states that at the time of our visit income tax was one per cent. Oh, blessed isle!

Christmas Island is the breeding place of several species of sea bird including boobies, frigate birds and bo'sun birds. The golden bo'sun with the lovely golden apricot plumage does not nest anywhere else in the world. But to us the most remarkable and interesting inhabitant of the island is the red land crab, *Gecarcoidea humei natalis Pocock*, which in great numbers inhabits the jungle where it lives largely on a diet of decaying leaves. Once a year these crabs migrate in mass to the shore to spawn. It is estimated that over one hundred thousand die of exhaustion while trying to cross the railway line. The first to reach the shore terraces are mostly males; they make their way to the sea to wash and then return a short distance inland where each digs himself in, making a shallow burrow. As soon as a suitable female passes, she is seized and dragged half-way into the burrow where copulation takes place. Afterwards the female continues to the shore where she lays her eggs, and eventually all the adult crabs return to the inland plateau. The young crabs begin to leave the water some thirty days after the spawn was laid, and if the season has been a favourable one they come up from the water in hundreds of millions, and sometimes the shore road through the palm grove at Flying Fish Cove has been bright red with them for a distance of 200 yards. The mortality is very high, for unless they remain in the shade they quickly die from dehydration.

We found the Europeans on the island so hospitable that during our stay of eight days we were not permitted to have any meals except breakfast on board *Wanderer*. Everyone seemed determined to make our stay interesting and pleasant. One evening we were taken to the open-air cinema where the closely parked Europeans' jeeps acted as stalls and the Chinese and Malays sat on the ground or on chairs they brought with them, most of them chattering unceasingly throughout the performance, for few could understand a word the screen actors said. The last evening of our visit we were invited to a big Chinese feast where we were plied with the richest of foods —plates of heaped-up mushrooms, roast duck and fat pork— and all the strange vegetables shredded in the manner beloved by the Chinese. Of course the meal was eaten with chopsticks, which were awkward tools in our unaccustomed hands. Late that night in the brilliant moonlight we made our way from house to house saying good-bye to our friends, all of whom pressed gifts upon us.

When next morning the pilot launch came to tow us seaward, for when the wind is in the south-east calm reigns in the cove under the high land, we were handed all the tinned provisions salved from a flying boat which had crashed there a short time before. Looking towards the shore as we slipped away, we could see little parties of people standing waving from beneath the palms, and in the District Officer's garden stood the kind Reeds waving also, while below the union flag on their tall, white flagstaff the code flags R.B.A. (adieu) stirred to a faint air.

Our next stopping place, Keeling Cocos, lay 527 miles to the westward and we made a fast passage with a wind of near gale force. It seemed strange when we started this trip to have to make no allowance for magnetic variation, but Christmas Island lies on the line where there is no variation. Ever since we were in the Caribbean we had been in the area of easterly variation; but now as we made our way to the westward, and in fact during the whole voyage home, our compass would point to the west of true north. So we crossed yet another of those invisible lines on the earth's surface which mean so much to the seaman.

The outstanding incident of the trip was the attempt of a booby to land on my head during one of the night watches. He missed his footing and fell into the cockpit between my bare feet where he immediately disgorged his last meal. When he had quietened down a bit I picked him up quickly, for I was frightened of his sharp beak, and threw him into the air.

He protested crossly, circled *Wanderer* once or twice, and then perched on the guardrail close beside me where he remained for several hours, quite unafraid and not in the least interested in the food we offered him. Birds were always a great source of interest and amusement to us when at sea. On the passage from Goulburn Island to Christmas Island we had five bo'sun birds as escort part of the way, two of them the golden bo'sun which I have already mentioned. They kept company with us for several hundred miles; while we were hove-to they alighted on the sea near-by and did not get under way again until we did, and then accompanied us all the way to the island.

The Keeling Cocos Islands consist of two atolls, the smaller one lying fifteen miles north of the other. The northern atoll is uninhabited and its lagoon cannot be entered. The southern atoll, for which we headed, is a horseshoe of coral enclosing a lagoon eight miles by six, and on it stand about twenty small, palm-crowned islands, none of them more than a few feet above sea level. Because of its small height Cocos is not the easiest of landfalls, and from our low viewpoint would probably not be visible more than six or seven miles away. The currents around it are said to be strong at times, and although they are believed to set mostly in a south-westerly direction one cannot be sure of that. If we missed the atoll, and others had done so before us including Voss in his canoe *Tilikum*, the next nearest land to leeward would be Rodriguez, 2,000 miles away. However, we were fortunate. In spite of the rough sea I was able to get observations of the sun the day before we expected to make a landfall. I would have liked some star sights as a check, but before sunset the sky became overcast and remained like that for the next seven days. By five o'clock the following morning, having run our safe distance, we hove-to to wait for daylight, and at dawn there ahead lay Cocos, a thin fringe of wind-bent palm heads lifting above the horizon every time *Wanderer* rose to a sea. We let draw and sailed into the lagoon where a

PLATE 23

Christmas Island. *Top:* The District Officer's house stands on the coastal terrace above the undercut cliffs. *Bottom:* A ship comes into Flying Fish Cove to load phosphate, while another fully laden departs for Australia.

wind and rain squall rushed upon us, blotting out the land and making the water smoke. So we turned and ran out to sea again until it had blown over. The only possible anchorage for a small vessel is in the lee of Direction Island at the north-east corner of the lagoon. To reach it we had to beat to windward and pass among some coral reefs and heads which we could not see properly as the sky was overcast. So we jilled about for a little while until a bearded member of the air-sea rescue launch crew put off to us in a rowing boat and kindly piloted us to a good anchorage in two and a half fathoms close to the white beach. By then we were quite ready for breakfast.

Only three of the Cocos Islands are inhabited. Home Island, where John Clunies-Ross, the owner of the group, has his remarkable teak and white tile house, is peopled entirely by his Malays. (*See opposite.*) Apart from boat building, which they do with great skill, the business of the Home Islanders is the making of copra. The Ross family has always looked after its people well, and the community, which has the unique distinction of being without money, struck us as clean, happy and well-ordered. But over-population had become a major problem shortly before our arrival and many of the islanders had gone to Borneo and some to Christmas Island to relieve the congestion.

On West Island, six miles away across the lagoon, one hundred Australians were running the air strip, the hospital, restaurant and passenger accommodation serving Qantas Airways, for Cocos is a refuelling point on the Australia to Africa air route. Susan and I spent a night over there and watched the Constellation air-liner take off on the flight to Mauritius, the longest non-stop over-sea passenger air route in the world. As the heavily laden silver plane with the red and gilt band roared down the runway and took off, her tail light winking, we felt a fellow feeling for her crew, for in a short time we also would be taking off on that long passage during which, should any trouble befall, there would be little chance of assistance, for the course crosses only one shipping route, that

PLATE 24

Top: At Rodriguez cattle are ferried off to the waiting steamer in sailing canoes.
Bottom: People of Home Island, Keeling Cocos.

from Perth to Aden. As the plane droned away into the lonely night sky, the palms were leaning steeply to the fierce south-east wind and a great swell was booming on the reef which lies beside the air-strip. We returned rather silently to our comfortable bedroom for the night.

But for us crescent-shaped Direction Island, only three-quarters of a mile long and three hundred yards wide, was the great attraction. That slender strip of coral then had a population of about one hundred. On it sprawled the long, low grey buildings of the cable relay station, run by a manager and seven young men, all of them English, with thirty Chinese and Malay servants. Here the cables from Perth, Singapore and Rodriguez meet, and in the 'office' a battery of intricate little machines which click, flash lights and ring bells, give the messages a fresh impulse on their long journey. On the beach near our anchorage stood the red-roofed mess and dwellings of the Admiralty-employed civilians manning a radio direction-finding station. They also had thirty servants, Malays and Sinhalese, who sometimes fought with knives. Right at the south end of the island lay the slipway and boathouse used by the Department of Civil Aviation for servicing the landing craft and air-sea rescue launches, but as all the men working there were Australian they employed no coloured servants or labour.

All these were bachelor establishments; their people were kind to us and particularly to Susan who was the only woman on their island. But when we think of Cocos our thoughts always fly back to the cable station. Never before had we met such a pleasant bunch of friendly young men as we met there. All of them quickly became our friends and we knew we were always welcome for a drink or a meal either at Top House, where Frank Bartlett (Bart), the manager, lived in solitary state, or in Long Mess where the others lived. In the mess Susan and I always sat on the right and left hands respectively of Long John, the mess president. There were appropriate drinks, even a choice of liqueurs; little speeches were made and everyone always dressed for the occasion, that is, all wore whites and shoes—for the rest of the day shorts and bare feet were the rig. As there is hardly any earth on Direction Island nothing much except coconut palms will grow there. But over a period of years the personnel of Cable & Wireless Ltd. (it used to be the Eastern Telegraph Company) have made a garden. All the soil for this has been brought ten tons at a time by the *Islander*, the little steamer which calls twice a year from Singapore and Christmas Island. Every day throughout our stay the *serang* brought out to us in a tiny canoe made of corrugated iron, which he skilfully baled with his bare foot as he paddled along, a box containing fruit and vegetables; this coming from the cable station was tied not with string but more appropriately with electric flex. There was also a well-stocked pigsty so that the station had a constant supply of bacon, ham and pork. All of this is very remarkable bearing in mind that the period of duty at Cocos is never more than one year, and it was in marked contrast to the methods of the Admiralty mess which lived entirely on a diet of tinned food—even the potatoes and carrots came out of tins—and never ceased to bewail the fact.

During our stay at Cocos the weather was bad. Week followed week of strong to gale force winds with much rain, and the little island and our anchorage were frequently enveloped in a fine mist of salt spray blown over from the great seas breaking a few hundred yards away on the windward side. Direction Island and adjacent Home Island are of course connected by the main coral reef of the atoll, most of which is awash at high water. All along this the seas thundered, rearing themselves up so high as they broke that at times it seemed incredible so low a barrier could possibly keep them from invading the lagoon where we lay at anchor. But in spite of the weather our four weeks at Cocos were most enjoyable. Never a day passed without us paying a visit to our cable friends or without some of them coming out to us; and many times each day we swam in the clear, warm water, wearing goggles and snorkels and enjoying the beauties of the marine scenery beneath us, or dived down to surprise the brilliantly coloured little fishes which with some crabs and clams inhabited a coral patch beneath *Wanderer*. Sometimes when we returned aboard late from Long Mess and the moon was shining, the yacht's shadow could be seen so clearly and sharply on the white sand two-and-a-half fathoms below her that she seemed to be floating not in water but in air, as at Ndravuni in Fiji. On such magic occasions the scene was so incredibly beautiful as almost to make one feel sad that it must ever be different or that one day we must sail away never to see it like that again. The transparent water of the wind-ruffled lagoon, pale in the moonlight with the dark patches of coral heads showing here and there like cloud shadows; ashore the graceful silhouettes of the palms standing out clearly against the star- and moon-lit sky, casting long black shadows across the glimmering beach; and to north and south of the little island which guarded us was the silver ribbon of the long-backed breakers thundering on the reef. In another situation it might have been a wild or lonely scene, but not there with the familiar shapes of the cable station buildings lying close at hand; in them were our friends, some of them on watch in the office, others sound asleep in their cool rooms along the verandah.

On 18 August we left Cocos with many regrets. We might have stayed longer, but we wished to see something of Mauritius and yet be clear of the southern end of Madagascar before November, when the hurricane season is due to start. Scarcely had we dropped the atoll out of sight astern than the wind, which had been only fresh during the past two days, piped up to a hearty force 8, a fresh gale, and the sky clouded over. We close-reefed the mainsail, handed the staysail and hove-to. After four days had passed and the weather still showed no sign of improvement, we realized that we might have to wait several weeks for better weather. So we took in the mainsail, a difficult and sometimes dangerous job which we do not like undertaking when the sea is as rough as it was by then; in its place we set the trysail and then gingerly bore away on the course.

To our relief we found that under her very small sail the yacht showed no sign of dangerously disturbing the over-taking seas, but the next fifteen days seemed like a nightmare of continuously bad weather. Under her storm canvas *Wanderer* moved along well, often at between five and six knots, and on one wild, nerve-racking day, when the wind must have been at strong gale force, we ran 154 miles in a smother of spray; yet the trysail is only 75 square feet in area and in normal weather we set about 500 square feet. At no time did there seem to be any serious danger of being pooped, but because the wind and sea were always well out on the quarter the helmsman was never dry day or night, for again and again crests broke aboard over the canvas dodgers to flood the cockpit. For a reason which has yet to be explained, one often finds in the open sea in bad weather a succession of two or three seas considerably higher and sometimes steeper than the others, arriving at regular periods of twenty minutes or half an hour. It was these that were so wetting, unless the helmsman took them exactly stern on, which was difficult at night when he often could not see them. The violent motion soon chafed holes in our elderly oilskins and after a day or two we had hardly a stitch of dry clothing between us. For the first eight days of the trip we had no glimpse of sun, moon or stars, and mostly it rained. The violent lurches as each great sea picked up our little ship and threw her cruelly to leeward made work in the galley almost impossible, though Susan still continued to cook simple meals without complaint.

Because of the direction of the wind steering was necessary for every mile of that passage, and unless the helmsman watched his steering carefully *Wanderer* would slew round and bring the wind abeam; then heavy water came tumbling aboard. Fortunately the wind remained steady in direction so we were not troubled with a cross-sea. It was an exhausting time for us; day by day we grew increasingly weary, and the effort required to keep our eyes open during the long, dark nights was really painful. We became so tired that we no longer cared about the finer points of civilized life. We gobbled our food out of the pot in which it had been cooked; we did not wash ourselves or even clean our teeth; the moment we got below at the end of a watch on deck, we just removed the wettest of our clothes and fell into our bunks to try to sleep; but sleep did not come easily because of the motion, the noise and our over-tiredness. Fortunately it was not cold, the temperature rarely falling below 75° F., and in spite of our wet condition all we needed were shorts, shirts and sweaters. One night when Susan relieved me at 2 a.m. she was so tired that she forgot to put her shorts on, and she did not discover this until, on going below three hours later, she tried to take them off. Because of their constant damp state our skins became wrinkled and puffy like a washerwoman's hands.

When the sun shone, as it did intermittently after the eighth

A.W.W.—P

day and continuously towards the end of the passage, navigation was more the work for a trapeze artist than a sailorman. Spray deluged the sextant, smearing the mirrors and shades, and the motion made it very difficult for me to wedge myself securely enough to leave both hands free to manipulate the instrument. To keep the sun in view in the sextant telescope was a constant struggle, and even when it was in view it was mostly buried in the flank of some great sea and only lifted clear for a split second occasionally. Working out the position down in the chart-room was just as difficult. The pencil, parallel rules, dividers and books of tables slid maddeningly to and fro as the yacht lurched drunkenly over to forty degrees and then flung herself back, and now and then water squirted in through the sliding hatch to soak the chart and books. But somehow the work got done, and the one thing we had to cheer us up was our consistently good progress; day's runs of 123, 119, 132 followed one another in spite of our tiny sail area, and we knew our period of wretchedness must end eventually. Once or twice on that passage we did set one of the small spinnakers on the opposite side to the trysail (*see p.* 212) but never kept it up for more than a few hours as even that snug rig was more than we needed.

We were surprised at such continuous strong winds, for the pilot chart indicated that force 4 was the average strength to be expected at that time of year. But on reading such accounts as we had on board of the few other small-boat voyagers who had been that way before us, Slocum, Voss, Pidgeon, Macpherson, Bernicot and the Holmdahls, we learnt that they also had experienced similar conditions. Slocum, who was never one to exaggerate, described the weather as 'rugged'; Pidgeon on his second crossing said that he was frequently up to his waist in water at the helm; Macpherson made almost as much use of his trysail as we did, and the Holmdahls reckoned the wind averaged force 7 the whole way across the Indian Ocean.

I had often thought that, so far as information about winds is concerned, the date of the pilot chart would not matter. With the sailing-ship routes now almost empty of shipping, I had assumed that so little new data would be available that the compilers of those charts would have no reason to revise the wind arrows. But in this I was wrong. Our chart was dated

1950 and showed, as I have said, winds averaging force 4 between Cocos and Mauritius; but on arrival at Mauritius we were shown a 1952 edition on which some of the wind arrows along our track had had their feathers increased to indicate winds averaging force 6; so presumably some recent information about the winds in that part of the ocean had filtered through to the American hydrographic office.

It had been our intention to sail direct for Mauritius; but on our seventeenth day at sea we had become so exhausted that we decided to put in for a rest at the nearer island of Rodriguez, which lay not very far south of our course. Originally we had not meant to stop there because the anchorage did not seem to be a good one.

Rodriguez is a high island, ten miles by four, with a population of 10,000; it is surrounded by a vast network of coral reefs which extend in places four and a half miles offshore. The anchorage is on the north side in a bight in the reef known as Mathurin Bay; it is more than a mile from the one and only landing place and is a rolly berth. There are two passes into the bay and we intended taking the most easterly one. But when we approached it Susan and I could not agree on the leading marks, which were indifferently shown in the sketch on the chart, so we kept away and entered by the western pass instead; but here again we found the marks misleading as a recently erected statue of the Virgin can easily be mistaken for one of them. The small steamer *Floreal* was lying in the roadstead and we brought up near her. Almost at once a boat put off from her and brought us a large box filled with fresh meat, bacon, fruit, vegetables and eggs, together with several bottles of beer and some tins of cigarettes. This most welcome gift came from her master, Captain Nicolin.

That evening we dined well in spite of the fifteen-degree roll and we drank one of the bottles of Pommard which had been given to us by the cable men of Cocos. Afterwards, feeling very sleepy and content, I stuck my head out of the hatch to have a look at the night before turning in and saw a signalling lamp calling us up from the cable station. In our bemused state neither Susan nor I could read the message, so I tried to send one asking for *Wanderer*'s arrival to be reported to Cocos. The signaller ashore was very patient, but eventually he sent something which I could understand: 'Sorry, I cannot read your morse.' In the circumstances that was hardly surprising.

Early next morning M. Rochecouste, the resident magistrate who governs the island, paid us a visit. He towed us to a quieter anchorage in the deep but narrow creek which winds through the reefs to the landing place, and then informed us that he had placed a house complete with servants entirely at our disposal for as long as we cared to stay. Isles of Hospitality, indeed! But we had to decline, for *Wanderer*'s berth in twelve fathoms closely surrounded by coral was no place in which to leave her unattended for long, especially at night when the wind tended to draw along the shore and blew with increased strength. But we had a fine lunch with the magistrate and then went to pay our respects to the manager of the cable station. He, we discovered, had learnt all about us by cable from Cocos, and he also offered us accommodation in a lovely little house overlooking the bay.

We remained at Rodriguez, which is British and a dependency of Mauritius, for four days. Having no air-strip and steamer communication with Mauritius only once every six weeks, it is quite unspoilt and unsophisticated and at that time possessed only two motor vehicles. The exports are cattle, goats and pigs; we watched the livestock being ferried off to *Floreal* in sailing canoes (*see p.* 202); these unhandy craft have little grip of the water and often blew on to the reefs where their patient crews had to resort to punting.

When we left the island our course for most of the first day kept us beneath the line of cloud which, like smoke, was streaming away to leeward of the island. Sometimes we had rain, but elsewhere the sun appeared to be shining brightly. We took only three days to reach Mauritius, and had we not hove-to for several hours so as to avoid arriving in the dark, we might have beaten *Floreal*; she started only a few hours after us and was capable of only seven knots even with the trade wind in her favour. But as it was she got in first and warned the port officials of our impending arrival, with the result that

PLATE 25

Left: Trysail and small spinnaker; a snug rig but often more than we needed in the boisterous Indian Ocean. *Right:* In smooth water at last; *Wanderer* at Mauritius.

when we reached Port Louis, Captain Aubrey Booker, one of the pilots, met us at the harbour entrance. He, being a sailing man, understood our needs. He offered us the choice of several berths and then, when the wind failed in the lee of the mountains, towed us to the best one off Blyth Brothers' private quay, where we were warmly welcomed by Rupert Knight and the other directors of that large and friendly firm.

It had been my intention to catch up with some of the long overdue writing and photographic work at Mauritius; but the number of visitors we had, and the great hospitality they extended to us, made this impossible; we even neglected *Wanderer's* needs, which in other ports had always come before anything else. Never a day passed without someone entertaining us to lunch or dinner in his up-country home. That sounds a strange term to use on an island which is not a great deal larger than the Isle of Wight, but none of the Europeans live in Port Louis, where at certain times of year the climate is not healthy, although malaria has now been stamped out. Most of them have their homes on the high ground at Floreal or Vacoas, set in neat gardens usually surrounded by thick, immaculately-trimmed, bamboo hedges. Motor tours and picnics were arranged for us; we were taken out to the sailing club at Grand Bay where, bless them, none of the members pestered us to sail, and to the races at the oldest racecourse in the southern hemisphere, set beautifully in a natural amphitheatre; twice we spent nights with the Blackhalls of the cable company in their house among the mountains where it was cool and the silence was profound.

Although Mauritius is a British possession the official language is French; the currency is the rupee; the bulk of the population is Indian and the most popular headgear is the fez. From the rich sugar-cane plains the jolliest little mountains, steep and sharp, rear up with surprising suddenness; because of their nearness there is no atmospheric recession, so that in the low evening light they look for all the world as though they

PLATE 26

Top: Jolly little mountains make the skyline for Port Louis; because of their nearness there is no atmospheric recession. *Bottom:* Lighters were being unloaded manually close to our berth in Port Louis' busy harbour where ships lie off on buoys.

have been cut out of cardboard to make some child's toy. The soil is red, orange or black, and the mud-walled, thatch-roofed huts of the people are the same colour as the soil. Many trees, often in fine avenues, grace the island: royal palms, casuarinas, flamboyants, eucalyptus and jacarandas, while the scarlet bougainvillea, clinging to walls and tree-trunks, is much in evidence. The Indian population is, as elsewhere, swelling to an alarming degree and in some families of ten there is only one wage-earner. The guaranteed price of sugar has been keeping the island going, but there must come a time when mass unemployment will be rife.

The port was full of life with a constant succession of ships entering and leaving. Quay space is so limited that most of the ships lie out in the harbour to anchors and buoys and the loading and discharging of cargo is done by wooden lighters towed in strings by small tugs and unloaded manually. (*See p. 213.*) Susan and I have always been intrigued by the skilful handling of merchant ships in confined spaces, so we were particularly glad when Aubrey Booker took me out one morning in his pilot cutter to see at close quarters how a large ship, the 7,500-ton *Tantallon Castle* is manoeuvred in such restricted space as Port Louis provides; at the same time he got Susan a berth aboard a tug which was to assist in the operation.

We went alongside the ship outside the harbour and, climbing the rope ladder, made our way to her bridge, where I was introduced to her master, Captain Lloyd. The harbour fairway is only 400 feet wide and that day was lined on both sides with moored ships with one vacant berth which *Tantallon Castle* was to occupy. As we approached the channel, Aubrey said quietly 'Stop'. The telegraph handles were moved and the reply gongs tinkled. But to my untrained eye we appeared to move just as fast and inexorably as before. No word was spoken and a cathedral-like silence reigned on the bridge.

'Slow astern,' came the order as we approached our berth, and then 'Let go starboard anchor'. There was a pause followed by the roar of running chain and a cloud of brown dust drifted over the forecastle head. Susan's tug then thrust her bluff, fender-protected bow against our quarter and started to push, and slowly, oh, so slowly, *Tantallon* swung round in the restricted space, her stern clearing by only a few yards one of the moored vessels. When eventually her bow was pointing seaward a wire hawser was run out from her stern to a mooring buoy. I breathed freely at last, for I was fond of Aubrey and for his sake did not wish anything to go amiss, but the business of mooring up was not yet completed. The ship's port anchor was lowered and slung from a mooring lighter and forty fathoms of cable were ranged on the lighter's deck. Then the tug towed the lighter away into shallow water where the anchor was let go and the slack of the cable was hove in. Never again ought either of us to say that there is not enough room to manoeuvre tiny *Wanderer* now that we have seen what the silently efficient merchant service can do.

The evening before our departure we invited twenty of our friends to a cocktail party which overflowed on to the quay. The following morning we were escorted seaward by several small craft carrying well-wishers who photographed our little ship until her boot-top blushed a rosier red.

The French island of La Réunion lies only 100 miles west-sou'-west of Mauritius, but, as we were anxious to get clear of the hurricane area before November, we passed it by and sailed direct for Durban, 1,700 miles distant. We made the mistake of passing to leeward of La Réunion for smoother water, but there found a large area of calm in the lee of the 10,000-foot mountains.

Four days out from Port Louis we lost the south-east trade wind, which had been our constant but much too boisterous companion for the past 7,000 miles, ever since we had rounded Sandy Cape on Australia's east coast six months before. Thereafter we had winds from all points of the compass in turn and the greater part of the passage was a rough one. Several times the wind reached gale force for a day or more and our little trysail came into use again. But sometimes we could carry only the 43-square-foot storm staysail, and on two occasions the gales were of such strength that even that tiny sail was more than the yacht could carry safely, and we stripped her to bare poles for a total of fifty-five hours. She then lay with wind and sea abeam, drifting to leeward at about one and a half knots, and the slick she left to windward of her robbed the advancing seas of their menace. It was fascinating to watch a big sea with upflung crest approaching. For a few moments it seemed as though it must surely break aboard; but then, as it came closer and felt the effect of the slick, its angry crest subsided to leave only a frothy scum, and *Wanderer* rode buoyantly up and over the sea, repeating the performance tirelessly with the next great sea and the next. . . . But sometimes in the fiercer squalls she forereached a little although the helm was lashed hard down; then the slick lay out on the quarter instead of abeam and a crest or two broke aboard to flood the decks and fill the cockpit. One of these invaded poor Susan's bunk by way of one of the water-trap ventilators, the cowl filling right up so that the small scuppers were unable to cope with the volume of water. Already everything below was damp and sticky to the touch, for the air was laden with moisture, and the sudden inrush of water through the ventilator added to our general misery.

Once a gale has risen to its full strength and everything possible has been done for the safety of the ship, there is a certain feeling of satisfaction as one changes into dry clothes, knowing that for the present there is nothing more one can do. Usually I then stand for a while looking out of the hatchway or one of the ports, watching the grandeur of the scene without, fearful as each great sea bears down on our small vessel, and elated each time she lifts swiftly up and over it, looking after herself so well, as most small craft will when stripped of sail or hove-to. But soon the novelty wears off. Susan is already in her bunk resting or reading and I follow her example. We carry about 150 books on board, but on these occasions I find I cannot concentrate on any informative or serious work; magazine articles or short stories are all that I can manage, and although they appear to occupy my mind at the time and keep it off the howling gale, I find that when I have finished I cannot even remember the subject matter. In bad weather Susan is better at concentrating than I am, but even she, I have noticed, spends most of the time just lying wedged in her bunk with the book or magazine face down on her chest.

There came a time, as the seas increased in size and steepness, when we seriously thought we should have to stream the sea-anchor as the yacht was fore-reaching too much for safety; but before we managed to spur our weary bodies to make the great effort, the shriek of the gale in the rigging dropped a note or two and the worst was over. Then, as the wind moderated, leaving us to flounder in the confused, left-over sea, the albatrosses, which had been our companions during the heavy weather, vanished.

Slowly we made our way to the westward, passing sixty miles south of the southern extremity of Madagascar. Our best days' run was 137 miles and our worst 45. As we approached the African coast we encountered yet another gale, which was accompanied by rain reducing visibility to about a mile, and by a very severe thunderstorm; each flash of vivid lightning was followed by crackling thunder almost instantaneously. We were reaching under the trysail only at the time and we experienced the strongest squall either of us can ever remember. I do not wish to exaggerate, but I judged it to be in excess of eighty knots. I was steering and bore away before the wind to ease the strain on the sail as much as possible, but every moment I expected to hear the stout flax canvas being ripped from its boltropes. I dared not attempt to hand the sail, for I knew that the moment I started sheet or halyard the sail would flap and that would be the end of it. *Wanderer* tore through the black night faster than I have ever known her go before; at times she carried marked lee helm which is a thing she never does in normal circumstances. Dimly I could see the bow-wave rising high each side of her as from a speed-boat. The squall probably lasted for ten minutes.

Running south-west along the south-east coast of Africa is an enormous body of warm water known as the Agulhas Current. The width of this varies considerably and so does its velocity; according to the October pilot chart it attains a rate off Durban of from fifteen to seventy-five miles a day. Of course we could only guess at the allowance to be made for it, and we wished to make our landfall north of Durban so as to have a fair current down the coast to the port. It was therefore unfortunate that a pall of nimbus should obscure the heavenly bodies for the final three days of the trip. We both disliked the idea of driving on blindly towards a lee shore, uncertain as we were of our exact position; but to heave-to and wait for better weather would be to place ourselves completely at the mercy of the current, with the likelihood of being set by it to the south of Durban. If that happened it might be impossible to work back against the current, and as the only large-scale chart of South Africa we had been able to obtain in Australia was of Durban, it was important to go to that port. So under the close-reefed mainsail we hurried on over the rough sea beneath the leaden sky, hoping all the time that our guess at the strength of the current would prove to be a good one, and steering a course that should, according to our reckoning, bring us to the coast fifteen miles north of Durban.

On our eighteenth day at sea, when by dead reckoning the coast should be only a few miles distant, we fell in with a motor fishing vessel. Putting our pride in our pockets we closed with her and asked for a bearing of Durban breakwater.

'West-sou'-west forty miles' is what we thought her skipper said. We thanked him and continued on our way and within a couple of hours the coast of Africa loomed up out of the rain less than a mile away. By then the wind had shifted to the south-west and for the rest of that day we beat slowly and wetly to windward, only catching occasional glimpses of the coast when nearing the end of each inshore tack. But at dusk, to our surprise and delight, the lights of Durban suddenly appeared as the rain stopped. Obviously we had mistaken the fisherman; it must have been fourteen, not forty miles he said. The wind, remaining persistently ahead, then fell light and our rain-soaked sails could make little of it, so we did not close with the breakwaters until dawn. There the wind died completely. We tried to start the motor, but water had reached the magneto through a leak in the copper floor of the self-draining cockpit, so we prepared to anchor and wait for a breeze. Just then an inward-bound tug came along and asked whether we wanted any assistance. I said 'No'.

'I will wireless for a pilot for you,' said the tug's skipper.

'We do not require a pilot,' I replied.

'Pilotage is compulsory,' was his rejoinder, and very soon a launch bearing pilot and medical officer came out and towed us in, clumsily parting a warp in the process and carrying away a section of our guardrail, and eventually berthed us with too much way on alongside a jetty in a corner of the harbour which is reserved for yachts.

We had learnt to dread our entry into a large commercial port because of the necessity for dealing with port officials and reporters before we have had time to collect our thoughts and tidy the yacht and ourselves. No sooner had we secured than we were boarded by four customs officers who, like most of their kind, were courteous and efficient, but they insisted that I must go that day to enter the yacht at the custom-house. Then tired, damp and unwashed though we were, a number of photographers and reporters insisted on coming aboard; not until they and the broadcasting people had done with us several hours later were we free to clean ourselves and the yacht and go ashore to collect our mail and buy fresh food.

But then, as is always the way, our troubles ended. The Royal Natal Yacht Club and the Point Yacht Club at once made us honorary members and their kind people could not do enough for us. This we found, was typical of all the British people we met in South Africa, and as a result we much enjoyed our stay in that country.

15

ROUNDING THE CAPE OF STORMS

WE remained at Durban until the end of December, a period of two and a half months, and found much to interest and entertain us there. Jimmy Whittle and his charming wife Jean, who together run Nicholls Shipyard, provided us with a set of fore-and-aft moorings in one of the two long rows of moored motor yachts which lie, well sheltered by a recently built breakwater, in the creek leading to the yacht clubs. (*See opposite.*) From there we had a fine view of the panorama of well-proportioned skyscrapers which are not so closely placed as to steal one another's light, and our berth was most convenient for the shops in the centre of the city; but for fruit, vegetables and meat we had to go to the markets, of which there are four—native, Indian, squatters and white— situated close together at the west end of the city. These are a riot of colours, noises, smells, people and goods of every kind.

So that we might have no dinghy work to do, Jimmy put at our disposal by day and night an outboard motor boat manned by two Zulu boys, Compass and Capstan. A blast on our fog-horn would bring the boat out to us immediately, and if we wished to go aboard *Wanderer* late at night, we had only to knock at the door of the little hut on the quay where Compass slept to get a cheerful 'coming, sah' from the willing boatman.

But the Whittles did more for us than this. They had *Wanderer* hauled out on their slip for repairs to her copper sheathing, which was again showing electrolytic trouble in places, and kept her there for several days while we painted her topsides

and gave her a general refit; they supplied us with all the paint, varnish and rigging wire we needed, for our own stocks were exhausted, and flatly refused to accept any payment. Each evening while the yacht was on the slip Jimmy or Jean picked us up by car, took us to their home on high ground overlooking Durban for baths, drinks, dinner, a luxurious bed, and returned us to the yard after breakfast as soon as the dew was off the work. Never before had we so enjoyed a refit.

Noel Horsefield, the owner of the ketch *Senta*, had his engineering firm remove our motor and give it a complete overhaul, while Jack Finlayson, another keen sailing man, had brass name plates made to replace our alloy letters, several of which had corroded and dropped off the stern.

And so we experienced once again that wonderful round of hospitality and kindness which nearly everywhere is extended to small-boat voyagers, and which does so much to recompense them for the discomforts of the long sea passages. We were invited to no fewer than three Christmas dinners while at Durban, fortunately on different days; one of them, eaten aboard *Senta*, was cooked entirely by the Captain of the Port, Captain Cox. We were specially glad to meet him because several people had informed us that we should not be allowed to go to sea again, for there was a rule that no yacht of less than thirty-five feet in length was considered seaworthy enough to be permitted to leave the harbour. Over the meal Captain Cox waived this rule for us and kindly exonerated us from all port and pilotage dues.

We were particularly fortunate to be invited to spend a few days inland with Geoffrey Luffingham who farmed at Winterton 4,000 feet above the sea and close to the Drakensberg Mountains, for it gave us an opportunity to see something of the countryside. Twenty years before Geoffrey had gone out to Natal with only £300 in his pocket. Disregarding all advice he bought with this a derelict farm, and when we visited him he was one of the most successful and respected pig-breeders in

PLATE 28

Top: We learnt to dread the appearance of the cloth on Table Mountain, sure sign of a coming sou'-easter. *Bottom:* A 92-miles-per-hour gale roars across the basin at Cape Town, whitening the water and setting the yachts sheering and snubbing at their moorings.

the state. The great rolling veldt with its immense distances, clear atmosphere, and teams of oxen ploughing or drawing wagons or sledges, sometimes eighteen oxen in one span, appealed greatly to us, as also did the native kraals, where several beehive-shaped huts huddle together within a stout wall.

Our stay at Durban was in the bad-weather months. The weather then was hot and, except when the berg wind was blowing, very humid. Most of the time the wind blew freshly from north-east, but once or twice a week this was replaced by a southerly, which arrived with startling suddenness and in a few seconds was blowing at forty or fifty knots. Sometimes the southerly arrived when dinghies were out racing in the wide, shallow harbour, and as it advanced swiftly across the water it capsized each little boat in turn, knocking them down like a row of ninepins. And there were thunderstorms, violent African thunderstorms, usually in the late afternoon or early evening; then Durban's skyscrapers were silhouetted against the vivid lightning and thunder echoed through the wide streets. Nevertheless we grew to like Durban.

When we were about to leave England at the beginning of our voyage, people told us that we should have a bad time in the Bay of Biscay, and we did. In Spain nobody was at all interested in the Bay, but all insisted that theirs and the Portuguese coast were particularly dangerous ones. The inhabitants of the West Indies told us of the roughness of the Caribbean when the winter trade set in, and the central Pacific islanders spoke of the hazards of navigation among coral (one even said that sailing at night was forbidden). When we got to New Zealand none of our acquaintances were at all impressed by the fact that we had crossed two oceans and had come through some bad weather and dodged a lot of coral. 'You ain't seen nothing yet,' they said. 'You wait till you've crossed the Tasman Sea; it's the roughest bit of water in the world and many a yachtie has come to grief out there.' It was rough, as I have told, but at Sydney few people cared about that. 'Mind how you go up the Barrier Reef,' they warned, 'that's the biggest coral structure in the world and the most dangerous.' At Thursday Island they begged us to take care along the Arnhemland shore which, they pointed out, had not been properly surveyed.

From all of this we had learnt that each coast and sea along our route was considered by those who lived near it, or sailed along or across it, to be more difficult and dangerous than any other. On reaching Durban we were therefore prepared to be warned about the Cape, and with good reason, for it has a world-wide reputation of ill fame and was known to early navigators as the Cape of Storms. On the general small-scale chart of the area there is a paragraph which reads:

'The severity of the gales off the Cape of Good Hope and the adjacent coast to the eastward, and especially in the neighbourhood of the Agulhas Bank, is well known to navigators, as also is the rapidity with which they succeed one another, and their violence.'

But, prepared though we were, we were shocked by the tales of shipwreck and disaster with which we were greeted on every hand. All those people who had been anywhere near the Cape wished to give us the benefit of their local knowledge, and even those who had only seen it from the land insisted that this really was the most dangerous place in the world.

Back in England we had made our plans with some care for the turning of this important corner. We had studied the sailing directions and the charts, and had read accounts of previous voyages; these had decided us to make the rounding in January, as that was generally considered to be the most favourable month for a west-bound sailing vessel. We had carefully overhauled the gear and had taken all possible precautions for the safety of our ship. But so pessimistic were our Durban friends—meaning only to impress upon us the need for the utmost care—that we felt depressed and apprehensive when we slipped our moorings on the morning of the last day of 1954, and ghosted out of the creek with a faint north-east air.

Most of our friends came to see us off from various vantage points and we were accompanied for a short distance by a boat packed with press reporters and photographers, who were determined to get what little copy they could from the occasion. As we rounded the end of T-wharf, all the tugs and most of the ships in port blew their sirens in farewell as little *Wanderer*, immaculate in her new coats of enamel and varnish, passed slowly down the harbour and out between the breakwaters to the open sea where an uneasy swell was running. The final farewell gesture came from Harold Evans who at lunch-time flew low over us several times in his own scarlet aeroplane, while we were sitting in the cockpit eating the cold chicken and salad which his kind wife had presented to us only a few hours earlier. Then we were alone.

We expected great things of the Agulhas Current, which at that season of the year can attain a rate in a south-westerly direction of between fifty and a hundred miles a day. Between Durban and East London the hundred-fathom line of the continental shelf lies ten to fifteen miles from the shore; but from East London onwards its distance from the coast increases steadily until, in the neighbourhood of Cape Agulhas, it lies about a hundred miles offshore. The current runs with greatest strength along the hundred fathom line and there, when the wind is contrary, a heavy, steep and irregular sea is encountered. It is this more than anything else which is reponsible for the Cape's bad reputation. A vessel bound westward round the Cape with a fair wind should obviously keep on the edge of the bank until that tails away offshore, so as to gain the fullest advantage from the current; but if the wind should come ahead she must get inshore to avoid the dangerous seas on the hundred-fathom line. If she stands too close inshore, however, she will probably find a counter current running against her. We looked for the current, but almost in vain. We stood obliquely out to sea for twenty miles, then back again, crossing and recrossing the edge of the bank, but nowhere did the current amount to more than twenty miles a day, which was a great disappointment to us. Commander Irving Johnson, who has made this trip on six occasions, has told me that in his experience the current runs with the greatest strength when the wind is opposed to it. This may sound strange, but I believe him, for currents are the oddest things and Susan and I have noticed that in the trades there is often least current when the wind is blowing strongly with it.

At Durban we had bent on a new mainsail which had been

PLATE 29

Top: On the Royal Cape Yacht Club slip Susan gives the finishing touches to *Wanderer's* new paintwork. *Bottom:* James Bay, St. Helena, from the top of Jacob's Ladder. The swell rolls in to break along the shore and at the landing place, top left of the picture.

sent out to us from England. We had ordered this while still in Australia as we thought that the old one might be growing weak by the time we arrived in Africa. In fact I believe it would have seen us home, but as the new sail was waiting for us we bent it on and sold the old one. The original sail was hand sewn, but as we could not afford the extra cost of this for the new sail, I had asked Cranfield & Carter to sew it by machine. It arrived hand sewn after all, the sailmakers having done this at their own expense because, as they said in their covering letter, they did not care for us to trust our lives to a machine-sewn sail on the kind of voyage we were making. Like the original sail, the new one was cut without any roach to the leech, so that battens, which in my opinion should find no place aboard an ocean cruiser, would not be needed except while the sail was being stretched. On our second day out the sail had to be reefed and the upper batten then came well below the upper crosstrees. The swell being heavy and the wind falling light for a little while, the upper part of the sail gybed repeatedly, though the boom was kept in position with a boom guy. When falling back into position after one of these gybes, the upper batten inserted itself between the topmast and intermediate shrouds, and there it stuck. All attempts to lower the sail failed, and I was contemplating with distaste the need to go aloft to clear it, when Susan said she thought another gybe might do the trick. We tried it; it worked, and fortunately no harm was done to the sail.

Two days out from Durban we were off East London. As the wind was still fair we sailed on past with mainsail and spinnaker set. A few hours later, chancing to listen in to the regional news on the radio set, we learnt that we had been sighted off the port and that a small tug had put out to tow us in. That was a kindly gesture for which we thank you, East London.

The night that followed was most unpleasant. Rain, which washed some of the tanning out of our new sail, deluged down, and squalls and calms kept me almost constantly at the reefing handle and Susan at the helm, so there was little sleep for either

PLATE 30

Top: Boarding a longboat at Ascension from the steps round which the blackfish (*bottom*) shoal in countless numbers.

A.W.W.—Q

of us. But dawn brought a clearing of the sky together with a brisk headwind, and the sun shone on the lively scene. The fresh breeze was right in our teeth, and as we beat to the westward we were surrounded by a great many sea birds— gannets, terns and black-backed gulls—all busy fishing and squabbling over their catches. To starboard lay the inhospitable coast consisting of gleaming white sandhills their caps of bush and the higher ground behind them almost black in contrast. Many rivers come down to the sea along this coast, but as all of them have shallow bars none is navigable, and some of them even reach the sea by tunnelling underground for a short distance. The motion was jerky and unnatural after the easy lift and roll of running free, and our progress was slow. As the glass was dropping it seemed likely that the headwind had come to stay for a time, so we had no hesitation about making Port Elizabeth to await more favourable conditions.

By evening the lights of that town lay not many miles ahead. For a time we were mystified by a flashing red light with the same character as the *Admiralty List of Lights* gave for the red light which is exhibited from one of the breakwater heads; but the position of this light in relation to another did not make sense. On closer approach, however, the breakwater light appeared and the other proved to be an advertising sign ashore. At midnight we beat in and anchored in the artificial harbour. Half of our journey to Cape Town was over.

In daylight we berthed at the South African Naval Reserve jetty, a clean and convenient spot where we were made welcome, and remained there for ten days while strong to gale force westerly winds blew. We had fourteen fathoms of chain out to a wooden dolphin ahead; at times the gusts were so strong that the full length of chain leapt out of the water to become bar taut with a clang that could be heard at the far end of the jetty, and we had to send a weight along it to act as a spring. The chain is $\frac{5}{16}$ inch and is tested, but on many occasions during our cruise we wished it were heavier, not for greater strength but for the greater catenary it would provide.

Port Elizabeth is a modern manufacturing town and it claims to be the windiest place in the world. The surrounding countryside looked parched and uninteresting after green and fertile Natal, but at Addo, where we were taken for a drive one day to see an orange farm, the soil, a clay sand, is fourteen feet deep and without a stone. At certain prearranged times the water supply is turned on to each farm in rotation and the trees are irrigated. Apart from that and the ploughing in of lucerne to provide nitrogen, the trees appeared to need little attention, but the picking of the oranges is a delicate matter if they are not to be spoilt by bruising.

On the very first breath of a south-easterly air we stole away and headed to the west once more on what, according to the Port Elizabethans who had not been lacking with tales of horror about the Cape, would prove to be *Wanderer's* greatest test. But as we had just had ten days of headwinds it seemed reasonable to expect a few days of fair winds, and in that assumption we were correct. For the first two days we could not have wished for better weather; a light to moderate breeze in which we carried the whole mainsail and spinnaker, and the blue sky was without a cloud. From Cape St. Francis to Cape Agulhas our course lay partly out of sight of land, for the bay between those headlands is a deep one, but there was plenty of shipping to keep us alert both by day and by night. One morning just before sunrise a Union Castle mailship passed close, eastward bound. Purposeful she looked as she hurried along, but terrifyingly impersonal, with no sign of human beings anywhere aboard. Later that same day a tanker overtook us. Aboard of her we could see no sign of life either, and no response came from her bridge or deck to our waves. Could it be possible, we wondered, in these days of radar, that no watch is kept except on the radar screen, even in coastal waters? Usually the people in the ships one meets are such cheerful, friendly folk, always ready to greet a small sailing yacht, with a wave or a dipped ensign.

On the evening of our third day at sea we rounded Cape Agulhas, the southernmost tip of Africa's blunt toe, in latitude 34° 57′ S., and nothing lay between us and Antarctica except icebergs. Although this was not our farthest south, for we had reached latitude 37° S. in New Zealand, it was a stirring moment and an important milestone on our voyage. The wind continued fair, but it freshened a lot so that double reefs were called for and the spinnaker had to come in. The barometer was falling steeply and the evening weather forecast warned us of a south-easterly gale at the Cape of Good Hope, a gale which, according to the radio news, had been blowing without a pause for the past ten days. It looked as though it was going to be a dirty night and we discussed the question of heaving-to and waiting for the gale ahead to blow itself out, for we never willingly go looking for bad weather. But at least this gale would be fair for our purpose, while in view of the falling glass we might well get a headwind if we missed this opportunity. So we continued on our way. The distance from Cape Agulhas to Cape Point is eighty-two miles, but before we had lost the loom of the Agulhas light astern, we could clearly see the triple beam of Cape Point light wheeling in the sky ahead, for that is the most brilliant light in the southern hemisphere with a candle-power of nineteen million.

Dawn found us eight miles south of the Cape of Good Hope, running at high speed in a rough sea with water sluicing along the side decks and cascading out of the scuppers, but although the sea was confused it was not dangerously steep. The panorama was magnificent, as the rising sun bathed the mountains of the peninsula and Cape Hangklip in a hazy, golden light. This spectacular piece of land would surely have made a more fitting termination to the great African continent than low and unimposing Cape Agulhas. Although the Cape of Good Hope is not the southernmost tip of Africa, most people are agreed that it is there that the waters of the Indian and Atlantic Oceans mingle. So now we had completed the crossing of our third ocean, and only the Atlantic lay between us and England. We felt we were almost home.

As we sailed up the western side of the peninsula the wind steadily took off, for the gale was of a local nature, and by noon we were only ghosting. We had seen no finer piece of coastal scenery than this. Bold and lofty stood the Twelve Apostles, and presently, as we made our way to the north, out from behind them peeped the flat top of Table Mountain and the steep cone of the Lion's Head. We made use of these natural signposts to fix our position, for the nearer objects along the shore were hidden or confused by a mirage. This consisted of a band of apparently quite smooth water hove up above the visible horizon, and on the top of it were perched the hotels, blocks of flats and other buildings, all of them upside down.

Although the day was sunny and hot the cabin was quite chilly, and condensation trickles ran down the sides of the yacht below the waterline, for on rounding the Cape of Good Hope the temperature of the sea had dropped from seventy-two to fifty-eight degrees.

In the evening when the sun was getting low we entered Table Bay and there were met by a stiff sou-'easter. We rolled in the reefs, set the second staysail, and with the spray flying and our flags standing out stiffly, we beat up to the weather shore and into Duncan dock. Apparently we had been sighted in the offing, for one of the local yachts came out to escort us in, and showed us to a mooring in the basin reserved for yachts. On the jetty of the Royal Cape Yacht Club beside the basin, waiting to welcome us as we stepped ashore from our dinghy, were members of the club and their wives. They congratulated us warmly on making the 430-mile trip from Port Elizabeth in three days nine hours, seemingly a record for so small a vessel; but they did not fail to point out, as they plied us hospitably with cold beer and hot meat pies, that we had been very, *very* lucky.

Since then, each time a yacht has been in trouble on that coast, one or other of our friends out there has written to tell us all about it. I quote from such a letter which I have recently had from Stephen Tomalin of Port Elizabeth.

'The enclosed cuttings will probably interest you. They show that we really do have bad weather along this coast. I know you were a bit sceptical about "the worst coast in the world" talk you heard around here, but you were lucky in that *Wanderer* happened to strike a fine spell.

'Referring to the cuttings: The case of *Windward*, a sturdy, gaff-rigged, straight-stemmed 20-tonner, was a real tragedy. I was in Cape Town recently and heard the whole story at the club. They were running before a westerly gale and carrying too much canvas. The helmsman was not wearing a lifeline, and when the yacht was pooped he was washed overboard. The yacht then broached-to, was knocked flat, inside ballast shifted and she made a lot of water. The loss of the skipper thoroughly demoralized the crew (his wife was aboard) and when a freighter loomed up they abandoned the yacht which has not been seen since.

'Then there is the case of the 6-ton *Marco Polo* which you met in New Zealand. She was just unlucky with the weather and being hit by a freak sea, but " turned over six times " is all journalistic rubbish. However, she was knocked down, the dinghy was smashed, the boom carried away and one of the crew was injured.'

We had a wonderful time at Cape Town where Geoff Guthrie, the popular and entertaining secretary of the yacht club, and Kit his wife, together with all the members, almost overwhelmed us with kindness. They made us feel not that we were visitors being courteously treated but that we belonged there, and if they could have had their way we would be there still.

Day after day the sun shone hotly down from out of a clear sky, and the atmosphere was dry and bracing after the great humidity of Durban. But unavoidably we were at Cape Town during the season of the sou'-easters. We learnt to dread the appearance of the 'table-cloth' on Table Mountain, for this layer of billowing cloud, dazzlingly white in the sunshine, is a certain sign of a coming sou'-easter (*see p.* 221), and within a short time of its formation, sure enough a gale would be blowing. This, sweeping across the Cape Flats, round the eastern side of the mountain and across the recently reclaimed land where trucks of granite chips were being unloaded and bulldozers were at work, roared out over the yacht basin, bringing with it clouds of sharp, grey dust and smoke and soot from the locomotives in the near-by shunting yards.

These gales occurred frequently, the wind usually attaining a speed of forty-five knots, and then died as suddenly as they had arisen. But on one occasion the wind continued to freshen all afternoon, and we spent a restless night with squalls of sixty knots striking *Wanderer* first on one bow, then on the other, to set her snubbing harshly at her mooring chain. In the morning the outlook was different. Gone was the blue sky, and the near-by mountain had vanished; in its place loomed a mass of grey swirling cloud. The gale had turned into a 'black sou'-easter', the worst wind Table Bay knows, and it was still increasing in strength. We shackled a second chain to our mooring and lowered a weight down it, for this was no weather in which to go adrift in a crowded yacht basin with the little seas breaking viciously on the rough stone wall to leeward.

Then, satisfied that we could do no more for the safety of our ship, we went to lunch with Commander and Mrs. Irving Johnson aboard the American brigantine *Yankee*, which was lying near-by in the Duncan dock just the other side of the yacht-basin wall. Quite a scend was running there and the 200-tonner was jerking sharply at her mooring wires, one of which she had already stranded. Though she was right up in the windward corner of the dock, her motion was such that at lunch the huge swing table in the mess-deck, at which her entire complement of twenty-two can eat at one sitting, had to be released so that it could swing. Susan and I were most interested to be aboard that famous vessel, then completing her third voyage round the world, and it was a pleasure to discuss with the quiet and unassuming Johnsons, who had made six circumnavigations, the many places we all had visited. But in spite of the cheerful company and the excellent meal, there was a noticeable feeling of tension. As each gust of the great gale roared across the dock Susan's thoughts and mine turned to *Wanderer*, and more than once Irving and Electa cast glances aloft through the skylight where the topsail and top-gallant yards, braced up sharply to offer the minimum wind resistance, stood out boldly against the grey sky. In *Wanderer*'s rigging the wind on such occasions screams; in *Yankee*'s it sounds a deeper note, like an organ with the *vox humana* stop out.

After lunch Irving and Electa came to visit *Wanderer*, and there again we sat and talked of ships and places, while the yacht heeled sharply over under bare poles and the squalls made the water in the basin smoke. We agreed that the gale must be between seventy and eighty knots, but we learnt afterwards that the anemometer at the meteorological station close by had proved us wrong—it recorded a wind speed of ninety-two miles per hour that day, well up in the hurricane zone. (*See p.* 221.) The port was at a standstill with no shipping movements, and the unloading of timber from a ship at the leeward side of the dock had to be stopped because too much water was finding its way into her holds through the open hatches.

That evening we and *Yankee*'s people were invited to a *braaivleis* (a supper of steak, chops and sausages cooked in the open on a wood fire) in the grounds of a house set beautifully amidst the mountains. We motored there by way of the coast road. From that high vantage point the sea presented the strangest sight. It appeared to be lying under a patchwork of snow-drifts; areas of many acres in extent gleamed silvery-white. These were patches of spindrift raised by the hurricane and blown low across the surface of the sea. The *braaivleis* was a fine one, but was spoilt for the yacht owners by anxiety, and we were greatly relieved on returning to our respective ships to find that all was well with them.

During the night the gale died, and in the morning Table Mountain stood out innocent and clear with every detail sharply defined under a cloudless sky. But *Wanderer* was a sorry sight. The sharpness of the grit from off the shore and the violence with which the wind had driven it, had sand-blasted all our recently applied varnish and enamel, leaving it dull and filthy. Before leaving we had to repaint, for which purpose the club kindly had the yacht hauled out on its electrically-operated slip (*see p.* 224), and nature thoughtfully provided two quiet and windless days for us to do the work in.

16

TWO DOTS IN THE SOUTH
ATLANTIC

THE yacht club was dressed over all for the occasion when we left Cape Town in mid March, and as we slipped our mooring and sailed out of the basin its ancient saluting cannon was fired. All our friends came to see us off; some were aboard Norman Goodall's motor yacht *Ancilla* and others were at the dock head. Parting from these good people who had been so very kind to us during our long stay in their port was a severe wrench, and as *Ancilla* turned for home and dipped her ensign in final salute we were in tears.

At sea there was so little wind that it was hardly worth while to persist in an attempt to make an offing; so we crept into Robben Island's conveniently situated little harbour eight miles from Cape Town, and there spent two peaceful nights in silence except for the cries of the waders, and we removed most of the grime of the city from the yacht's rigging.

Lying right on the sailing route between the Cape and England are the islands of St. Helena and Ascension. In the immensity of the otherwise almost empty South Atlantic, they are indicated on the chart merely as small dots. Though neither has a harbour and each is subject to rollers, we hoped to call at both of them for refreshment on our way north. St. Helena, the most southerly of these islands, lies 1,700 miles from Cape Town, and as soon as a fair wind tempted us away from Robben Island we shaped a course for it. We had four days of light to strong variable but mostly fair winds, and the nights were so cold that we were glad of all the clothes we could struggle into during the dark hours. On the fifth day, after a gale had kept us hove-to for seven hours, the wind settled down to blow steadily from the south-east. We knew then that the days of uncertain and variable winds were over for a time, for once again we had reached the area of the south-east trade wind out of which we had passed on our way from Mauritius to Durban; the trade should now be our constant companion all the way up to the Equator, 2,600 miles ahead, or even a little beyond it.

We soon had the twin spinnakers set, and *Wanderer*, steering herself for most of the time, rolled happily along on her homeward way, making good an average of 120 miles a day for the next nine days. After the recent cold nights it was pleasant to feel the temperature rising, and it rose so quickly as we made northing that very soon we no longer needed blankets on our bunks, and when I left my bunk now and then to see that all was well on deck, the night wind felt only pleasantly cool on my naked torso. With the hatches wide open the trade wind blew cleanly right through the ship, humming its friendly, powerful and unforgettable tune as it pushed past the forepeak door and out of the fore hatch to join forces again with its other part which sang gaily in the taut rigging. Night by night the Southern Cross rose less and less high in the sky, while ahead the Plough climbed higher; these were marks of our steady progress on the curve of the world's surface. By day the scene was brilliant with light and colour; blue predominated, but the sea was dappled with the white flashes of breaking crests, and the wide arrowhead of our bow-wave fanned out broadly on either side to mingle with the cascade of the overtaking whitecaps. This was sailing at its best; this, surely, was what our brave little ship was fashioned to do, to run unhindered across the kindest ocean in the world, an ocean where there are no coral or other reefs and where hurricanes are unknown. Day after day the crosses marking her noon positions on the chart advanced across the blank paper, each one almost equidistant from its neighbour and all of them in a nice straight line. The twin spinnaker rig is certainly the ideal one for short-handed little ships making long ocean voyages; it relieves the crew from the tyranny of the helm, and they then have time and inclination to enjoy the beauty of their surroundings and the exhilaration of their progress, and are able to make up their lost sleep, cook and eat elaborate meals and even read or write letters.

On this passage we had remarkably few birds with us once

we had entered the tropics and seen the last of our albatross escort. Sometimes there were several days at a stretch without any birds, not even a stormy petrel, of which species there had usually been several in sight previously wherever we had been, both in the tropics and out of them. Flying fish were scarce, and even the puffy little clouds which we had learnt to expect in fine trade wind weather, were mostly absent, the sky either being clear or streaked with cirrus. The red-letter day of the trip was 29 March. On that day we crossed the meridian of Greenwich, and our watches and the cabin clock, which during the past two and a half years had shown every time in the world in turn, were back once more at Greenwich mean time; and we, with 26,000 miles astern of us, had completed our circum-navigation of the globe, though we would not cross our outward track until we had sailed another 3,000.

By 5 a.m. on our sixteenth day at sea we had run our distance; so we hove-to, for the morning was dark with heavy rain squalls about. At dawn the island of St Helena emerged from a black cloud just where it ought to be; its tremendous cliffs had a forbidding appearance in the grey light. We remained hove-to for breakfast and to have a general tidy up, then let draw and sailed close round the east and north coasts of the island to James Bay on the north-west side. (*See p.* 224.) There off Jamestown, where the grey houses are packed tightly into a steep-sided valley running down to the sea, we secured between two vacant mooring buoys, for the bay is uncomfortably deep for anchoring, the bottom is foul with several wrecks and the best berths are taken by the lighters' moorings. Although the bay is on the island's leeward side, the swell was breaking quite heavily along the shore with a deep roar followed by a screech as the undertow dragged at the pebbles. The doctor, harbour-master and police superintendant came off to give us pratique, but remained only for a few minutes and then were glad to go ashore, for *Wanderer* was rolling heavily.

The island's only landing-place consists of a flight of stone steps at the seaward end of the quay which runs along the north side of the bay. The local long-boats, beautifully handled under oars, back in stern first towards the steps, choosing the comparative quiet following a succession of heavy swells. The person who is to land stands in the sternsheets facing aft and holds on to a stout post fastened in the stern. Then, as the boat rises on the swell, the oarsmen back a little, he grasps a rope which is hanging from a horizontal steel bar overhead on the quay, and jumps ashore. Landing like this from a properly handled boat is not at all difficult; but when the time comes to leave the island, jumping back into the boat, which may be lifting and dropping five or six feet vertically, requires better judgement. We wished to employ a boat and crew to look after us and our needs, but the charge of 25s. a day was rather more than we were prepared to pay, so after the first day we did our own boat work, though indeed our 7-foot pram dinghy was hardly suitable for the purpose. With care it was not too difficult for one of us to land the other, but when we wanted to go ashore together, as we usually did, we had to haul the dinghy up the steps as there was no safe place in which to leave her afloat, and there was always the risk that on our return we might find the swell had increased enough to prevent us getting off to the yacht.

No doubt we saw the island in indifferent circumstances; the sky was mostly overcast and there was much rain. We felt we could well understand Napoleon's feelings when he first set eyes on his gloomy prison from the deck of H.M.S. *Northumberland* in 1815. From seaward the place looks barren and uninviting with its towering cliffs rising 1,200 feet, and its lack of sand beaches or visible vegetation. But inland the scenery is different, as we discovered when His Excellency the Governor kindly sent his car to the landing place to bring us to lunch with him and Mrs. Harford at Plantation House, his beautiful Georgian residence 2,000 feet above sea level. There we saw the other face of St. Helena, well timbered and with fertile green valleys not unlike those of South Devon. In a paddock in front of the great house we were introduced to Jonathan, the 240-year-old giant tortoise from the Galapagos, who has lived there most of his life. His Excellency told me that Jonathan has no endearing habits; he does not recognize people, but he does enjoy bananas, and once a year, in the spring, he wanders off searching fruitlessly for a mate.

Apart from flax rope and lace, the island is unable to produce anything for export; but a little money is made out of the visitors who land for a few hours from the ships which call on their passages between England and the Cape. Most of these people hire cars to take them to Longwood, where Napoleon lived, the house having recently been overhauled and reopened to the public. The island must, however, be a considerable drain on the British taxpayer, for, apart from the cost of administration, £1,000 is paid for every intermediate liner calling there, and £500 for each cargo ship. About twenty-four ships call each year.

Climbing almost vertically up the steep south side of the valley in which Jamestown lies are the 699 steps of Jacob's Ladder. We did not climb these, but we did once make the descent and our sea-weakened legs took a week to recover. The more usual way of reaching the summit of Ladder Hill is by car. The road is cut diagonally in the almost sheer side of the valley; it has blind corners, is barely wide enough for two cars to pass and is guarded from the precipice only by a thin stone wall. Never have Susan or I been so terrified as we were when being driven down this at forty miles an hour by a reckless driver who, without the slightest foundation, assumed that nobody would be coming the other way. As each blind corner was approached we really thought our voyage was going to finish at St. Helena.

During our stay the S.S. *Braemar Castle* came in early one morning for a stop of a few hours. Seeing *Wanderer* rolling in the roadstead, her master, Captain Cambridge, at once sent over a boat to bring us aboard for breakfast with him in his ship's air-conditioned dining saloon. We much enjoyed the freshness of that meal, in such cool and civilized surroundings, and when we left we were the richer by four pounds of butter (we particularly appreciated that gift as all the butter on the island was badly tainted), apples, Jaffa oranges and up-to-date magazines. As *Braemar Castle* left she signalled 'A pleasant voyage' to us, and both she and *Wanderer* dipped their ensigns.

The perpetual rolling and the dismal noise of breakers on the shore were so wearying that we decided we might just as well be at sea, where we would be no more uncomfortable and could be making progress towards home. So after only four days at St. Helena, of which we wished we had been able to see rather more than we did, we sailed away bound for the island of Ascension, 700 miles farther on. This very easy passage took us six days, mostly under twin spinnakers, and the yacht steered herself a lot of the time.

Again we arrived by night and hove-to for daylight before approaching Clarence Bay, which is the island's best anchorage, on the leeward side. The sea had been particularly rough during the final two days of the trip although there had not been a lot of wind, and as we entered the bay we could see the swell breaking heavily on the beach and at the landing place. All the mooring buoys were occupied by lighters, so we anchored close to but outside them in eight fathoms; but the bottom there is of loose volcanic clinker and the bower anchor was reluctant to hold. We therefore dropped the kedge as well and then veered thirty fathoms of cable on one anchor and fifteen on the other; that was all the chain we had.

Almost at once a boat put out to us bringing the resident magistrate, who is also manager for Cable & Wireless Ltd., which concern rents and administers the island. He came to invite us to live ashore with him and Mrs. Harrison. But we were not entirely happy to leave our uninsured floating home together with most of our worldly possessions in that open anchorage until we had made sure that all was well; for the wind blows hard there, and had *Wanderer* dragged out into deep water while we were ashore, she would quickly have blown away to sea and there was at the island at that time no suitable vessel in which we could have given chase. So we spent a night aboard and then, satisfied that the yacht was safe, landed in the same manner as at St. Helena from a shore boat which had been sent out to fetch us.

Now that we have explored Ascension and lived on it for three enjoyable days, I do not think that Susan or I will ever again say that anything is impossible. The island, about seven miles in diameter, is of volcanic origin and geologically is comparatively new; it is said that the British took possession of it before it had even cooled off. The island has forty cones of lava, pumice and cinders, some of which are crimson in colour; this dark red, contrasting with the vivid blue and white of the sky and the bright gold of the sand beaches, makes Ascension one of the most colourful of islands, and in this respect it is in striking contrast to its grey neighbour, St. Helena.

With the exception of Green Mountain, a peak which, exceeding 2,000 feet, is high enough to pierce the trade-wind clouds as they go sailing by and therefore gets plenty of rain, the island is dry and barren and has not so much as a blade of grass growing on it. The only landing on this hot and arid cinder, isolated in the South Atlantic, is at a small rock-and-stone quay which is provided with two cranes and a flight of steps round which the blackfish swim in countless numbers; because of the constant swell, nothing except small lighters and rowing boats can approach it. (*See pp.* 225 *and* 240.) This island, like St. Helena, is subject to rollers. These, which are believed to be caused by great storms many thousands of miles away in the North and South Atlantic, occur without warning, break in a depth of from five to seven fathoms, and thunder in on the islands' leeward sides. The unbroken rollers may be as much as ten feet in height and they sometimes continue for two or three days at a time, but vessels anchored in deep water ride them out in safety. Occasionally there are double rollers, that is, rollers coming in from north-west and south-west at the same time; then landing is impossible as indeed it had been during the two days prior to our arrival. The rollers arrive suddenly and with no warning, and for this reason the landing of passengers from ships calling there is not encouraged as they might get marooned and the island has only enough food and water for its own use.

In spite of the landing difficulties this tiny speck of land was garrisoned by a company of Royal Marines in 1821 and was rated then as one of H.M. ships. First the marines had to build the quay, which was no mean feat having regard to the conditions under which the work had to be done, and then they proceeded to land all the things they needed for the building of forts, barracks, a church, club, hospital and stores, most of them massively constructed of stone. They built a road up Green Mountain, so steep and sharply zig-zagged that a jeep can only just turn the corners in one, and at the summit constructed a great stone farmhouse and outbuildings, as well as a cement water-catchment on the windward side (the island has no springs) with a 500-yard-long tunnel to carry the pipe through the mountain on its way down to the settlement at Georgetown.

Ascension is an important cable station with five cables landing there and is inhabited now only by the employees of the cable company: thirty English people, including wives and children who live in bungalows in Teapot Alley and Scandal Terrace (relics of marine days), and about one hundred servants and labourers from St. Helena. But during the war the island was used as a fuelling point for aircraft flying between America and Africa. Again great physical difficulties were overcome but this time by Americans. Fuel, food, water, building materials and machinery, together with a thousand men, had to be landed from lighters at the one small quay when the swell permitted; a hill was removed, a valley filled in, and the airstrip was completed in ninety days.

The clock on the roof of the Exiles Club chimes the quarter hours and is known as 'Oh, God!' To newcomers recently arrived for their three-year tour of duty on the island and lying sleepless in their beds, it seems to chime 'Oh, God! Another two years and three-hundred-odd days to go before we can leave.' Yet after a short time most people grow to like this colourful and healthy little island and are sorry to leave, though a few do get an attack of what the doctor there calls 'Ascensionitis', a nervous complaint which he thinks is caused by the never ceasing wind that day and night booms across the island and through the houses.

The Harrisons took us by jeep all over the island and even to the summit of Green Mountain, where we walked for hours in the cool, damp air, looking at the fertile kitchen gardens and the lush meadows with cattle grazing in them, and we marvelled that this place should be on the same latitude as the mouth of the River Congo. As I looked out from that point of vantage under the mountain's cloud cap, across the barren lowlands of the island to where, beyond the golden beaches and the line of surf, the great ocean stretched away to the far horizon, I experienced again that feeling of excitement and uncertainty which always besets me at some time or another

PLATE 31

Top: Ascension, tiny dot in the South Atlantic, has forty barren cones of grey and crimson ash rising from plains of cinders, lava and pumice. *Bottom:* Farewell from Ascension's one and only landing place.

when I find myself on a small ocean island. In the roadstead I could just make out the tiny speck of *Wanderer*, and it seemed just then presumptuous and almost a tempting of fate that in a day or two we should be setting out in her to cross that vast ocean to look for another small island more than three thousand miles away. I felt very small and nothing worth in the presence of such immensity, and I wondered as I had done more than once before whether we should succeed.

Our host and hostess seemed thoroughly to understand the needs of small-boat voyagers. In their comfortable home, in front of which the union flag always flew during the days of our visit, they gave us a bathroom to ourselves in spite of the water shortage, and a huge cool bedroom through which, by way of wide louvred windows, the trade wind poured; and they fed us superbly on the best and freshest of food. Therefore, when we returned to our overheated little yacht which all the time had been rolling madly in the bay, we felt strengthened and refreshed both physically and mentally, and were ready for the next long passage on our homeward route. We have never ceased to wonder why it is the people we have had the pleasure of meeting during our circumnavigation have been so uncommonly kind to us.

PLATE 32

Top: The doldrum belt proved to be 650 miles in width instead of the expected 240. *Bottom:* The harbourmaster welcomed us home when we returned to Yarmouth in the Isle of Wight at the end of our voyage.

A.W.W.—R

17

FIFTY-TWO DAYS AT SEA

THE passage of 3,400 miles from Ascension to Fayal, one of the Azores, which group of islands lies in the middle of the North Atlantic, promised to offer more variety of weather than any other of our long ocean passages. Starting in the south-east trade wind, we should have to pass through the doldrums and then through the full width of the north-east trade wind belt and across the greater part of the area of sub-tropical calms and variables, which used to be known to seamen as the horse latitudes because of the occasional need for sailing ships becalmed there to jettison their cargoes of horses in order to conserve the drinking water.

The recommended sailing route for the Channel crosses the equator in about 25° west longitude. Had we been bound direct for England, no doubt it would have paid us to follow that route as closely as possible, leaving the Azores well away to starboard. But as we intended to call at the Azores, we wished to be as far up to windward as possible when we reached the north-east trade wind, for we would have to sail right through the area of that wind close-hauled for perhaps 1,600 miles. But the farther one is to the eastward on crossing the equator, the wider is the belt of doldrums likely to be. After much discussion we decided to cross the equator in 20° west longitude, thus following in the track of *Viking*; the previous year in the same month she had found so narrow a belt of doldrums there that she got through it in two days.

But, of course, winds do not always perform as the pilot charts and sailing directions suggest they will, and instead of the wind being fair and fresh for the 650-mile run to the equator, it fell light after we had been at sea only three days. So all too soon we found ourselves in the doldrums, which is a most unpleasant place, especially for a small and short-handed sailing vessel. The weather was hot and very humid, often with an overcast sky; strong squalls of wind from any direction raised a short and confused sea which retarded progress and was hard on the sails and gear; these squalls alternated with calms and light airs while torrential downpours of rain were common. It was necessary to make use of every puff of wind if we were not to be held up there indefinitely, so we were for ever shifting sail. At one moment we might be running under whole main and spinnaker, the next be close-hauled under reduced sail in a fierce squall, and a few minutes later the ghoster would have to be set to take advantage of a faint air. As we could not endure the terrible slamming of the rain-soaked mainsail in the calms, we handed it many times but often had to reset it soon after doing so. It was tiring work and we learnt to dread the approach of the great rain-filled black and purple clouds which plagued us day and night, for they always brought with them a calm or a sudden shift of wind.

Although the risk of collision out in the broad oceans is very small, it had always been our custom to hang the paraffin riding light in the rigging when at night we were both below at the same time; but between the squalls the nights in the doldrums were so damp and airless that the light refused to burn as soon as its lid was closed. With the cabin temperature well above 90° F. there was little comfort to be had in our bunks where, almost naked, we lay sticky with sweat, tossing restlessly from side to side. During those long damp nights when *Wanderer* lay rolling without steerage way waiting for the next squall to drive her on half a mile or so, we sometimes wondered whether our provisions would be exhausted or our water tanks run dry before we could reach port. No doubt it was stupid to worry about such things so early on the voyage, but that was one of the effects the enervating weather in the doldrums and the lack of progress had on us.

In the vicinity of the equator we encountered a current setting in a north-westerly direction, and it carried us over the equator in 23° west longitude, which was farther to the west than we had intended. The night we crossed the equator after two years in the southern hemisphere, Father Neptune sent along an escort to see us over, a great party of phosphorescent porpoises, swimming all around and frequently breaking surface to take their short gasps of breath. We like these friendly playful people who appear to get such tremendous enjoyment from life. The current we were in was alive with big fish, notably dolphins and sharks. On one occasion our patent log rotator was taken by a dolphin which, no doubt surprised at the hardness of its catch, jumped clear out of the sea with the line in its mouth. Susan, who was steering at the time, saw this happen, and fearing that the log recorder might be torn from the rail to which it was secured by two brass screws, grabbed the line. But the strain was too great for her, so she called me. With a struggle I managed to haul in about forty feet of it; then it went slack in my hands and I felt sure the line had parted. But on continuing to haul I found the rotator intact, so it must have been taken and then disgorged by the fish. We were glad of this because it was an old friend which had not only circumnavigated the world with us but had seen many years of service in *Wanderer II*.

Sharks were a nuisance. These sinister-looking beasts approaching slowly from astern, came right up alongside and then, turning over on their backs so that we could see their evil little eyes and rows of sharp teeth, rubbed their bellies along *Wanderer's* bottom, presumably in an attempt to rid themselves of the parasite fish adhering to them. That was all very well, but as our copper sheathing had lost some of its anti-fouling properties owing to oxidization, we had given it a coat of paint at Cape Town, and the sharks usually managed to remove a considerable quantity of this before we succeeded in driving them off with shots from our 12-bore gun, which is not a very effective weapon for that purpose.

One afternoon when we lay completely becalmed and Susan and I were resting down below, we felt something strike the yacht a hard blow. Hurrying on deck we saw in the clear water a fish of great size swimming swiftly round and beneath the yacht, now and again striking its body against her. At least ten feet in length, this fish was black except for tail fins of vivid electric blue, and from its upper jaw, projecting three feet or more, was a great spear or ram. We did not care for the proximity of this creature, and, fearing it might do the yacht an injury, we brought the gun on deck and were awaiting an opportunity for a shot when we heard a tremendous clatter aft and were horrified to see the fish's head and spear appear over the taffrail. I could not shoot then as there were too many obstructions. The fish had come up between the twin bobstays which brace the bumkin to the hull, the force of its great body bending those half-inch-diameter rods sharply outwards; there between them it remained wedged for a few moments while its powerful tail thrashed the water furiously. Then one of the rods broke and it fell back into the sea. The fish then approached for another attack, but that time I got a shot in it and drove it off. As it swam away we noticed something white adhering to its spear, and on investigation discovered that it had ripped a piece twelve inches long and half an inch deep from the side of the hard-wood rudder stock, the scar extending right up to the brass cap on the rudder head at deck level. Fortunately it had given us a glancing blow and the damage was only superficial; but we could not help wondering what might have happened to the yacht and to us had the spear pierced the transom or planking, for then the fish's struggles to release itself might have torn away a section of woodwork.

At the time we gave the fish the benefit of the doubt and assumed it had been chasing some of the small fry which swam beneath us, and had misjudged its distance or its aim. But we have since learnt that this type of spearfish, which may weigh anything between 700 and 1,000 lb. and has a speed of sixty-eight miles per hour, does attack whales. In the days of wooden ships it was not uncommon for a vessel to be attacked, and in the British museum there is a piece of timber twenty-two inches thick completely transfixed by the spear of one of these powerful and belligerent creatures.

We could not tell whether the remaining bobstay had been weakened when it was bent, so we rigged a tackle in place of the broken one; but as the lower block of the tackle had to be fastened to the copper plate at the waterline with a steel shackle, we had little faith in the repair, and so did not dare to use the masthead genoa for the rest of the passage except in the lightest of airs, for we did not wish to have the singular distinction of being dismasted, even indirectly, by a fish. Our caution was justified, for on arrival at Fayal the shackle had been reduced by electrolytic action to the thickness of a darning needle and broke the moment I touched it.

This handicap added to our delay and we took two weeks to work through the doldrum belt, which proved to be 650 miles in width instead of 240 as shown on the pilot chart. (*See p.* 241.) Had it not been for the favourable current we should have taken even longer, but even with the current to help we made a day's run on one occasion of only seventeen miles.

It was a wonderful relief when, after we had struggled mile by mile to latitude 4° north, a breeze made from north-east and steadily freshened—the trade wind at last, and it never faltered once during the next eighteen days. Much of the time it blew at force 5 but often increased to 6 and on occasions even 7. *Wanderer* obligingly steered herself on the starboard tack about six points off the wind for nearly the whole of that time, and she made runs of between 90 and 100 miles a day. Usually the strength of the wind called for several rolls in the mainsail, which then nicely balanced the No. 1 staysail, and a tiller line was not necessary. We were glad of that because *Wanderer* will never hold her course for long with the tiller lashed; if the wind freshens she luffs and if it eases she tends to bear away. But with the helm free and the balance achieved by the sails, changes in the strength of the wind do not cause her to deviate from the course. When the wind was strong and we had to change to the No. 2 staysail, we rolled down more of the mainsail until balance was again achieved. Several times when the sea became too rough for sailing we jilled slowly along under the close-reefed mainsail only.

We led a strange life during those eighteen days. Nearly always the motion was too violent to permit us to do anything beyond the necessary daily tasks of sweeping out the cabin, trimming and filling the lamps and the galley stove, cooking, eating and navigating. For the rest of the time we wedged ourselves in our bunks and dozed or read—we read everything on board, even the advertisements in the magazines. And what a dreadful waste of time that seemed to be with nothing to show for it except 1,600 miles made good on the earth's surface. In a larger or steadier vessel we might have put that time to some useful purpose; but as it was we lived a kind of hospital existence—bedridden, but fortunately free from bed-sores. At times the motion was almost indescribably violent, though Susan got fairly near to it when she said it was like sailing among a lot of concrete blocks. The strain on the gear must have been severe, and through many a sleepless night we lay and listened to the noise as *Wanderer* pounded her way to windward and water sluiced along the deck overhead, waiting apprehensively for something to carry away through fatigue; but, as is usually so, the yacht was stronger than her crew. A constant deluge of spray drove over her and the sails became stiff with caked salt. Sometimes at night when the wind veered a few points and she headed more directly into the old sea, she shipped heavy water.

The one compensation for the miserable discomfort was our steady progress. Day after day our game little ship burst her way through the crests and plunged down into the troughs, but always she pressed on without a pause to windward, always to windward. Nightly the heavens changed. In latitude 8° N. we saw Polaris for the first time in two years and three months. In theory this star should become visible soon after one crosses the equator, but because of atmosphere and the clouds which so often hang above the horizon, it is rarely seen until six degrees or more of north latitude have been made. Meanwhile the Southern Cross, our companion during so many nights in the southern hemisphere, dropped lower and eventually sank, almost unnoticed, out of sight. We felt a little sad when we realized it had gone for good, and we wondered whether we should ever again be so fortunate as to make another voyage south of the line to renew our acquaintance with the lovely places and the charming people there.

On 15 May we passed beneath the sun and thereafter faced south when taking the noon latitude sight. The next day we crossed our outward track at the position we had occupied on 23 October 1952, and so at last had put a girdle round the globe. That evening was not as rough as the previous ones, so we celebrated the occasion with a bottle of Stellinheimer Stein from the Cape with our supper. Two days later we crossed the tropic of Cancer and from then on the days, which already had shown signs of lengthening, drew out quite rapidly. The milestones along our lonely track were slipping past.

On 24 May in latitude 30° N. the wind died and *Wanderer* stood upright and shook herself. She had hammered her way through the whole width of the north-east trade wind belt and had surfaced on the other side of it. Thankfully we opened the ports and hatches and had a great drying of our personal belongings, and we noticed with surprise that a large area of the white enamel on the port topside, which had been constantly submerged for the past eighteen days, had grown a crop of green weed and embryo barnacles. It did seem strange to be able to move about without having to hold on with both hands.

All the time we had been in the trade wind the weather had been peculiar; often the sky was heavily clouded or overcast, and rarely had we seen any of the small cumulus clouds which usually predominate in that area. But on reaching the horse latitudes the weather became really lovely except, of course, for lack of wind. The days were bright blue, cool and crisp with the thermometer down to 70° F. (that seemed really cold to us) and by night the dear old Plough and Polaris glittered in a clear sky.

The north-east trade wind had been without mercy. Instead of becoming more easterly as we made northing, as indeed it should, it always persisted in heading us away to the westward of our course, so that by the time we had finished with it we had sagged away to 37° W., while Fayal lay in 29° W. and was then distant about 600 miles. It may seem hard to believe, but we actually took another fifteen days to cover that distance, for we had long spells of absolute calm and such little wind as there was persisted in coming from dead ahead, while the short popple into which we pitched jerkily stopped us badly; once again, as in the doldrums, we made a day's run of only seventeen miles. Whichever tack we were on always seemed to be the wrong one, and again and again we went about but with no improvement. Here the pilot chart shows wind arrows from all directions, though the longest ones are from west and south-west; but always the wind remained persistently in the north-east. We worked hard to get the utmost out of the fickle airs and almost came to prefer the calms, for then there was nothing we could do except hope that when the wind did come again it would be fair.

In those calms *Wanderer* lay without a stitch of sail set (on that passage we handed the mainsail no fewer than nineteen times to save it from chafe) rolling heavily above her own reflection. Towering masses of cumulus stood all around above the almost invisible horizon, but usually the sun set clearly, tumbling down to meet his own reflection in the oily sea. The silence was profound. It did not cheer us up at all to read that in this area Voss in *Tilikum* made good only twenty miles in one fourteen-day period.

For several days we were on the low-powered steamer route between the Mediterranean and Gulf ports, and several ships altered course to close with us, dipping their ensigns and blowing their sirens. The master of one of them, which was flying the Panamanian flag, hailed us through a megaphone and asked: 'Do you vant for anyting?' Such kindly contacts gave us something fresh to think and talk about, and we were grateful, but we never accepted offers of food as we feared that damage might be done in going alongside. With three exceptions these were the first ships we had seen when out of sight of land during our entire circumnavigation, for the sailing-ship routes are almost empty of shipping today, and the chance of a meeting during the quick crossing of a narrow steamship route is very slight.

We had with us a party of little blue-and-black-striped pilot fish swimming in our shade. They always used to pop out and investigate with insatiable curiosity everything we threw overboard. Quite by accident we discovered their favourite diet was drop-scones and canned crayfish, and on this they visibly grew larger day by day. In the lonely wastes of the ocean we became quite attached to these amusing little creatures and to the porpoises which used often to visit us. Some of the latter were of an unusual kind with speckled bodies and white tips to their noses. The sea was dotted with thousands of Portuguese men-of-war, all bright pink and all of them like us making very little progress. The only birds we saw until close to the Azores, where we met fulmars and terns fishing, were a few storm-petrels.

The continued slowness of our progress caused us to take careful stock of our provisions and fresh water. Susan had laid in a great store of provisions at the Cape, so we never had occasion to ration ourselves, but unfortunately all the corned beef she had bought there was of such poor quality as to be uneatable; even in the cooler weather we were getting it was almost liquid. Our lockers were, however, becoming very empty by the time we approached Fayal. The water was lasting well, but of course the only washing we did was in rain water caught in the doldrums or in sea water using a detergent.

Not until we had with infinite labour and patience worked our slow way to a position 200 miles south-west of Fayal did we pick up a decent breeze, and that quickly hardened into a gale which we rode out a-hull under bare poles for two days. The swell was as large as we had ever seen, and the gale soon whipped it into a really heavy sea which, with crests breaking everywhere beneath the leaden sky, certainly looked magnificent and had a real savour of the North Atlantic about it. But this further delay was exasperating, for again we could do little but lie in our bunks waiting for it to blow itself out.

As soon as wind and sea had moderated sufficiently we made sail, and skirting the Azores Bank, where there is a reported ten fathom patch which would probably be breaking, headed for the first time since leaving Ascension directly for our destination.

On the evening of our fifty-second day at sea out of sight of land, the western tip of Fayal appeared indistinctly from out of the mist and rain in which the rest of the island was shrouded. This was a tremendously exciting moment for us both; but my own relief at such a perfect landfall was probably the greater, for I as navigator had been suffering all day from a severe attack of 'landfallitis', fearing, as perhaps other navigators had done before me, that some cumulative error might have crept unnoticed into my daily calculations. Under the reefed mainsail and spinnaker we hurried along the southern shore, one misty headland after another looming out of the drizzle and gathering darkness.

At ten o'clock that evening *Wanderer* lay snugly in Horta, Fayal's walled harbour, silent and without a movement for the first time since she was at Robben Island, now nearly 6,000 miles away. A friendly pilot came out to see if all was well with us, and while I filled in the few simple forms he had brought with him, the crew of his launch helped Susan to stow the stiff, wet sails and make all snug on deck. Then we were left in peace, surrounded by the strangely unfamiliar sounds and smells of the land, to sleep and sleep.

18

THE HOMECOMING

THE Azores are attractive islands, mountainous, but green and fertile, and their Portuguese inhabitants are friendly, helpful, courteous and pro-British. There are two harbours in the group: Ponta Delgada on the island of San Miguel and Horta on the island of Fayal; both are formed by massive breakwaters. We had visited Ponta Delgada on a previous cruise, and on this occasion called only at Horta which is, I consider, the more comfortable of the two. There, with the gay little pink, white and cream houses of the town crowding the hill one side of us, and the 7,600-foot cone of Pico thrusting out disdainfully above the clouds which masked its foothills, on the other, we remained for two pleasant weeks, resting, writing and attending to the yacht's needs. We called on the Captain of the Port, as is our custom in a foreign harbour, and he at once placed the port and its facilities entirely at our disposal free of charge. The Fayal Coal and Supply Company repaired the damage done by the spearfish and not only refused to accept any payment, but entertained us to dinner and helped us with our shopping, as did the manager and staff of the cable station. The proprietor of the Café Sport and his son went out of their way to assist us in many little matters and obtained for us daily supplies of sweet mountain strawberries.

The town with its narrow, cobbled streets, patterned pavements and buildings decorated with wrought-iron balconies is, like the rest of the island, unspoilt and charming. Mule-drawn carts form the bulk of the traffic, and these are frequently piled high with firewood brought over in boats from the neighbouring island of Pico, for Fayal has few trees and nobody would think of using coal for cooking purposes. Horta means 'kitchen garden', and the surrounding countryside is a patchwork of tiny, well-tilled fields, while along a high ridge overlooking the harbour stands a row of little windmills with triangular roller-reefing sails, all busily grinding corn. Vegetables and fruit are cheap and of excellent quality and so, strangely enough, is tinned ham and tinned butter; but such few other tinned foods as are available are about three times the English price. The local wine, or the Portuguese wine, can be bought in five-litre wicker-work-covered bottles at about 1s. a litre, and we laid in a good supply of it.

One of the most important exports from the Azores is whale oil, but I doubt whether it is generally realized that the whales, of which about a thousand are caught each year, are harpooned and killed from open boats propelled by sails or paddles. High speed motor launches, which are in radio communication with the lookout stations ashore, tow the whale boats out to the position where the blow was seen—this may be anything up to thirty-five miles from the land—and tow the dead whales back to the factory. But the dart is made and the lances thrust from the bows of the open boats, which carry a crew of seven; they often approach in the whale's blind sector and make the dart 'wood to blackskin', that is, with the bow of the boat actually touching the whale. It is a hazardous occupation, and sometimes a man is killed when caught in the coils of the fast-running line as the whale sounds, or a boat is smashed to splinters by the whale's flukes.

We had previously regarded whales as benign and harmless creatures, as indeed they generally are; but now that we know more about them and their habits, it seems to us that when sailing through a pod, especially at night, there is some risk of a yacht, approaching silently in the blind sector, striking one, and the result might then be serious. We kept a more careful lookout than usual on our way home and we saw a large number of whales.

We left Horta towards the end of June, hoping to make our home port of Yarmouth in the Isle of Wight direct. To start with we had light headwinds mostly from ahead, and during the first week we did not make a day's run exceeding 100 miles. We thought we might have done better to have stood away in a north or nor'-nor'-west direction on the starboard tack until we picked up a fair wind, for that is the recommended course for a sailing vessel homeward bound from the Azores and faced with a headwind. But the weather forecast we had received at Horta had promised freshening south-west winds, so, expecting a change of wind at any moment, we kept as close to the great-circle course as possible, for that is the shortest route. Generally the sky was overcast with a low, foggy type of cloud, and for navigation we only got occasional snapshots of the sun when he appeared mistily for a few moments now and then. The damp atmosphere made the sails as stiff as cardboard so that they flogged badly in the light airs, for all the time there was a swell running from the north-west to keep the yacht rolling.

As we were sailing for much of the time along the low-powered steamship route between the Channel and New York, we saw many ships; but as we had no arrangement with Lloyd's for the passing on of messages, we never attempted to communicate with them, though several approached us closely and dipped their ensigns. For the first time since leaving the Cape we had our navigation lights shipped ready to be switched on.

From Horta to the Lizard is a distance of about 1,200 miles, a comparatively short hop for us, and as that was the last leg of our long voyage we were naturally enough anxious to have done with it for we were excited at the prospect of getting home. But the time passed all too slowly, for once again we were unfortunate in finding north-east winds in an area where the pilot chart indicated there should be a large proportion of winds with a westerly component. We learnt later that the area of north-east winds was an enormous one spreading at that time over most of the Atlantic, and we should not have improved matters by standing away to the north. Because of our slow progress our estimated time of arrival was of a pessimistic order. But there was one compensation. As we increased our latitude the nights grew shorter and shorter until there were no more than five hours of darkness and we had only to take one two-and-a-half-hour night watch each. This, after nearly three years of tropic nights which everywhere are about twelve hours in length, was a great comfort.

It was not until we were a day's sail from the 100-fathom line of the continental shelf that we got a fresh, fair wind which brought with it a fine drizzle to reduce visibility to a mile or less at times. As *Wanderer*, with mainsail and spinnaker pulling hard, strode out at six and a half knots for England, we looked forward eagerly to a fast run up Channel and a landfall on the Needles at the end of it. And then, of course, for such is human nature, our estimated time of arrival was changed extravagantly, for always one tends to base it on the conditions prevailing at the moment. During a calm we feel we shall be at sea for ever, but, given a fair wind and a day's run of 130 miles or so, we immediately jump to the conclusion that we shall continue at that speed for the rest of the passage.

After two days of fast sailing in weather that seemed so cold to us that we were glad of all our thick clothes, which had a strong smell of mildew about them, the wind fell light and came ahead once more and the sky cleared as though a giant hand had drawn a curtain aside. Observations of the sun then placed us thirty miles south-west of the Lizard. As those were the last sights we should have to take, I cleaned the sextant with loving care before putting it away in its box. I had bought the instrument in 1937 for £5, and it had served us well. As though to confirm our observations, the clean, fresh smell of the English countryside—new-mown hay and honeysuckle—drifted out to us; then at dusk the brilliant light on the Lizard flashed its welcome. What a wonderful moment that was!

Dawn found us almost becalmed in the shipping lane with our destination still 150 miles away. Suddenly the longing for a new, crusty loaf, a crisp lettuce, a pound of cold, firm butter and a long uninterrupted sleep became too much for us. So we gave up our objective and worked our way into Falmouth Bay, which looked as lovely as we had remembered it with its rounded green hills and fishing boats jilling about under sail off the Manacles. Presently we reached an anchorage at St. Mawes where the customs cleared us and we were welcomed by old friends.

There we rested for a little while and then sailed on, mostly with airs so faint that scarcely a ripple showed on the glassy surface of the Channel. It was an enjoyable trip; for the first time since she was in New Zealand *Wanderer* sailed in water where there was no swell, a sensation Susan and I had almost forgotten. The genoa stayed round and full and the yacht ghosted silently through the water.

Visibility was so poor that we sighted the familiar landmarks, Start, Portland, Anvil and the Needles, only faintly through the heat-haze, and so we arrived unannounced in proper sailing-ship fashion at Yarmouth.

There *Wanderer*, with her brown sails faded by the tropic sun, her ropes bleached almost white, and the ensigns of the countries she had visited flying in a colourful string from the starboard crosstree, slipped quietly into the harbour at the conclusion of her 32,000-mile voyage round the world.

As Susan and I moored our little ship stem and stern between the posts which she had left just under three years ago, we were filled with a strange mixture of exultation and humility. We rejoiced that we had succeeded without mishap in doing what we had set out to do; we had proved our seamanship and judgement to our own satisfaction, and we had seen something of the world and its people. But we were deeply conscious of the untamed might of the vast oceans and the hazards of their shoals and shores, and we were grateful to Providence for bringing us safely home.

EPILOGUE

SHORTLY before Christmas 1955, *Wanderer III* made what Susan and I considered to be her most hazardous journey. This was on a ten-ton trailer through the busy streets of London, where her guardrails reached as high as the top of a double-decker bus. Her architects and builders, in collaboration with Beaverbrook Newspapers, had asked us whether we would permit her to be exhibited in the Second National Boat Show at Olympia as a good example of British workmanship. With some misgivings, for we are of the opinion that boats should remain in their natural element and not be subjected to the unnatural strains and stresses of an overland journey, we agreed. It was decided not to overhaul or refit her, but to show her as she was at the end of her long voyage. As she was one of the largest exhibits, she was one of the first to arrive at Olympia, and in a corner of the cold, grey, empty hall she sat in her cradle waiting while the complications of the show took shape round her.

The next time we saw our little ship the show was in full swing. Olympia was a maze of attractively laid-out stands on which were shown a number of yachts, new and shining from their builders' yards, together with everything appertaining to the sport and industry of yachting. From the loud-speakers came the sounds of gulls crying and seas breaking, and over the low partition, which separated the show from the menagerie next door, came the loud trumpeting of elephants and the roaring of lions. One hundred and forty thousand people visited the show, and most of these followed the signposts directing them to *Wanderer*. Beyond the display of photographs telling her story and the giant chart illustrating her track, steps and a staging had been erected across the stern and along the starboard side, so that visitors could look down on the deck and into the cabin, which was brilliantly lit by electric lamps.

For ten days Susan and I took it in turn to stand on deck answering the many questions asked by the passers-by. In anticipation we had dreaded our appearance at the show because of the publicity this would entail, but apart from that publicity it proved to be a most enjoyable experience. From 10 a.m. until 9 p.m. each day a constant stream of people came to look at our yacht, and often the patient queue extended a long way. These people, many of whom were married couples or young men with their girl friends, were charming. Some shook us shyly or enthusiastically by the hand, others asked questions about the yacht and her gear, what we ate, how we managed at night or in bad weather. But the majority had a far-away look in their eyes and a smile on their lips; some stroked the rail, others fondled the rigging or slapped the topsides as they filed past. These we believed were dreaming of wide oceans and distant, sunny places; imagining themselves far away out there in small boats of their own, living the life of their choice and putting into practice the quotation from one of Arthur Ransome's books which is carved in *Wanderer*'s companionway. This reads 'Grab a chance and you won't be sorry for a might-have-been.'

Appendix 1

A DESCRIPTION OF *WANDERER III*

As the yachtsman reader may wish to have some more technical information about *Wanderer* than has been included in the body of this book, I include here a brief description of her and her gear.

Her dimensions are: length over all 30 ft. 3 in.; length on the waterline 26 ft. 5 in.; beam 8 ft. 5 in. and designed draught 5 ft.; but throughout the voyage she was drawing between 6 and 8 inches more than that because of her rather heavy construction and the weight of food, water and other things she had on board. Her Thames tonnage is 8 and her displacement in seagoing trim about 9 tons. In most respects she is an orthodox British yacht; we would, however, have preferred greater beam and a short, sawn-off counter, but could afford neither.

Keel and deadwood are of elm. The ballast keel, about 3 tons, is of lead because the yacht's bottom is copper sheathed; there is no inside ballast. Stem, sternpost, frames, carlines and deck beams are of English oak. All the frames are steam-bent and some are doubled; the floors on the doubled frames are of oak, and on the single frames of wrought iron. Keel bolts and chain-plate bolts are of steel, but all other fastenings are of copper, brass or bronze. Planking is of iroko, a West African timber which has some of the properties of teak, and is finished 1⅛ in. thick. Coamings, cockpit, hatches, rail and cabin sole are also of iroko. Decks are of tongued-and-grooved western red cedar covered with canvas and painted pale green.

The internal joinery work is of light African 'mahogany', varnished up to sideboard level and painted white above. At the after end a large galley with stainless-steel-covered bench and swinging two-burner Para-Fin stove (Primus type) faces the oilskin locker and the navigation space, which has a chart table and room below it in drawers for about 400 Admiralty charts stowed flat. The cabin has a Dunlopillo settee-berth each side of a fixed table with hinged leaves; above the settee backs are shelves for 150 books. The forward ends of the berths extend beneath sideboards to take the sleeper's feet at night and the bedding in the daytime. Canvas bunkboards lie flat beneath the mattresses when not in use. Each side and forward of the sideboards are really large lockers with shelves for clothes, photographic equipment, medical supplies, typewriter, etc. The forepeak houses a Baby Blake w.c., the chain locker and four water cans, and has stowage space for all sails, warps, spare rope and navigation lamps; there is a bench each side for use when it is converted into a photographic darkroom and a large bin for tinned food.

Seventy gallons of fresh water were carried in three tanks, one under part of each settee and one under the galley floor; these can be shut off from one another by means of cocks, so that if one were to spring a leak or its contents were to go bad, all the water would not be lost. Provisions for 90 days were stowed away in the many lockers with which the yacht is provided; each was numbered and a list of its contents made. Ventilation is by six opening ports in the coachroof coamings, four large cowls (the forward two are of the water-trap type) and a mushroom vent at bow and stern. In port in hot weather we spread an awning to shade the deck between mast and stern, and we rigged a large canvas wind-sail to blow down the fore-hatch.

The auxiliary motor, a 4-h.p. Stuart Turner two-stroke running on petrol, is installed beneath the self-draining cockpit. The two-bladed propeller is placed on the centre line and is driven through a centrifugal clutch; it is not possible to go astern. When under sail the propeller can be clamped with its blades vertical abaft the sternpost. In a calm and absolutely smooth water the motor gives a speed of three knots. It charges a 12-volt battery at 4 amps, but electricity is only used for dark-room work and navigation lights; all other lighting is by paraffin. Right aft are tanks holding 10 gallons of petrol, and 10 gallons of paraffin in cans are stowed in one of the cockpit lockers.

The steering compass was made by Henry Browne & Sons
A.W.W.—S*

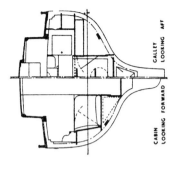

GALLEY LOOKING AFT

CABIN LOOKING FORWARD

STARBOARD SIDE FACING GALLEY

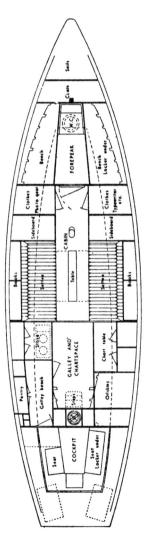

Seats

Gear

W.C.

FOREPEAK

Berth

Bench Locker under

Clothes Photo gear

Clothes Typewriter etc.

Sideboard

Sideboard

CABIN

Berth

Table

Settee

Settee

Berth

Pantry

Galley bench

Shelf

GALLEY AND CHARTSPACE

Chart table

Oilskins

Stops

Seat

COCKPIT

Seat Locker under

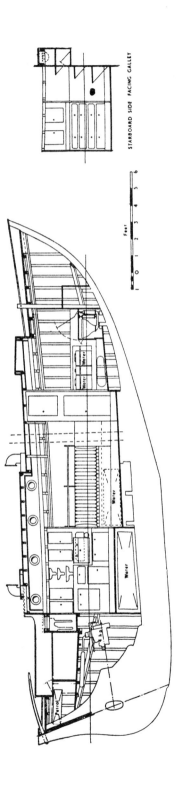

Water

Water

Water

Water

Petrol

Feet

0 1 2 3 4 5 6

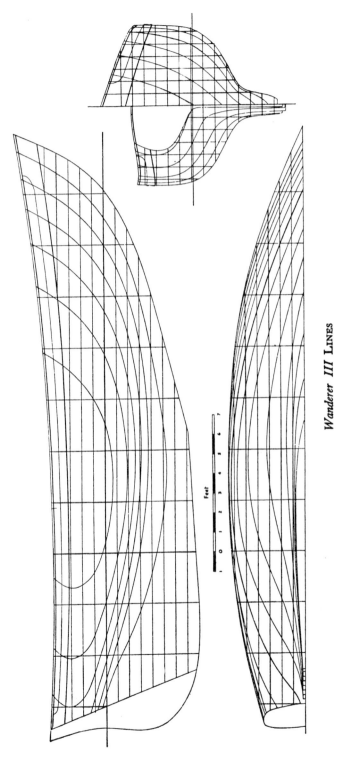

Wanderer III Lines

Dimensions: L.O.A. 30 ft. 3¼ in.; L.W.L. 26 ft. 4¾ in.; beam 8 ft. 5 in.; draught 5 ft. 0 in.; Thames measurement 8 tons; displacement 16,000 lb.; lead keel 7,000 lb.

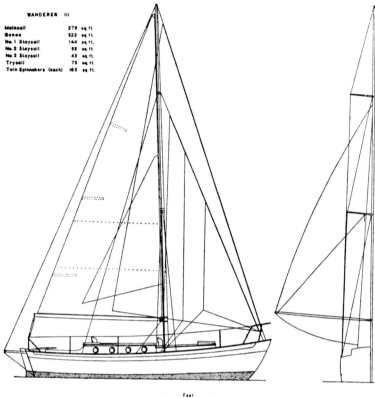

WANDERER III

Mainsail	279	sq. ft.
Genoa	322	sq. ft.
No. 1 Staysail	144	sq. ft.
No. 2 Staysail	92	sq. ft.
No. 3 Staysail	43	sq. ft.
Trysail	75	sq. ft.
Twin Spinnakers (each)	165	sq. ft.

Feet
1 0 1 2 3 4 5 6

and is of the grid type, the grid being luminous so that no light is needed. It is installed beneath a hinged pane of unbreakable glass in the bridge deck where, after correction, it had no deviation or heeling error. A hand-bearing compass is shipped in a bracket on the after leg of the cabin table where it serves as a tell-tale.

Wanderer is rigged as a jib-headed sloop; the maximum sail area, with mainsail and genoa set, is 600 square feet. The mast of silver spruce is hollow and has two pairs of crosstrees; the main boom and twin spinnaker booms are solid. To keep the mast and spars as cool as possible to preserve the glue, they are painted white. Gibbons' slides with large thimbles are used for the upper two-thirds of the mainsail luff, a rope lacing

3

being used on the lower third for convenience when reefing. Worm type roller reefing gear is fitted. The working staysails, of which there are three, are set hanked to the lower forestay; the cotton genoa and the nylon ghoster are set hanked to the top-mast stay. A flax trysail of 75 square feet, and twin spinnakers of 125 square feet each are carried, the latter enabling the yacht to steer herself down wind. The sails were made by Cranfield & Carter and all except the nylon ghoster and the twin spinnakers, which also are of nylon, were tanned a rich red-brown to make them easy on the eye in bright sunshine and to protect them from mildew. All the standing rigging except the forestay and topmast-stay, which are stainless, and the bumkin bobstays, which are of bronze, is of galvanized plough steel wire; we protected it against damp by frequent applications of boiled linseed oil. Halyards are of galvanized steel flexible wire with hemp falls, the final setting up being done with winches; all other running gear is of white Italian hemp.

The yacht is fitted with guardrails supported by Reynolds' alloy stanchions 30 inches high; there is a steel tube pulpit forward and a high mainsheet-horse aft. At sea we laced canvas dodgers to the guardrails in way of the cockpit.

Two 35-lb. C.Q.R. anchors were carried and 45 fathoms of $\frac{5}{16}$-in. chain, together with a 28-lb. weight and traveller. There were also two 30-fathom 2-in. warps of Italian hemp. No windlass is fitted, but a pawl mounted over the stemhead roller holds each link of chain as it is hauled in and is, in my opinion, the equal of a windlass in a vessel of this small size.

A 7 ft. 3 in. Viking Marine alloy pram dinghy is carried bottom up on chocks on the coachroof between the mast and main hatchway.

The yacht with all her gear, fittings and equipment cost £3,300 to build. The total cost of the voyage, including food, drink, tobacco, clothes, fuel, travelling and the maintenance of the yacht and her gear to a high standard, was £500 a year, but this sum did not include the cost of charts and sailing directions.

Appendix 2

TABLE OF TIMES AND DISTANCES

	Time on passage in days and hours		Distance in sea miles
24 July to 4 Oct. 1952 Yarmouth to La Palma via ports in France, Spain, Portugal, Madeiras			1,857
11 Oct. to 6 Nov. La Palma to Barbados, West Indies	26d.	8h.	2,662
21 Nov. to 28 Dec. Amongst the West Indies			342
28 Dec. 1952 to 7 Jan. 1953 Antigua to Cristobal, Panama	9d.	17h.	1,160
15 Jan. Transit of canal to Balboa		14h.	46
26 Jan. to 4 March Balboa to Marquesas	36d.	22h.	3,972
19 March to 25 March Marquesas to Tahiti	6d.	9h.	769
18 April to 29 May Amongst the Society Islands			166
29 May to 11 June Bora-Bora to Pago Pago, Samoa	13d.	2h.	1,070
27 June to 7 July Pago Pago to Matuku, Fiji	10d.	3h.	722
12 July to 31 Aug. Amongst the Fiji Islands			211
31 Aug. to 18 Sept. Suva to Russell, New Zealand	17d.	0h.	1,097
18 Sept. 1953 to 12 Jan. 1954 In New Zealand waters			442

12 Jan. to 23 Jan.			
Whangaroa to Sydney, Australia	10d.	18h.	1,156
4 March to 4 June			
On the east coast of Australia			1,940
9 June to 14 June			
Thursday Island to South Goulburn I.	5d.	3h.	532
19 June to 4 July			
Goulburn I. to Christmas Island	15d.	12h.	1,658
13 July to 17 July			
Christmas I. to Keeling Cocos Is.	3d.	23h.	527
19 Aug. to 7 Sept.			
Cocos Is. to Rodriguez I.	19d.	2h.	1,986
11 Sept. to 14 Sept.			
Rodriguez I. to Mauritius	3d.	5h.	360
2 Oct. to 21 Oct.			
Mauritius to Durban, South Africa	18d.	23h.	1,655
31 Dec. 1954 to 3 Jan. 1955			
Durban to Port Elizabeth	3d.	12h.	411
14 Jan. to 17 Jan.			
Port Elizabeth to Cape Town	3d.	9h.	431
15 March			
Cape Town to Robben Island			8
17 March to 2 April			
Robben Island to St Helena	16d.	1h.	1,691
6 April to 12 April			
St Helena to Ascension I.	5d.	23h.	704
17 April to 7 June			
Ascension I. to Horta, Azores	51d.	11h.	3,444
22 June to 6 July			
Horta to St Mawes, England	14d.	0h.	1,261
10 July to 13 July			
St Mawes to Yarmouth, Isle of Wight			153

Total distance made good in sea miles   32,433

Duration of voyage   2 years 50 weeks 4 days
Best day's run   157 sea miles
Number of places visited   153

An Explanation of some of the Nautical Terms used in this Book

Abaft. Nearer the stern than some other object mentioned.

Abeam. At right angles to the fore-and-aft line amidships.

About. A sailing vessel is said to go, come, or put about when she stays from one tack to the other.

Aft. Towards the stern; behind.

Ahead. In front of, in the direction of the bows.

A-hull. Lying without any sail set in a gale and usually beam on to wind and sea.

Amidships. The middle part of a vessel; sometimes refers to the fore-and-aft line, e.g. put the helm amidships, i.e. neither to port nor starboard.

Asleep. Sails are said to be asleep when they are full of wind and make no noise.

Athwart. Across; at right angles to fore-and-aft.

Backstay. A wire rope support leading aft from a mast to prevent it from bending forward.

Bar. A shoal at the mouth of a river or harbour.

Bare poles. Without any sail set.

Batten. A semi-flexible wooden stiffener sometimes fitted to the after edge of a mainsail, to prevent curling or flapping.

Beam. The extreme breadth of a vessel. *On the beam*: in a direction abeam of the vessel (see *Abeam*).

Bear away, to. To turn a vessel farther away from the wind.

Beat, to. To tack, i.e. to make progress to windward by a zigzag course with the wind first on one bow and then on the other.

Bobstay. A rope, chain or rod bracing a bowsprit or bumkin to the hull.

Bilge. The curve of a vessel's bottom where it merges into the side. Also the space beneath the floor boards.

Bolt rope. A rope sewn along the edge of a sail to strengthen it and take some of the strain off the canvas.

Boom. A horizontal spar for extending the foot of a sail.

Bows. The sides of the forepart of a vessel, from the stem to amidships.

Bulkhead. A partition below deck.

Bumkin. A spar, to which the backstay is attached, projecting horizontally from the stern.

Butt. Where two planks or other parts of the vessel's structure touch one another end to end.

Carline. In the construction of a vessel, a fore-and-aft member at the side of a coachroof or hatch.

Catenary. The curve or sag of the chain between a vessel and her anchor.

Chronometer. An accurate clock used in navigation.

Close-hauled. Sailing as close to the wind as possible.

Coachroof. A part of the deck raised to give increased headroom.

Cockpit. The well near the stern in which the helmsman sits.

Companionway. The entry from the deck to the accommodation below.

Course. The direction in which a vessel is sailing or wishes to sail, measured in degrees or compass points from her meridian.

Crosstrees. Struts fitted to a mast to spread some of the shrouds so that they make a greater angle with the mast.

Dead reckoning. The account kept of a vessel's position when out of sight of land, having regard to the course made good and the distance sailed.

Fathom. A nautical measure of depth; 6 feet.

Fore-and-aft. In the direction of a line drawn from stem to stern.

Forepeak. The triangular space below deck in the bows.

Fore-reach, to. To make headway when hove-to.

Fother, to. To fix canvas or other material over a hole in the vessel's bottom to reduce the inrush of water.

Gasket. A short length of rope or canvas used for securing a sail when not in use.

Genoa. A large triangular headsail used in light or moderate winds.

Ghost, to. To make headway with a very faint breeze.

Ghoster. A sail similar to a genoa but made of very light material for use in light airs.

Great-circle course. The shortest distance between two points on the earth's surface.

Gybe, to. When running, to bring the wind from one quarter to the other so that the boom swings across.

Halyard. A rope used for hoisting a sail.

Hand, to. To lower, take in, or stow a sail.

Head wind. A wind which prevents a vessel from laying the desired course, compelling her to beat.

Heave-to. To trim the sails and helm in such a manner that the vessel lies almost stationary.

Helm. The tiller used for steering.

Hoist, to. To haul something, usually a sail, aloft.

Knot. A measure of speed; one nautical mile (6,080 feet) per hour.

Landfall. Sighting land at the end of a passage.

Latitude. Distance north or south of the equator expressed in degrees.

Lead. A weight on a marked line used for taking soundings.

Leech. The aftermost part of a sail.

Lee helm. A vessel is said to carry lee helm when she tends to turn her bow away from the wind and the helm has to be kept to leeward to prevent this.

Leeward. The side opposite to that on which the wind is blowing.

Leeway. Sideways movement made through the water.

Log-book. A book which contains a record of a voyage.

Longitude. Distance east or west of the meridian of Greenwich expressed in degrees.

Mainsail. The fore-and-aft sail set on the aft side of the mainmast.

Meridian. A true north-and-south line.

Offing. Position at a distance from the shore.

Patent log. An instrument for recording distance sailed through the water.

Port. The left-hand side of a vessel when facing forward.

Pram dinghy. A small rowing boat with a flat transom instead of a pointed bow.

Quarters. The sides of the after part of a vessel, from the stern to amidships.

Reach, to. To sail with the wind on the beam.

Reef, to. To reduce the area of a sail (in *Wanderer* by revolving the boom, thus rolling part of the sail round it).

Roach. The outward curve sometimes given to the leech of a sail.

Run, to sail before the wind.

Scend. The vertical rise and fall of the water in a harbour caused by the swell outside.

Scupper. A hole in the bulwarks to allow water to drain from the deck.

Sea-anchor. A conical canvas bag or other contrivance, secured to the bows or stern by a warp, for reducing the speed of a vessel in bad weather.

Set, to. To hoist or make sail.

Sextant. An instrument used in navigation for measuring angles, usually the angle between a heavenly body and the horizon.

Sheet. A rope by means of which a sail is trimmed.

Shroud. A wire rope giving athwartships support to the mast.

Slick. The smooth patch left on the surface of the sea when a vessel is driven broadside to leeward by the wind.

Sounding. A depth of water as found by the lead or marked on the chart.

Spinnaker. A triangular sail set on a boom and used on the opposite side to the mainsail when running. Twin spinnakers, as used in *Wanderer III*, are similar sails set one on each side of the mast when running without the mainsail.

Starboard. The right-hand side of a vessel when facing forward.

Stay. A wire rope giving fore-and-aft support to a mast. A vessel is said to stay when she changes from one tack to the other by coming head to wind.

Staysail. A triangular fore-and-aft sail set on a stay forward of the mast.

Stem. The foremost part of the bows, to which the plank ends are fastened.

Stern. The after-end of a vessel.

Swell. Long, easy waves, the crests of which do not break.

Tack, to. To make progress to windward (See *Beat*).

Tail in, to. A vessel is said to tail in when the wind blows her to the full scope of her anchor chain with her stern towards the shore.

Take in, to. To hand or stow a sail.

Tiller. The wooden bar secured to the rudder head for steering.

Topside. That part of the side which is above the water when the vessel is not heeled.

Transom. The type of bow or stern which is flat instead of round or pointed.

Trysail. A small sail of strong canvas sometimes set in place of the mainsail in bad weather.

Variation. The difference between true and magnetic north.

Vigia. A possible danger marked on a chart, the position, or even the existence, of which is doubtful.

Warp. A strong rope used for mooring or when riding to a sea anchor.

Weather shore. A shore to windward of a vessel; therefore one which offers shelter.

Weather side. The side of a vessel on to which the wind is blowing.

Windward side. The same as weather side.

INDEX